The Kingdom Field Guide

Keys to Finding God's Really Real Kingdom

Brian C. Steele

Renown Publishing
www.renownpublishing.com

The Kingdom Field Guide / Brian C. Steele
ISBN-13: 978-1-952602-17-7

This isn't an ordinary book—it's an extraordinary series of field trips with geologist-turned-pastor Brian Steele. With infectious enthusiasm, he guides you on a walk with Jesus through scriptures, stories, streets, and skies to discover the really, real kingdom of God where you live. Right away in the opening pages, heaven's joy will open to you as you discover the hidden treasure of King Jesus befriending you and empowering you to join with him and do great things.

Bill Gaultiere, PhD, Psychologist, Founder of Soul Shepherding, and author of *Journey of the Soul*

This is the most relevant book of our time on the realities of the kingdom of God. The pages of this book are packed with practical tools, inspiring stories, and captivating truth from God's word! It answers basic questions like: "What is the story of the King and his kingdom?" "How is God acting as King in our everyday lives?" "How do I discover the gospel of the kingdom in a personal way that changes my life and the world around me?" I believe God will use this book to help "ordinary" believers discover and demonstrate the kingdom of God in extraordinary ways, and all for the glory of King Jesus!

Dr. Jason Hubbard, Chaplain, Arizona Christian University

Brian Steele does a masterful job awakening our senses to the kingdom. A must-read by a gifted writer with a fresh, unique voice and a compelling message. Relevant, clear, logical, thought-provoking, and practical, [this book] delivers on the promise of its premise and is not only enjoyable, but a treasure that draws the reader in, inviting them to seek, find, and experience the kingdom in their everyday lives.

Candy Marballi, President of The Prayer Covenant

Have you ever had the thrill of a treasure hunt? Here's a book that *is* one. The prize for your search is the most marvelous treasure one could ever uncover. Helpfully, the book is laid out in a way that reading it turns into such an adventure! Brian Steele's highly interactive *The Kingdom Field Guide* offers you hours of discovery about one of the most important questions you could ever tackle: "What is Christ's kingdom really all about today?" Brimming with fresh insights, it keeps you awake and active in your heart—and sometimes even with your feet (true!). The chapter on what God's kingdom is *not* is nearly worth the price of purchase in itself. Get ready to be ushered into the riches of Christ in ways you've never experienced before.

David Bryant, author of *Christ Is NOW!*, President of Proclaim Hope!, Director of ChristNow.com

Years ago I remember watching Brian Steele, like a kid in a candy shop, awaken to the reality of the kingdom of God. This vital and overlooked aspect of the gospel has been his passion for the last decade—and it has made him an excellent spokesperson to put kingdom teaching in bite-size portions for the everyday Christian. I believe if you allow this field guide to penetrate your heart and soul, you will discover what has been right in front of you all along!

Todd King, Lead Pastor, Mercer Creek Church

Some authors point us in a direction and then hope that we find our way. Pastor Brian Steele is not that author. Instead, Brian invites us to join him on a journey, with *Field Guide* in hand, to experience the exhilaration and challenge of discovering the kingdom of God. The path, the views, the incline, and the weariness in all of our souls all contribute to a moment when we see all that Jesus has for us, wants for us. More than just reading the book, I have watched Brian walk this journey out personally. Walk with him; it's worth every step!

Grant Fishbook, Lead Teaching Pastor, Christ the King Community Church

The Kingdom Field Guide is based on the bedrock of Scripture, taking the reader on a journey of discovery to find the hidden treasure in our lives. To live today in this ever-changing world, we need structure to go deeper in searching out truth—"Your kingdom come on earth as it is in heaven." If you want more of Christ's *love*, take the adventure of a lifetime through this guide to open up locked doors within. Then share your experience with others!

Peter Friend, President of Peter Friend Corporation

Brian has an amazing heart and an unwavering love for the hidden treasure—both of which really show up in this book. Business leaders tend to be moving so fast that we forget to stop and look around. "Jesus stops for those who stop for him" resonated with me, and I found myself thinking about it throughout the book. *The Kingdom Field Guide*'s invitation to seek and experience the kingdom in our lives is spiritually refreshing.

Jesse Nelson, Co-Founder of Overflow Taps

As Christians, we know we are told to "seek first the kingdom of God." In *The Kingdom Field Guide*, Brian Steele provides a guide to understanding what the kingdom is, where it is, and most importantly, how we find it in plain sight and experience the joy and goodness it offers now. This book is packed with gems and is sure to be the beginning of a great adventure for anyone willing to accept Jesus' command to seek the kingdom as if it is the most important thing you can do.

Tony Larson, President, Whatcom Business Alliance, and Founder, Illuminate Northwest

As a pastor, I thought that I had a simple job: lead people to the cross to be saved. However, after exploring the concepts laid out in this book, I realized that was an incomplete picture. I was selling fire insurance this whole time. I was not helping people experience the depth of the life now and the life to come that Jesus invites us to live.

This book has completely changed how I preach, teach, and lead my church. Most importantly, though, it's changed how I encounter Jesus personally as my savior and King as I live out my role as a co-regal in his already-but-not-yet kingdom. It's not just another textbook. It's not a story of how the author got it right. Rather, it is an invitation to an adventure. In the same way C. S. Lewis invites his readers to climb into a wardrobe, Brian invites you to take a walk through a field where you will inevitably stub your toe on a treasure. This book is that toe-stub moment.

Chad Hoffman, Executive Pastor, Alderwood Community Church

The kingdom of heaven is often a mysterious concept, far out into the realms of the unknown. But it doesn't have to be that way. Brian exposes something missing in the American culture. His understanding and journey into the concepts of how people can live in the kingdom of heaven here and now, on earth, will transform both business and community.

Bruce Barlean, President of Barlean's: Pathway to a Better Life

For Katie, my Beloved.

For Kai, my Son.

CONTENTS

Foreword by Josh Yates

I remember sitting in Brian and Katie's living room as Brian shared with a group of pastors what he had discovered about the kingdom of God. His eyes lit up, animated with wonder and curiosity. Brian's love for scripture is profound, and his teaching style is full of practical, real-life illustrations that cause us all to pause, think, and fix our eyes on Jesus. For two years, I made the six-hour drive every month as our group of ministry leaders explored what it meant to follow Jesus and make disciples. The treasure for me was the six-hour drive home. I would ruminate on what the "really real kingdom" actually meant. Month after month, my heart grew, and my eyes began to open. This book will prove to do the same for you.

Imagine for a moment that you are sitting on an overstuffed leather couch surrounded by rock piles in Brian's living room. Sit back with a warm cup of freshly brewed coffee and feel the infectious hospitality as if you've been lifelong friends. This is a safe place to engage with your soul. But don't just sit on a comfy chair while reading *The Kingdom Field Guide*. Go on the field trips, get out of the house, get dirty, and explore. The best learning will be found outside of any living room.

I spat into a tube out of curiosity.

There is a cultural phenomenon happening. We long to know who we are and where we come from. We have a fundamental desire to discover lost family connections and fulfill the longing for cultural identity. My wife and I joined the bandwagon and sent our DNA off to a company to receive a report on our ancestral heritage. This is a fascinating process and a little concerning, to be honest. My DNA is on record someplace in the archives of history.

Within a few weeks, we received our reports breaking down the percentages with nice little pie charts full of colorful sections. I discovered that I am more British than many of the Brits living in the United Kingdom (80% England and Wales, 20% Ireland and Scotland). My ancestral line is filled with knights, kings, nobility, chicken farmers, and truck drivers. Just your everyday, bland minced-meat pie found at the corner pub.

Knowing our identity and purpose here on earth is mission-critical. This cannot be overstated. It informs our story. It tells us the role each of us plays in the grand narrative that shapes our lives. Understanding the kingdom narrative is one thing; however, living it is another.

Jesus modeled this for us. He said, "I must preach the good news of the kingdom of God to the other towns as well; for I was sent for this purpose" (Luke 4:43 ESV). Kingdom is a significant message of Jesus', as it appears throughout the Gospels 124 times in 116 verses.[1] The relevance is the same today as it was 2,000 years ago. Jesus would often explain to his disciples how the kingdom of God worked because it was so radically different from the world in which they lived—and the world in which we live today.

The kingdom of God is a kingdom of *Shalom* (the Hebrew word for peace).[2] It means that nothing is lacking, missing, or broken. God is rescuing his family and inviting them to trust him. God delivered his people from Egypt (under the kingdom of Empire) to become his messengers of his kingdom rule and reign. Not only did God have to rescue them out of Egypt, but he also had to purge Egypt out of their hearts in order to restore things to their proper place.

The kingdom of God is completely upside down compared to how the world operates. That is why we need the good news of the kingdom to restore us to his original design. However, the kingdom is foreign to us, and we need someone to explain it. Just like the disciples were hard of hearing, we, too, struggle with being kingdom tone-deaf. We need to train our senses to come fully alive and experience life as God intended. If we're honest, the kingdom of God is a bit mysterious. We don't always know how it works. It is full of surprises if we are ready for the adventure.

This past summer, I took my family on a heritage journey. We traveled through parts of the United Kingdom, exploring our family tree. Our last stop before our return flight was the Windsor Castle outside of London. This has been the home of British royalty for almost 1,000 years. Being that my family line descends from a reigning monarch, you'd think that I would have special access and treatment or at least get a button that says, "I am royalty."

Nope. Nada. Nothing.

We scoured the great halls, looking for family crests, and peeked behind curtains to see our name scratched into the walls, but to no avail. My DNA report amounts to nothing, at least to the royal guards.

I am just your average bloke, with no castles to inherit. This is my reality, and this is how most of us live, with a sunken view of our royalty and opportunity to live the greatest adventure, serving the King of Kings.

As followers of Jesus, we have a glorious calling. By putting our faith in him, we become part of his body, members of royalty (1 Peter 2:9). The kingdom reality painted in the Bible casts a noble vision and corporate entity as his royal family. In Exodus 19:5, the Hebrew word *segullah*,[3] translated as "treasured possession," encapsulates this with magnificent beauty:

> *"Now if you obey me fully and keep my covenant, then out of all nations you will be my treasured possession. Although the whole earth is mine, you will be for me a kingdom of priests and a holy nation." These are the words you are to speak to the Israelites.*
> **—Exodus 19:5–6** *(NIV)*

Carmen Imes talks about *segullah* in her book on Exodus, *Bearing God's Name*.[4] This word refers to the king's personal treasury, but when it is applied to people, it refers to those who have a high status with the king. It is a partnership between the king and his people, which imparts kingly responsibilities. God rescues his family and has empowered them to partner with him as his treasured possession. God's people are to be a kingdom of priests to the entire world, living on mission as ambassadors with the keys to the storehouses of God's riches and resources.

This is not just a different reality.

This is not just our reality.

This is the *only* reality.

The *Kingdom Field Guide* is more than just a book. It is a treasure map to living as God intended. Brian's work on the kingdom is a fresh voice with powerful illustrations that make you rethink the trap of living a safe, domesticated, ordinary existence. This book is dangerous. Taken seriously, it will cost you everything, but the return of investment is endless.

I "stubbed my toe" on the really real kingdom with Brian's help almost eight years ago. I had no idea how boring and truncated my faith was prior to this. Sadly, even with growing up in the church, attending Bible schools, and being a "professional pastor" for twenty-five years, I didn't realize what it meant to live with an awakened adventure of serving the King. I am your average bloke, and I have the paper to confirm it, but I am now living as a vice regent in God's kingdom.

The invitation is yours.

Are you ready to explore God's really real kingdom? It's breathtaking.

Your average bloke (well, sort of),

Josh Yates
Associate Director of Sonlife Ministries
July 12, 2020

Something Missing

I am the man who with the utmost daring discovered what had been discovered before. ... It recounts my elephantine adventures in pursuit of the obvious.[5]

—G. K. Chesterton, *Orthodoxy*

All your works shall give thanks to you, O LORD, and all your saints shall bless you! They shall speak of the glory of your kingdom and tell of your power, to make known to the children of man your mighty deeds, and the glorious splendor of your kingdom. Your kingdom is an everlasting kingdom, and your dominion endures throughout all generations.

—Psalm 145:10–13

Something was missing. He knew it. The Christian life is supposed to be good, abundantly good. Jesus said so. But as I sat with a church member at lunch, his body language told a different story—head bowed, shoulders slumped, eyes down. We'll call this man Glenn, but he could very easily be you or I.

Glenn had been faithfully attending our church for years. He read his Bible, he prayed, and he volunteered from time to time. He believed in Jesus, but he considered his faith a fraud. He was checking all the right boxes, but his inner life was plagued by stress and depression. While we continued eating lunch, I listened to his anguish. It was real, and I had seen it before. Something was missing— something big.

I asked Glenn if he was familiar with Jesus' parable of the hidden treasure from Matthew 13:44:

The kingdom of heaven is like treasure hidden in a field, which a man found and covered up. Then in his joy he goes and sells all that he has and buys that field.

He'd heard it before. The words were familiar, like front-page headlines of old news that no longer grabbed his attention. Glenn had a good family, a good job, and a nice house. He confessed that there was nothing in his life of faith that would motivate him to "sell all." Then I asked him two questions that changed everything:

1. What is the kingdom?
2. Why is it worth selling everything to acquire?

Over the following months, we looked at the "something" that was missing from his life. We peered inside that dirt-covered treasure box in the field to see the magnitude and wonder of what was hidden inside. You see, Glenn had walked past that hidden treasure for decades of his Christian life. He had been happy enough. He'd been content, but he wondered if he was missing out on something more. Then one day, while walking through the field, he stubbed his toe. Looking down, wondering what could have possibly gotten in his way, he found the treasure that had been buried there all along.

That treasure changes everything.

At this point, we want a happy ending for Glenn. In a Hallmark movie, his problems would dissolve, and his life would take a blissful upward trajectory. But his life got worse—much worse—because Glenn faced a peril that lies before all of us. We might find a treasure, ponder it, even understand its value, but then leave it right where we found it. Glenn hadn't yet moved from kingdom *finding* to kingdom *living*.

This often happens with a myriad of treasures we find in our lives. We find a great exercise machine, but then it gathers dust in a closet. We find a new resolve to reduce social media, but a week later, we are still scrolling through our feeds. That new diet plan gets shoved aside by that new bag of chips. Valuing something does not always lead to life change. Even a treasure with the eternal worth of God's kingdom can lie dormant, even forgotten, right at our feet.

The Kingdom Field Guide is for all of the Glenns who need not only to find God's kingdom, but then to live within the goodness and beauty that Jesus offers in that kingdom. Glenn's story is not finished, and neither is yours.

This book is for the parents, pastors, people in the workforce, leaders, teachers, and students who have been faithful in practicing the Christian life but feel like their inner life with Christ has a void. They feel like something is missing.

This book is for the "nones" and "dones" who have discarded "that religious stuff" because it is too judgmental and hypocritical. They find churches to be more like hollow shells than hallowed halls. Something is missing; they can feel it.

This book is for the person serving in Christian ministry. She brings the gospel to others but would be hard-pressed to describe the "gospel of the kingdom." She senses the void, the lack of full understanding. She knows that there is something missing.

This book is for the business owner who knows that her influence for good in the world is about more than just increasing sales. She's convinced that her leadership with employees and clients has a greater significance than the bottom line, but the daily grind has ground down her hope. Something is missing in her leadership.

This book is for parents who know that they hold the primary responsibility for showing their children the best life in Christ. But in the frenzy, they struggle just to get their family to church before the sermon starts.

This book is for the pastor who has offered communion to others hundreds of times but has never connected that practice to God's kingdom. He may not even know that something is missing from this most sacred ritual.

This is for the person who has heard of and may even know Jesus, yet has no idea what his kingdom is.

If any of these examples is you, keep reading.

Continue with this book if you have prayed the Lord's Prayer countless times but can't begin to describe what "your kingdom come" really means (Matthew 6:9–13).

Living in a Void

The Apostle Paul identified something missing in the church at Rome. They were arguing and bickering over religious food laws, ceremonies, and holidays to observe. Divisions and power struggles were tearing them apart. As an antidote, he told them this:

> *For the kingdom of God is not a matter of eating and drinking but of righteousness and peace and joy in the Holy Spirit.*
> **—Romans 14:17**

The kingdom is a matter of righteousness, peace, and

joy. Not nitpicky rules. Not oppressive religious duty. And certainly not squashing others to climb the religious version of a corporate ladder.

Are you experiencing a good life because you are well-aligned with God's good order? Is there clear evidence of flourishing and thriving as God's peace invades your daily activity? Is there an overriding joy that weaves through your inevitable failures, pains, and struggles? If not, then you may be missing the kingdom.

I've felt that terrible void as a follower of Jesus. Even as a Christian, I have had significant periods of my life held captive by darkness, chaos, and misery. My life was unintegrated—dis-integrated, if you will—with some of my most important relationships suffering most. I was a Christian on Sunday, less so from Monday to Wednesday. By Thursday and Friday, I was practically a pagan. On Saturday, I repented so that I could be a Christian again on Sunday morning at the worship service. Then the weekly cycle of sin management began again. My life was missing God's reign as a real King over his real kingdom. I could often check the boxes for prayer, Bible reading, giving, serving, and worship, but I could not describe my faith as having found hidden treasure worth "selling all" to acquire. Not by a long shot.

Many Christians are missing the kingdom of God, but not in the way that you lose car keys or are late for an appointment. God's kingdom is missing in a different way. The kingdom of God is hiding in plain sight. It's right outside our door, waiting. The reason we miss it is because we aren't seeking it. You can't see what you don't seek.

Jesus commanded his disciples to set their highest priority on searching out the kingdom:

*But **seek first the kingdom of God** and his righteousness,
and all these things will be added to you.*
                                                    —Matthew 6:33

What if the kingdom of God is missing because it is lost among your other priorities, languishing way down at the bottom of the list? What if the kingdom is hidden because *anything* else comes before seeking it? Jesus wants us to invert our upside-down priority list. He commands us to seek the kingdom as if it were of the utmost importance. If you do this, I promise you that what is missing will be found right at your feet. It's been there all this time, and it is real.

Jesus taught his disciples to pray, "Your kingdom come, your will be done, on earth as it is in heaven..." (Matthew 6:10). My hope is that this prayer becomes as normal as breathing. My prayer is that *The Kingdom Field Guide* will help you to see God's really real kingdom coming in and through your life right here and now. May you stub your toe on the treasure hiding right at your feet. And when God's kingdom comes, it will be your deepest joy to meet a most desperate need and bring the greatest good in the world around you.

A Synagogue Hidden in Plain Sight

In 2018, my wife, Katie, and I travelled to Israel. Before joining a guided tour group, we rented a car and drove around the Sea of Galilee. Our jet-lagged bodies were starving, and we were getting cranky. We needed food ASAP!

Desperately meandering around a foreign landscape, we found ourselves on a dead-end road with signs in Hebrew and English for "Magdala Archaeological Park." A quick glance showed some old ruins, but clearly no food.

I whipped the car around, and we left in a huff of frustration. Eventually, we found a restaurant and enjoyed a delicious Mediterranean meal. What we didn't realize was that meal was merely an appetizer for a much greater feast waiting for us at Magdala, the place we had so irritably left behind.

A few days later, we joined the tour group. Our local guide, Sam Makarios, brought us back to Magdala. Sam was born and raised in Israel, and he is an expert in the history of the region. He speaks five languages fluently, including Hebrew, and after twenty years of guiding tours in the Holy Land, Sam knows Israel.

Sam knew that our tour group *must* visit Magdala. What my wife and I had casually dismissed out of our ignorance (and hunger) turned out to be a hidden gem waiting to be discovered.

Accidentally uncovered in 2009, Magdala is a synagogue and village on the shoreline of Galilee that had been buried for two thousand years. Jesus almost certainly spent time in the area of what was believed to be the hometown of Mary Magdalene. In this place, a woman was miraculously healed by Jesus with only a touch of his garment (Mark 5:21–34). Our tour group meditated on this encounter in the Duc In Altum chapel, which was built to honor the women of the New Testament, those dedicated disciples.

Below a massive painting by Daniel Cariola of this healing encounter, our group had a powerful sense that we were in the presence of the Jesus who still heals, the Jesus who still looks on the overlooked, the Jesus who still calls the outcast "Daughter" (Mark 5:34).

At the risk of sounding sensational, we really met Jesus in that chapel on the shore of Galilee, and our lives were forever changed. At that easily overlooked site, we learned that Jesus stops for those who stop for him. Were it not for our guide, Sam, we would have completely missed the experience. Magdala was hiding in plain sight, but we needed a guide to help us see it.

God's kingdom is just like that. It's a treasure hidden in the field. This book is about finding what's hiding in plain sight. My hope for *The Kingdom Field Guide* is that you will see what's always waiting at your feet.

CHAPTER ONE

Using This Field Guide

Many people who profess faith in Jesus Christ, the King, can't begin to describe his kingdom, let alone enjoy most of the goodness that kingdom offers. That was me for much of my life as a follower of the King.

Why not just read a book that describes God's kingdom? Couldn't we curl up on the couch with a cup of coffee and the book to discover the kingdom as a hidden treasure? I suppose if you want to discover the thrill of roller coasters, there is some value in watching YouTube videos of people riding them. But isn't that missing the whole point? And isn't that part of the problem of our phone-addicted culture?

Our lives are being lived through screens, but these screens can only take us so far. We need direct personal encounters with the real world. That's how we will find God's real kingdom.

God's kingdom is really real. And God's really real kingdom needs to be seen, touched, heard, experienced, and lived. King David said, "Oh, taste and see that the LORD is good!" (Psalm 34:8). *The Kingdom Field Guide* is a launching point to get you to do just that: taste and see.

Long before I was a pastor, I was a geologist. When I was a geology student, the professors used field guides to help us explore volcanoes, fault zones, and landslides. The time spent on those field trips was valuable beyond words and provided me with experiences that could not have been gained from just shoving my nose in a geology textbook. The field guides unveiled the world of rocks that had been hiding in plain sight all around me.

The Kingdom Field Guide is meant to be lived out. Any field guide—whether for birds, travel, or rocks—is designed to get dirty through experiences and journeys. This book will have failed miserably if in five years it sits pristinely on a shelf without dings, stains, and ripped pages.

Rather, cram this book into a backpack and visit the suggested locations. Get out of the church classroom. Escape from your living room. Open your eyes and search out God's kingdom. Pray often that God's Spirit will show you what has been hidden. Jesus said that the search for the kingdom is to be of the utmost importance in our lives, our highest priority, our most vital motivation (Matthew 6:33).

Explore with Others

The Kingdom Field Guide is also intended to be read and experienced with a few close friends or family. The disciples learned about God's kingdom in community with one another. They ate together, walked together, grew exhausted together, laughed together, cried together, and fought together. Gather a few people and embark on this journey as a small group. Spend time with them on the field trips. Do not be afraid to confront ideas which seem out of place, strange, or even wrong. Challenge one another.

You could read this book and go on the field trips

alone, and there would be good value in that. But to really maximize the experience and life change, go with friends or family.

Don't limit your company to people who are just like you or share your world view and faith. Jesus' disciples were an assortment of people who had no natural reason even to be in the same room together. It was in *this* context that Jesus taught them about God's kingdom and commanded them to love one another as he loved them (John 13:34–35).

This book is also meant to be read and lived out with children. Because children haven't gathered too much baggage, they will most likely understand God's kingdom far easier than adults will. Their delight in a rainbow, butterfly, or waterfall hasn't yet been squashed. While parents need to teach their children about the kingdom, often children have a greater capacity to delight and wonder in what they see and hear. They just might become your greatest instructors, so include them on your field trips.

Bible Trips, Side Trips, and Field Trips

The Kingdom Field Guide has three kinds of trips. The trips are designed to provide you with practical experiences to help you seek and see God's kingdom.

Bible Trips

Bible Trips lead you to explore the sprawling landscape of scripture. As you find the kingdom story of scripture, you'll find the kingdom coming in your life. Pay careful attention to themes related to God's rule and reign. This includes elements common to any kingdom: crowns, thrones, kings, power, authority, laws, militaries, etc. Look for them. When you read the Bible through the lens of the kingdom story, you'll be able to see what you couldn't before. Even familiar passages will become brand new. When kingdom themes leap off the page, you know that you're on the right track. Small groups are an ideal setting for exploring the Bible Trips. Your small group will be enriched by focusing on the kingdom narratives of scripture.

Side Trips

The Side Trips are found within each chapter, reflecting its content. These mini-excursions are short breaks in your day and require only five to ten minutes. They are intended to interrupt the hectic pace of life. They almost always involve going outside and engaging all of your senses. The side trips are opportunities to reorient your attention and will help train you to "seek first the kingdom of God" as you slow down (Matthew 6:33). You'll find that when you stop for Jesus, he is already waiting for you.

Please don't skip the Side Trips. *Prioritizing these experiences will greatly help you to seek and see God's kingdom.* The side trips are personal encounters with Jesus that allow you to explore the depths of God's goodness. Here is an example of a Side Trip:

Side Trip: Breathe

"Thus says God, the LORD, who created the heavens and stretched them out, who spread out the earth and what comes from it, who gives breath to the people on it and spirit to those who walk in it…" (Isaiah 42:5). Take a few minutes to go outside right now. Breathe slowly and deeply. Pay attention to each breath. That breath is a gift from God. Conclude by thanking him for this incredible kindness and goodness.

Field Trips

Field Trips require more time and effort than the Side Trips, but they will be worth it. Field Trips take you to familiar territory. You will explore spaces that you've traveled dozens of times, but you'll be training your eyes to see what's been hiding in plain sight. Remember that you can't see what you are not seeking.

Be willing to go out of your comfort zone. Try all of the field trips, even if it doesn't initially seem to be "your thing." When you adopt new modes of looking, then new modes of thinking will open up.

Your brain is wired to say "pass" on leaving your comfort zone. Do whatever is needed to override the reflex that compels you to stay in familiar routines. I can't say that your life depends on it, but I *can* say that the fullness of abundant life in Christ depends on it.

The more you establish habits of seeking, the more you will see God's kingdom all around you. And the more you see God's kingdom all around you, the more you will see that you are called to play a part in the greatest kingdom story.

A few of the field trips are solo ventures, but most of them will yield the best value when you explore with a few friends or your small group.

Field Trip Design

In order to see the kingdom, you'll need to get out and actually *see* the kingdom. You'll have a lot of good reasons not to do it. Too often we stop short by only taking in information. Transformation comes from rearranging your priorities, changing some life habits, and being stretched as you engage not only your mind, but also your body and your senses.

Destination

All of the destinations in *The Kingdom Field Guide* are likely within a short drive of where you live. Be creative in finding a destination that is the best fit for each field trip. Keep your eyes open for great locations and keep your ears open to people describing places they've been.

Type of Setting

Settings are both urban and wilderness. Some of the settings require you to find the highest point of your region with the best view. Others take you to low places of your environment, the places of sorrow or despair that we usually try to avoid. Some settings are isolated; some are crowded. In some settings, you'll be keenly aware of God's goodness. Other places will give you a sense of the competing kingdom of darkness.

We don't need to be alarmists, but at the same time, in the regular course of our day, we *do* bump into the various aspects of the dark kingdom: the porn shop on the corner, the shopping chaos in the aisle of Costco, the rage on the freeway on-ramp. Even more alarmingly, as we seek God's kingdom, we will see that there are outposts of the dark kingdom marking dark corners of our own hearts.

Length of Time

Dallas Willard famously said, "Hurry is the great enemy of spiritual life in our day. You must ruthlessly eliminate hurry."[6] When you explore God's kingdom, try not to be pinched for time. Carve out time and protect it. Some of the destinations in *The Kingdom Field Guide* can be explored in a few hours. With others, you may want to take a few days. But by all means, start searching for God's kingdom with the time that you have. Begin with a half-hour lunch break and adapt a trip to the time you can spare. If you have a weekly Sabbath (or rest/play day), these field trips are a wonderful way to play and delight with God on your day off.

One way to find the time for these trips is to "steal" time from your normal day. Instead of looking at the Instagram picture of your third-grade classmate's dinner, take your dinner to an ocean overlook. Instead of binge-watching Netflix, walk your neighborhood to see how God's throne is more compelling than *Game of Thrones*. I can hear my friend, Pastor Todd King, saying right now, "We *do* have time for our priorities."

Gear

At a minimum, I encourage you to take a journal, *The Kingdom Field Guide*, and a Bible or Bible app. Both iPhone and Android phones have excellent free Bible apps. I recommend beginning with the YouVersion.com apps. When you travel to backcountry or wilderness areas, you'll need to take reasonable hiking gear. Otherwise, adapt the setting to your comfort level and abilities. Many locations are logistically simple and don't require much preparation or many provisions.

Key Scriptures

Every field trip has a set of key scriptures that tie into the biblical kingdom narrative. I suggest that you bring a Bible on every trip so that you can pause, read, reflect, and pray. Some of your most powerful and intimate moments with God may come when you are outside, moving around and exploring.

Seeing the Kingdom Connection

Each field trip will focus on a key element of God's really real kingdom. Push yourself to see what is actually right in front of you, not just what you think you see right in front of you. Pay attention to what you are paying attention to. God's kingdom will remain invisible as long as it's not a priority in your life to seek it out. Jesus' command to seek his kingdom is imperative to accessing the abundant life he promised you. As I mentioned earlier, you can't see what you don't seek.

Questions for Personal Reflection

Each field trip will offer questions prompting you to reflect on your experience. Spend time during and after each field trip to write out your answers. Something happens when you put pen to paper. It accesses a different part of your brain than when you are just thinking.

The reflections prompt you to consider new ideas, difficult questions, kingdom connections, and life application and then turn it all into a conversation with God in prayer. Ask the Holy Spirit to guide you. Invite the Spirit to show you what you don't or can't yet see.

Set a Date Right Now

Before reading any further, I'd like you to get out your calendar and mark a day and time for your first field trip. Create an event for at least two hours that says, "Kingdom Field Trip." This trip will be in your hometown and won't require extensive travel or logistics. It doesn't matter if the event doesn't happen for a week or a month. It's just important that you write down the day and time of that trip and commit to it. This will help you actually to do the trip and to avoid the dreaded "Trap of Inaction" (which we'll talk about later in the book). As a bonus, invite a friend or family member. Now write down the details of your first field trip here:

My commitment for the first kingdom field trip:

Day: _____

Time: _____

Trip companion(s) invited:_____

Using the Small Groups Guide

When people follow Jesus together, they grow in ways that are simply not possible alone. I strongly recommend that you gather together with a few people to learn about God's kingdom in community. Here is how I recommend utilizing this book in a small group setting:

1. *Gather* a group of your friends, neighbors, or co-workers to meet on a regular basis.

2. *Go* on the field trips together.

3. *Discuss* the questions in the Small Group Guides.

4. *Learn* together with openness and curiosity.

5. *Eat* and share a meal together. Those who eat together will also grow together.

6. *Share* your story with others by taking risks of vulnerability. As you do this, avoid judging those in your group and don't try to fix their problems. Be great listeners when you gather together.

7. *Pray* the Lord's Prayer together (Matthew 6:9–13) and pray for one another between your gatherings.

8. *Practice* living your faith together so that God's kingdom comes in and through your lives.

You don't need to be a world-class teacher or superstar pastor to facilitate a small group. The biggest need for a great small group is hospitality—creating a safe environment and helping people feel like they belong. The best small group host isn't the "Bible Answer Man"; it's somebody who makes sure that everybody has an opportunity to contribute.

If you can host a Super Bowl party, then you can host a small group. Why? You don't need to be a former NFL player or an expert football analyst to host a gathering where you watch others play the game. Instead, you invite some friends over, create a comfortable setting, chuck out some snacks, turn on the game, and talk about it.

That type of hospitality is what's most needed for a small group that goes through *The Kingdom Field Guide*. Read together. Do Bible Trips together. Go on Field Trips together. Talk together. Learn together. Grow together. Also, don't feel pressured to discuss a whole chapter each time you meet. Agree on what is doable each time you gather. If you only get through a few pages, that's much better than trying to cram too much in.

As you meet in small groups, I'm certain that you will find God's kingdom and, together, stub your toes on a hidden treasure.

CHAPTER ONE FIELD TRIP

A Walk Around Town

Walk through your hometown and search for evidence of your city's government. Take a notebook and record the evidence of the local power structure at work. Look for street signs, pavement markings, utilities, infrastructure, and law enforcement. The "invisible kingdom" of your city will immediately pop into existence when you start paying attention to it.

Look also for evidence of county, state, and federal *government*. For example, when you pass a mailbox, notice that it is a function of the United States government.

Look for evidence of the county, state, and federal *power* all around you. Carefully notice signage stating laws, guiding traffic, and indicating city, county, or state parks.

Note: What government services are provided? How do officials use their authority? How do citizens exercise their rights and responsibilities? How does local and federal authority show up in everyday life (think about the FDA, the FAA, etc.)?

After looking for human authority, make the shift to looking for similar evidence of God's kingdom authority. How is the government of Jesus manifested all around you? What is the evidence of his power? How does his rule and reign show up in the world? Who are the representatives on earth of his kingdom authority? What is the result of their work to carry out the royal agenda of Jesus?

Field Trip Details

Travel: Walking around your hometown

Cost: Zero

Time: A few hours

Physical Demands: Put on your walking shoes.

Gear: Journal, Bible, pen

Key Scriptures to Guide Your Trip: Psalm 21:1–7; Psalms 145–150; Isaiah 60:1–22; Matthew 13:10–17; Matthew 28:16–20; Romans 13:1–7; Colossians 1:16; Titus 3:1

Seeing the Kingdom Connection

Read Psalms 145 through 150. These songs were written to praise the King for the works of his kingdom. Move slowly through the list of the evidence of YHWH's reign.[7] The Psalms include weather, food, security, clouds, and mountains among the list of the manifestations of the King's rule. When you are seeing snow, you are seeing an outworking of the kingdom.

What has the King created that you can see right now, right before you? Weather? Shelter? Food? As you look for what sustains and nourishes life, you are seeing the goodness of God's kingdom.

Questions for Reflection

1. What new ideas did you encounter in this field trip?

2. What questions have come out of this field trip? What doesn't make sense to you?

3. How do you see Jesus and his kingdom in this experience?

4. How can you apply this to your life and take a next step?

5. What have you learned or experienced today that you will talk to God and others about?

Chapter One Discussion Questions

> **Key Scripture:**
> Parable of the Sower and the Seed
> Matthew 13:1–23

1. How would you describe what God's kingdom is? Is it something you've ever thought about before? Has your mindset about God's kingdom shifted at all after reading this chapter?

2. What are your initial thoughts and feelings when asked to leave your comfort zone? In what areas of your life do you think you've gotten too comfortable? Is there a particular area in which you sense God is leading you out of your comfort zone?

3. In the parable of the Sower and the Seed, why does Jesus tell his disciples, "To you it has been given to know the secrets of the kingdom of heaven, but to them it has not been given" (Matthew 13:11)? Why is the kingdom hidden to some? How can you know if you've discovered the "secrets of the kingdom"?

4. Where do you see governmental authority exercised

throughout your normal day? Are there regulations at work that you must follow? When you are driving, shopping, or going through daily life at home, how does the "kingdom" of your city or state rule over you?

5. Discuss your experience on the field trip. What did you learn? What surprised you? What challenged you?

Chapter One Notes

_____

_____

_____

_____

_____

_____

_____

_____

_____

_____

_____

_____

_____

_____

_____

_____

_____

_____

_____

_____

_____

CHAPTER TWO

Mapping the Journey

Jesus unveiled his extraordinary kingdom of God by using ordinary objects all around his disciples. Ordinary stuff like rocks, fish, trees, and seed became the stuff of profound teaching.

What is grand often lurks within that which seems bland. If Jesus were doing his public ministry in twenty-first-century North America instead of first-century Israel, he would use the normal stuff of our world to explain the wonderful stuff of his kingdom.

But the world around us is more than just sermon notes for Jesus. When we look at the ordinary material world around us, we are, in fact, looking at what belongs (or will eventually belong) to the kingdom of the Christ. When Jesus said that he has "all authority in heaven and on earth" (Matthew 28:16–20), that means that everything in heaven and on earth is ultimately under his rule and within his kingdom realm. The God who said, "...all the earth is mine," on Mount Sinai (Exodus 19:5) was incarnate in the King who was crucified to restore all of his creation.

Anything we see can teach us about God's kingdom because everything we see is—someway, somehow—part of God's kingdom. The ordinary points you to the extraordinary; the bland declares the grand. God's kingdom is actually quite normal and has always been all around us.

Jesus spoke at a simple level with basic, single-syllable words. If you add some rhymes, his sayings could fit nicely in the Dr. Seuss *Cat in the Hat* book:

- "I am the light of the world." (John 8:12)
- "You are the salt of the earth." (Matthew 5:13)
- "I am the bread of life." (John 6:35)

You could mistake his simple language for simple meaning, but Jesus' teachings are profound and have challenged academics and philosophers for millennia.

There are only thirty-four English words in the Matthew 13:44 hidden treasure parable (the original Greek text has only thirty-one words), but after eight years of studying this parable, these thirty-four words still continue to change my life.

Matthew 13:44 is like a clown car from which the whole narrative of God's coming kingdom spills out. All of the Old Testament covenants, prophesies, and grand stories are somehow packed into that treasure hidden in the field.

The parable poses two critical questions to consider:

1. *What exactly is this treasure?* What is the kingdom of heaven? Is it really real, and is it still possible for people in the twenty-first century to find it?

2. *Why is this treasure worth the sum total of all the man's possessions?* Why is it logical for the man in the parable to sell everything he has and to sell it "in his joy" (Matthew 13:44)? Is God's kingdom really worth all that we have? Is God still calling people to trade everything in their lives for the sake of acquiring the hidden treasure?

The Path to Finding Hidden Treasure

This parable is far more than a metaphor for God's good work or your need to search for him. We must press this teaching further. In the graphic on the following page, I have adapted a popular theory of learning from Benjamin Bloom and Peter Scazzero to chart the journey of Jesus' treasure seeker in Matthew 13:44.[8]

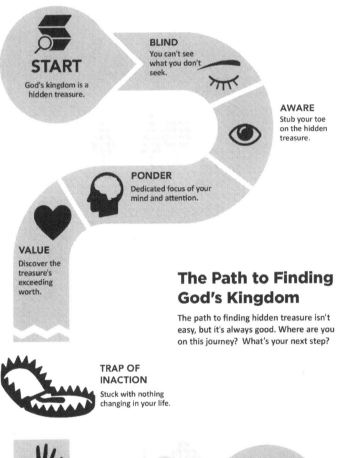

START
God's kingdom is a hidden treasure.

BLIND
You can't see what you don't seek.

AWARE
Stub your toe on the hidden treasure.

PONDER
Dedicated focus of your mind and attention.

VALUE
Discover the treasure's exceeding worth.

TRAP OF INACTION
Stuck with nothing changing in your life.

PRIORITIZE
Arrange your life so God's kingdom comes first.

OWN (SELL)
Delight in God's kingdom coming and sharing it with others.

The Path to Finding God's Kingdom

The path to finding hidden treasure isn't easy, but it's always good. Where are you on this journey? What's your next step?

This map identifies stages on the path toward discovering God's kingdom. It's not a straightforward, linear journey. One step doesn't always lead directly to the next. Sometimes you move forward, then backward. How many times have you discovered something of great value, only to lose it and then rediscover it later in your life? But eventually, in order for God's kingdom to come in and through you, all of the stages of this journey will be taken.

Here is an example of what that journey map looks like when you are in search of God's hidden treasure. Place yourself in the parable. Imagine walking back and forth across a field on your way to work for years. There's a well-worn track.

1. *Blind*: You have crossed the field hundreds of times. You can't see what you don't seek.

2. *Aware*: You stub your toe on a box and are suddenly aware that a hidden treasure exists. Your eyes are open.

3. *Ponder*: Opening the box, you ponder the treasures inside. Your mind is engaged; your attention is closely focused.

4. *Value*: You realize that the treasure is worth more than everything you have. Your heart is captured. Looking up, you see that the field is for sale!

5. *Trap of Inaction*: You face a horrible peril. Though you value what you've found, the Trap of Inaction could swallow you up, preventing any life change, if you do nothing.

6. *Prioritize*: After you make it through the Trap of Inaction, your highest priority becomes rearranging your life and liquidating all you have so you can buy the field and acquire the treasure. You engage your hands, and your values are translated into action.

7. *Own/Sell*: You buy the field and acquire the treasure. You enjoy and delight in God's kingdom coming in you and through you. But soon after taking possession of the hidden treasure, you put up a "For Sale" sign in the field. You are excited to share the discovery and tell others about it.

With surprising accuracy, this maps a journey you must take if you want to enjoy the full life in God's kingdom and acquire the hidden treasure for yourself. Let's dive deeper into each phase.

Living Blind

You begin blind. The treasure at your feet is invisible, and you don't even realize that you're missing out.

For decades, I've studied geology. I've spent the majority of my adult life with my head down, looking at rocks. I love the stories that rocks tell. I can read narratives of cataclysm, volcanic explosions, and plate movements by looking at rocks. When I hike the North Cascades, I see a drama unfold with the passing miles along alpine trails. But often my hiking partners are blind to the wonders I see. They only see *rocks*. Where I see stories and beauty, others see just dirt. They are blind, but my intentional focus has allowed me to see what's invisible to most other people.

However, my focus on rocks left me blind to what was above the ground. After decades of looking at rocks, I discovered that I was blind to birds. In 2016, I moved to a new house with my wife, Katie. One day, I was gazing at the stunning view of Mount Baker from our backyard, and suddenly my gaze was diverted from a gorgeous volcano on the horizon to a bird that landed on our fence.

I wondered, "Hmm, what kind of bird is that?" I was curious enough to buy a "Birds of Washington" field guide and found out that the mystery bird was a Black-capped Chickadee. Then I noticed a different kind of bird land on the fence. Again I thought, "Well, what kind of bird is *that*?" My bird book said that it was an American Goldfinch.

And then something popped. I realized that there were dozens of different birds flying by and landing in my yard. The next obvious step was to download some bird apps on my phone and really dig into trying to identify birds in my yard. I became a birder! I realized that I had been blind to birds my whole life. They'd been around me, but because my attention was turned toward rocks on the ground, I did not see them.

You can't see what you're not looking for. Obvious landmarks are hidden. Abundant things get overlooked. Treasure in a field is missed. God's kingdom is hidden to anybody who is not looking for it, but it's hiding in plain sight.

Be Aware

The journey to acquiring the hidden treasure begins with sight. In Matthew 13, a trove of kingdom parables, Jesus identified those who find the kingdom as those who see:

Then the disciples came and said to him, "Why do you speak to them in parables?" And he answered them, "To you it has *been given to know **the secrets of the kingdom of heaven**, but to them it has not been given. For to the one who has, more will be given, and he will have an abundance, but from the one who has not, even what he has will be taken away. This is why I speak to them in parables, because **seeing they do not see**, and hearing they do not hear, nor do they understand. Indeed, in their case the prophecy of Isaiah is fulfilled that says:*

*"'"You will indeed hear but never understand, and you will indeed see but never perceive." For this people's heart has grown dull, and with their ears they can barely hear, and **their eyes they have closed, lest they should see with their eyes** and hear with their ears and understand with their heart and turn, and I would heal them.'*

***But blessed are your eyes, for they see**, and your ears, for they hear. For truly, I say to you, many prophets and righteous people longed to see what you see, and did not see it, and to hear what you hear, and did not hear it."*
—Matthew 13:10–17

God's kingdom needs to be looked for. Awareness of God's kingdom comes through sight—and not just metaphorical sight. The distinction between those in the kingdom of darkness and those in the kingdom of light is what they can see:

And even if our gospel is veiled, it is veiled to those who are perishing. In their case the god of this world has blinded the minds of the unbelievers, to keep them from seeing the light of the gospel of the glory of Christ, who is the image of God.
—2 Corinthians 4:3–4

It's easy to over-spiritualize this teaching or turn sight into a metaphor for being aware of God, but physical sight plays a more important role than you may imagine. You must train your physical eyes on the world around you to see the kingdom of God. Jesus often directed his disciples to focus their sight on the concrete, physical elements of their real world.

> Look at the birds of the air: they neither sow nor reap nor gather into barns, and yet your heavenly Father feeds them. Are you not of more value than they?
>
> **—Matthew 6:26**

Our first step in finding the kingdom is seeing—being aware—that there is a kingdom to be found. I call that moment when you become aware of the kingdom "stubbing your toe." You've been walking the same field for years, but then, one day, you stub your toe on a box in the ground. Looking down, you see a treasure at your feet for the first time ever. *Now* you are aware of the really real kingdom.

Have you stubbed your toe yet?

Side Trip: "Ordinary" Objects

Jesus taught about the extraordinary kingdom using ordinary objects, such as a net, bread, a vineyard, and seed. Take five minutes to go outside right now. Imagine that Jesus is present with you and is teaching a kingdom parable with something in your immediate surroundings. What can you see that he would pick up or use to explain the kingdom? What lesson would Jesus draw from this ordinary part of your world to uncover an extraordinary part of his world?

Ponder

Think of the man who stubbed his toe and became aware of the box at his feet in the field. He pried open the rusty hasp and lifted the lid. Peering inside, he began to ponder the treasure. He pawed through the assortment of jewels, coins, and gold baubles.

Whether this lasted for a moment, an hour, or days, the man engaged his mind and pondered the bounty. The path to owning the hidden treasure requires your thinking to be focused intently on God's kingdom.

There are a million distractions in your world that claw for every square inch of your thought life. Your Netflix queue, Amazon wish list, iPhone notifications, TV, radio, Facebook, and Instagram are only the tip of the iceberg. A constant battle is being waged for your mindshare. Your ability to concentrate and think deeply has been dangerously eroded.

Here's an example. By some measures, the average adult spends over five hours per day on his or her smartphone.[9] In a moment of honesty, consider how much of your thought life is dominated by your phone.

If you expect the fullness of God's kingdom to be at your command after you digest 120-character tweets, then you will miss the treasure. You must develop the discipline of *pondering more than scrolling*. Your brain literally needs to be rewired with new mental pathways. The good news is that neural scientists believe that new neural loops can be formed within three to four months of focused attention and habituated practices.[10] The bad news is that you need to be willing to dedicate three to four months of focused attention and habituated practices. But that journey begins with small steps of turning your attention away from a screen and keeping your mind from being scattered by the distractions all around you.

In an apocryphal account, Walt Disney is reputed to

have said, "There is no magic in magic; it's all in the details."[11] While he might or might not have actually said this, there is no doubt that Disney's "Magic Kingdom" is rich with minutiae—intricate details that create awe and wonder. God has infused this world with wonder and awe, but most of that majesty is encapsulated in the small details all around you. That's where the "magic" is. Author Mike Cosper beautifully identifies the enchantment of God's rule in his book *Recapturing the Wonder*:[12]

> All is accomplished in Jesus. Once we accept that finished work, we'll find an ancient path that allows us to walk more and more deeply into the remade world of God's kingdom. As we take up ancient practices like prayer, Scripture reading, and fasting, we will see the way they confront our disenchanted way of knowing the world. **The kingdom is an enchanted place, and by God's grace, we can experience the kingdom's mystery and wonder throughout our lives.**

Jesus often prompted his disciples to think deeply about the details—the profound beauty—in the world around them. He was not being trite when he told us to consider the lilies (Matthew 6:28–30) and the ravens (Luke 12:24).

The Apostle Paul certainly encouraged other believers to engage their minds, to focus their thinking. We are to "be transformed by the renewal of" our minds (Romans 12:2) and "to be renewed in the spirit of [our] minds" (Ephesians 4:17–24). He even goes so far as to say that we are to "take every thought captive" (2 Corinthians 10:5).

Side Trip: Think About These Things

Read Philippians 4:8. Now go outside and find

something in your yard, street, or neighborhood to ponder. It could be a tree, a flower, the skyline, a cloud, or a blade of grass. Spend time looking at it. Pay attention to the small details. Look at the textures, colors, and patterns. Think about what is true. Consider what is honorable and lovely as you focus and hold your attention. Find the excellence lurking beneath the surface. God has infused the ordinary with a grandeur that is extraordinary. Mull over what is worthy of God's praise hiding below the veneer of "normal." Think about these things.

God's kingdom is well worth your attention. It deserves to be pondered frequently. When you open the treasure box hidden in the field, you'll find that there is no limit to the greatness of the kingdom. Don't speed past this part. Allow God's kingdom to recapture the territory of your mind away from YouTube binges and the tyranny of your Twitter feed.

When Jesus told the parable of the sower and the seed, he said that the seed is "the word of the kingdom" (Matthew 13:19). Most people living in a technological culture don't understand the value of a seed—it's just a seed. But in an agrarian society, people know that seeds are exceedingly valuable. Their very livelihood is hidden inside that tiny seed. Farmers understand something most others miss.

Consider what Jesus said can happen to this seed, the word of the kingdom. When people hear and understand the word of the kingdom, that is the good soil; those are the ones who bear fruit thirtyfold, sixtyfold, or a hundredfold (Matthew 13:18–23). Hearing and understanding the word of the kingdom, that's the nourishing earth. Hearing and understanding the word of the kingdom is what staves off the birds who would pluck it away. Hearing and understanding is what allows the taproot to grow deep and survive a scorching sun. Hearing and understanding is what rids the garden of the choking weeds.

God's kingdom is magnificent beyond description, but it is also understandable. You can't fully comprehend the fullness of his kingdom, but you can truly understand it. Why? Because God's kingdom is a really real kingdom.

Bible Trip: The Big Bag of Seeds

Take a tour through the Gospel of Matthew. With your journal, record the different kinds of parables Jesus used so that people could hear and understand "the word of the kingdom" (Matthew 13:19). Pay close attention to the small details of his parables. Make a list of the many ways Jesus helped his audience to ponder the greatness of his rule and reign by offering them various "seeds" of wisdom, insight, or challenging thoughts.

Begin by reading Matthew 13, which is like a little stack of seeds, but also look at Matthew 18:1–4, 21–35; Matthew 19:23–26; Matthew 20:1–16, 20–28; Matthew 22:1–14; and Matthew 25:1–13. The entire Gospel of Matthew seems to be a big bag of seeds, with the word of the kingdom spoken in many different forms so that people can hear and understand. Perhaps some of these seeds will find good soil in your heart as you hear and understand.

Small Group Guide

Spend a few gatherings of your small group digging into and discussing the kingdom parables of Matthew 13. With which parable do you connect most? Which parable is the most difficult to understand? What parables might Jesus tell today if he did his public ministry in the twenty-first century? How would he draw from our culture, workplaces, entertainment, and physical settings?

Value

In the hidden treasure parable, the man's heart was eventually captured by the tremendous value of the hidden box at his feet. Pondering the treasure with your mind leads to valuing the treasure with your heart.

Just before Jesus commanded us to "seek first the kingdom of God" (Matthew 6:33), he taught that our hearts are inseparably connected to what we treasure:

> *Do not lay up for yourselves treasures on earth, where moth and rust destroy and where thieves break in and steal, but lay up for yourselves treasures in heaven, where neither moth nor rust destroys and where thieves do not break in and steal. For where your treasure is, there your heart will be also.*
>
> *—Matthew 6:19–21*

If you treasure your investment portfolio, your heart will be located on the New York Stock Exchange. If you treasure a football team, your heart will be located in the stadium. If you treasure the prestige of a job, your heart will be located in the corner office.

If you've ever wondered where your heart is, simply look at how you spend your time, money, and energy. Consider what dominates your calendar. That is what you value. Open your wallet and watch what claims most of your dollars. That is what you value. Where are you willing to spill your blood, sweat, and tears? There is where your heart is. Make a quick survey of your thought life over the last few days. What dominates your attention? There you will find your heart.

Side Trip: Crashing Thoughts

Grab your journal and go outside. Clear your mind and stand in silence for a few minutes. As you try to be quiet, pay attention to the thoughts that crash into your head. Is there a nagging worry? A looming deadline? A persistent fear? A deep longing? Record the intrusive thoughts in your journal. They are pointers to what may be holding your heart hostage.

You can know that you've found the treasure hidden in the field when your heart—your will and your deepest affections—are captured by the kingdom. When you open your eyes and see the really real kingdom all around you, when you open your mind and ponder this truth, then you'll start to value what's in the box. Remember that you can't see what you don't seek. You'll see that the kingdom is a treasure of incalculable worth. You'll know that you've found God's great kingdom when you are ready to sacrifice, with joy, everything in your own little kingdom. Only then will you find your heart set on the kingdom.

The Trap of Inaction

In a perfect world, you would move seamlessly between valuing something and making it a priority in your life. However, we don't live in such a world.

How many sermons have you *loved* but then never acted on? How many New Year's resolutions have you broken before February? How many lofty goals have been torn down by the whirlwind of your daily life?

Danger lurks between what you value with your heart and what you put into practice in your life. This is the "Trap of Inaction."[13] This dark chasm holds the ruin of a million good ideas that never saw the light of day. It's where innovation and creativity languish. The Trap of Inaction is a vast collection of discarded twelve-step guides and five-year plans. None of them were ever put into motion. They were valued at one time, but not enough to matter. A value that doesn't make it beyond the Trap of Inaction is merely an aspiration, a dream. It will vanish like a vapor because it isn't embodied and lived out.

I've attended numerous leadership conferences with world-class speakers. My eyes have been opened to game-changing solutions to problems I didn't even know I had. I've sat in the conference seats, pondered the principles, and taken furious notes. Leaving the conferences, my to-do lists have been filled to the brim. But only weeks or months later, I've completely forgotten the things that were sure to change the world.

What happened? That fire hose of great ideas from the conference went directly into the Trap of Inaction. Not one of the ideas made it into the working of my daily life, and it wasn't from lack of value or pondering.

For many of us, the kingdom of God has fallen into that trap. We may see, ponder, and value God's kingdom, but then we sweep it into the yawning chasm where nothing actually happens, nothing changes, nothing grows. Other priorities pull us into the Trap of Inaction. It is a black hole with a nearly irresistible gravity of its own.

The Gospel of Luke records people who encountered Jesus but got sucked into the Trap of Inaction. They failed to establish his kingdom as their highest priority. They always had a convenient excuse or urgent conflict (Luke 9:57–62). Sadly, these people were aware of, pondered, and valued the kingdom, but they failed to establish a new, singular priority in their lives.

Later in Luke's gospel, Jesus told a similar story about a wedding banquet. This time, however, the warning is even more stark. Jesus taught that people would miss the splendor of the kingdom because of excuses and life circumstances (Luke 14:15–24). In the story, one person had bought a field. Another was newly married. Another had bought some oxen. These people were not ready to sell all, so they were swallowed by the Trap of Inaction. In Jesus' sobering parable of the wedding banquet, there were some who traded the kingdom for cattle.

In the journey to find God's kingdom as the hidden treasure, you certainly need to engage your sight, mind, and heart, no doubt. But you can't move beyond the Trap of Inaction until you engage your hands by establishing new habits, new ways of living, and new priorities that get worked into daily life. Habituated practices allow you to cross the Trap of Inaction. Your pursuit of the kingdom moves from sight, thought, and heart into the very work of your hands. God's kingdom comes in your life when his rule becomes embodied in your practices and shapes your priorities.

Prioritize

The parable of the hidden treasure is remarkable because the man was able to cross over the Trap of Inaction. He did this by reprioritizing his life and selling his possessions. This detail is crucial:

> *The kingdom of heaven is like treasure hidden in a field, which a man found and covered up. **Then in his joy he goes and sells** all that he has and buys that field.*
> **—Matthew 13:44**

At this point, the man had one priority. His world had been turned upside down, and he came out of that realizing that only one thing mattered: getting rid of what doesn't matter.

Every other goal, dream, and drive was swept aside for

the single priority of selling all. He crossed the Trap of Inaction, and the value of his heart energized the work of his hands. He was prioritizing.

This was no drudgery for him. He was not weighed down by the drab tyranny of duty. "In his joy" (Matthew 13:44), he sold all that he had. Perhaps he felt some sense of loss for what was being sold, but he most certainly found the thrill of what was to be bought.

He didn't let people talk him out of it. He didn't let aspiration get in the way. His calendar was cleared. All other commitments fell to the wayside. He had one priority, a singular focus, and he acted with joy.

Joy is a major marker that you've found the kingdom of God. Perhaps it is *the* marker. If you're not willing to sell everything in your life for the sake of acquiring God's kingdom, then you haven't found the kingdom. Or, if you're following the parable, then you haven't pondered it and understood the full value of the treasure at your feet.

If the sum total of your spiritual life is a laundry list of religious duties to check off, then you haven't found the kingdom. A list of obligations isn't worth selling all for, is it? And it certainly doesn't have the mark of joy; it's just drudgery. Joy is the signal of a person who has found God's kingdom as an unexpected treasure.

Imagine that you got a phone call from a global titan of technology. He said, "Listen, I want to offer you a deal. I'll give you the full contents of my bank account, but in return, you need to give me the full contents of yours."

Assume that the phone call is not a scam. You would instantly have a new priority in your life. You'd make a beeline to your bank to set up the wire transfer. Nothing would get in your way, and you wouldn't move as if there were some boring duty before you. In your joy, you'd skip to the bank to swap accounts with the billionaire.

We may laugh at this scenario for how ridiculous it is, yet God makes us this very offer every day. Jesus is not scamming you when he tells the parable of the hidden treasure. The kingdom of God is *really and truly* available, and it's better than anything we could ever know or expect.

*And the kingdom and the dominion and the greatness of the kingdoms under the whole heaven **shall be given to the people of the saints of the Most High**; his kingdom shall be an everlasting kingdom, and all dominions shall serve and obey him.*

—Daniel 7:27

*Therefore let us be grateful for **receiving a kingdom** that cannot be shaken, and thus let us offer to God acceptable worship, with reverence and awe....*

—Hebrews 12:28

Inside the treasure hidden in the field are all of "the kingdoms under the whole heaven" (Daniel 7:27). God intends to give you everything he has in return for everything you have. He is asking everything from you: to have no possession more important to you than he is, to hold no goal higher than his goals, to have no priority more urgent than his priorities, to worship no god other than him.

Side Trip: Under the Whole Heaven

Grab your journal and go outside to a spot where you can get the best view of the sky. Take a few minutes to scan the wide expanse of sun, blue sky, and clouds above. Really look. Pay close attention to the small details of color and texture. Now consider again Daniel 7:27, which says that "the greatness of the kingdoms under the whole heaven shall be given to the people of the saints of the Most High." Everything you see under the heavens above is part of your inheritance in the kingdom. Soak that in. Record a few of your thoughts that this incredible promise evokes. Give God thanks for his tremendous kindness in this gift.

It doesn't matter what you lose if everything you gain is worth far more. The parable of the hidden treasure is even more outlandish than the phone call from the tech billionaire because God isn't just offering us the stuff of a material kingdom. It's not just crowns, thrones, power, resources, or territory that's crammed into that hidden treasure box (although those things are included). Jesus himself is part of the hidden treasure. God is giving us his Son!

He who did not spare his own Son but gave him up for us all, how will he not also with him graciously give us all things?
—Romans 8:32

For God so loved the world, that he gave his only Son, that whoever believes in him should not perish but have eternal life.
—John 3:16

A loving, personal, eternal communion with the King of kings is included in the hidden treasure. The very Son of God has already been given for you. How could you not sell all in your life for this treasure?

God is right now calling you to a new priority in your life. Jesus said, "Seek first the kingdom of God and his righteousness, and all these things will be added to you"

(Matthew 6:33). This commandment is imperative because you can't see what you don't seek, and what you don't see can never drive the priorities in your life.

Own (Sell!)

We've reached the end of the parable of the hidden treasure. The man joyfully sold all, then went and bought that field. The treasure and everything that went with it was all his.

A few years ago, I was teaching the parable of the hidden treasure to some young adults. At this point in the parable, a student asked me a question that stopped me dead in my tracks.

He said, "But what about grace? How does God's grace fit into the parable of the hidden treasure? Because acquiring the kingdom can't be based on a financial transaction like a real estate deal."

This is a brilliant question because it points to a real tension. If you press the parable of the hidden treasure too far, it becomes just a business deal. But the parable is about grace. The Greek word for grace is χάρις (pronounced *charis*), and it has the meaning of a gift or kindness given freely.[14] Grace is unearned favor given freely.

So where is grace in a kingdom that we have to buy? Consider this. Everything that you have belongs to God—all of it. He already owns everything—every penny, every car, every home. Anything you have has been given to you out of kindness as a stewardship, not an ownership. For a while, he entrusts all you have to you, by grace.

When you sell all to acquire the kingdom, you move from one grace to another. You are not losing anything if you don't have anything to begin with. A gambler would say that you are playing with house money.

When you sell all, you are merely returning to God

what already belongs to him. Then, in return, he gives you the kingdom—by grace! None of it is earned. None of it is merited. All of it is a gift. From beginning to end, the parable of the hidden treasure is a grand story of the God who is so generous that he only wants to give and give and give.

When you understand that the sum total of everything in your life is a gift, then you can joyfully relinquish that to receive an even greater gift. When you "own" the kingdom as a treasure hidden in the field, it comes purely through a gift exchange, by grace, from first to last.

If I haven't done so already, I now need to take a little liberty with the parable. I think that there's an unspoken ending that Jesus had in mind but didn't express. The parable should really end with the man putting up a "For Sale" sign. He has acquired the kingdom. He knows that it's a gift that's not to be hoarded, but given away. When you live in the kingdom of God, you become his real estate agent who seeks to bring others into the kingdom.

Don't you wonder about the foolishness of somebody selling a field that has a treasure? The parable only makes sense if the treasure is inexhaustible and is meant to be shared, not hoarded. When the man purchased the field, he took a moment to relish the "Sold" sign. He delighted in the treasure that was now his. Then he realized that he could have an even greater treasure if he made it possible for others to find the treasure hidden in the field. He took down the "Sold" sign and put up a "For Sale" sign to give away what he had been given.

This is the character of God's really real kingdom. He is supremely generous. His desire is for all of "the kingdoms under the whole heaven [to] be given to the people of the saints of the Most High" (Daniel 7:27). Owning it really means selling it by giving it away to others walking up and down the field.

Evangelism is not just telling people to believe in Jesus

so that their sins are forgiven and they can go to heaven. It's far greater than that. As evangelists, we are agents of the King who bring the good news that the kingdom of God is available to one and all. The good news far surpasses a message of repentance. The good news is that King Jesus really is reigning and wants to include you in his coming kingdom. When that kingdom comes, it will be given to us! *That* is the good news of the kingdom. And when we own that kingdom, that hidden treasure, we shall joyfully seek to pass on that gift to others. In the economy of God's kingdom, you don't lose what you give away. You only gain it to an even greater degree.

Journeying to the Kingdom

The writers of the New Testament frequently drew on the images of Israel being delivered from slavery and led to the promised land. Their journey out of Egypt and crossing the Red Sea was their "baptism." After forty years of wandering in the wilderness, they miraculously crossed the flooded River Jordan and were led by YHWH in a military conquest of the promised land.

When they entered the promised land, there was territory to explore and capture in order for Israel to become the "kingdom of priests" (Exodus 19:6) that would bring God's blessing to all of the families of the earth (Genesis 12:1–3). All of this was to be beneath the rule of the Son of David, sitting on an eternal throne (2 Samuel 7:16).

In many ways, your journey of faith mirrors Israel's journey of faith. You, too, need to be set free from the slavery of sin, being baptized into the new life of Christ (Romans 6:3–4). You, too, face temptations of falling away before you enter the goodness of a restful Promised Land (Hebrews 3:7–19). You, too, are called to a kingdom of priests that brings the blessings of God to all of the families in the world (1 Peter 2:9; Revelation 5:10; Matthew

28:16–20).

Finally, you, too, face personal and corporate battles in order to come into the fullness of God's kingdom in your life (Romans 8:37; Romans 12:21; 1 Corinthians 15:57; 2 Corinthians 10:3–5; Ephesians 6:10–20; 1 Timothy 6:12; 1 John 4:4).

You have territory to explore, land to conquer. When God's kingdom comes, it must displace other kingdoms that are established against it. The heart of the question is not "How can I get victory over my sin?" That's only a small part of God's kingdom coming in your life and sphere of influence.

God wants to do something much greater in you and through you than just conquer your sin habits. There are five main territories he will partner with you in conquering. In this way, his kingdom will come in your life, and you will find a fuller, more satisfying, more thrilling life of faith than you could ever have imagined.

Territory 1: Seeing the Really Real Kingdom All Around You

The first territory to conquer is "Seeing the Really Real Kingdom." We've already given considerable attention to this, but it's worth a recap.

We all start by being blind to God's kingdom, but we're commanded to "seek first" that kingdom (Matthew 6:33). Seeking the kingdom begins with becoming aware that it exists, stubbing your toe on that box in the field. If you don't seek God's kingdom, you won't see it in your life. Your pondering of that kingdom will require paying attention to the real world around you. With diligence, you can find that God's kingdom is on full display in practically every nook and cranny of your life—if you know what to look for.

You know what I'm talking about if you've ever looked

at one of those blurry posters at the mall. What initially seems to be a mishmash of nonsense suddenly leaps out at you with the proper focus. The image has been there all the time, but if you don't know what to look for or how to look, it's hidden. That's similar to God's kingdom.

Territory 2: Living in the Kingdom Story

The next territory to conquer is changing the personal narrative of your life. You are called to *live in* that real kingdom. The Lord's Prayer of "Your kingdom come" (Matthew 6:10) is so much more than a rote ritual to mutter before bedtime. This is the narrative of all the Bible, and it's to become the narrative of your life. You may be a professional athlete, an engineer, a student, a gardener, a stay-at-home parent, or a politician. Regardless of your vocation, the story of your life as a Christian must be shaped by your citizenship in God's really real kingdom.

The personal story you tell yourself has immense power over practically every aspect of your life. Some personal narratives are centered on achievement: "I'm trying to become a successful businessman." Others focus on key relationships: "I'm devoting my world to my kids as a good parent." Other narratives are aimed at a lifestyle: "I can't wait until I can get a season's pass to ski this winter." All of these are good, but if the story of your life is not wrapped up in the story of God's kingdom coming, then you'll miss out on the greatest endeavor of all time.

Something happens when you adopt a kingdom narrative as the personal story of your life. You wake up in the morning and understand that every breath, every word, every action, every connection has eternal implications. A kingdom narrative shatters the boredom of ritualistic religious duty.

If you are a follower of Jesus, then you've been baptized into *him*. That means you have been submerged and immersed into his story, and his story is centered on his kingdom. For God's kingdom to come in your life, the territory of your personal narrative must be conquered by the narrative of God's kingdom.

Territory 3: Trading in the Kingdom Economy of Abundance

God owns everything—not most things, but everything (Psalm 24:1). Everything under the sun and over the sun and in the sun is his. Every resource is his. Every blade of grass bears his name. Every dime in every bank account ultimately falls under his claim.

Real kingdoms have real economies, systems of exchange and allocation of scarce resources. Since God's kingdom is a really real kingdom, it also has an economy. But God's economy is based on abundance, not scarcity.

As a citizen of God's kingdom, you have access to resources that are not limited. This isn't a cheap version of a false "prosperity gospel," which views faith as a ticket to wealth, ease, and comfort. But with God's abundance, there is a rich life even in poverty, pain, and suffering.

As you conquer the often hostile territory of your money, resources, and time, you become more and more generous, like your King. Trading in God's kingdom economy means that you trust that he will always give you what you need to be generous. No matter how much you have, you will always have enough to give. Beware of the greed, envy, and fear that will oppose you every step of the way. A scarcity mindset must be overcome in order for you to flourish in the economy of God's kingdom.

Fear not, little flock, for it is your Father's good pleasure to give you the kingdom. Sell your possessions, and give to the needy. Provide yourselves with moneybags that do not grow old, with a treasure in the heavens that does not fail, where

no thief approaches and no moth destroys. For where your
treasure is, there will your heart be also.

—Luke 12:32–34

Territory 4: Following the Kingdom Law of Love

The next territory to conquer is following the kingdom law of love. Real kingdoms have real laws, and because God's kingdom is really real, it also has a real law: love.

Jesus summed up all of the Old Testament law and prophets with love as the Great Commandment (Matthew 22:34–40). Jesus also issued a New Commandment that we are to love in the same fashion as he has loved us (John 13:34–35).

Without love, seeing the kingdom of God all around you makes no sense. Without love, it's impossible to live a kingdom narrative in your world. Without love, you won't have the drive to be generous as an active trading partner in God's kingdom economy of abundance.

Love is the action that brings Christ's goodness to others around you. As his rule and reign increase in your life, his love captures the territory of your thoughts, motives, desires, and ambitions. Then his love will overflow to others around you as his goodness increases. This is how his kingdom comes.

Territory 5: Stewarding Kingdom Authority

Finally, after you learn to see God's kingdom, live an active role of love in the kingdom story, and trade in the kingdom economy, then you will be empowered more and more with the King's authority. The character of his throne is to share and delegate responsibility. This is clearly seen in the Great Commission of Jesus:

Now the eleven disciples went to Galilee, to the mountain to which Jesus had directed them. And when they saw him they worshiped him, but some doubted. And Jesus came and said to them, "All authority in heaven and on earth has been given to me. Go therefore and make disciples of all nations, baptizing them in the name of the Father and of the Son and of the Holy Spirit, teaching them to observe all that I have commanded you. And behold, I am with you always, to the end of the age."

—Matthew 28:16–20

The authority of Christ delegated to his followers enables Christ's kingdom to come. It's not your own strength, but you are entrusted with a measure of authority from the King of kings to act on his behalf. You are granted vice-regent status from the Son of David, who sits on an eternal throne. You are befriended by the person who holds the highest authority in the universe, and he lends you some of that authority to steward in his name on his behalf. In fact, the Apostle Paul says that we are seated with Jesus (Ephesians 2:6) and join him at the very top of the universal organization chart, "far above all rule and authority and power and dominion, and above every name that is named" (Ephesians 1:21).

As you see the really real kingdom all around you and live a kingdom narrative, you will grow into the authority entrusted to you. Pride is the great enemy you face in this battle because as you receive authority, you'll be tempted to claim it for your own and establish your own kingdom apart from God.

The Wrecking Ball

Seeking God's kingdom poses a risk that may be more serious than a grizzly bear encounter or downtown traffic. Let's call this danger "The Wrecking Ball."

When you seek God's kingdom, you aren't just sight-seeing as a passive passenger on a tourist bus. You are seeking for God's kingdom to become established in your life, and this is an invitation to disaster.

The Lord's Prayer is a wrecking ball. Caution must be used when praying this in genuine faith.

> *Our Father in heaven, hallowed be your name.* **Your kingdom come, your will be done, on earth as it is in heaven.** *Give us this day our daily bread, and forgive us our debts, as we also have forgiven our debtors. And lead us not into temptation, but deliver us from evil.*
> **—Matthew 6:9–13**

In asking God to establish his rule and reign in your life, you are asking for the progressive destruction of all things that are currently outside of God's rule and reign.

When one kingdom conquers another kingdom, the new ruler removes all signs of the power and authority of the deposed ruler. Portraits and statues are taken down, tossed into a heap, and burned. The coat of arms on the royal letterhead is changed. The old signet ring is melted. All tokens of the old monarchy are obliterated. Then the new ruler places his emblems of authority throughout the realm. The old kingdom is demolished to make way for the new.

What are the areas in your life that are not currently under God's rule and reign? Where have you reserved territory for yourself? Have you decided that the King may rule all of your life except for your place of work? Are you wanting God to leave that under your control? Then, by all means, *do not* pray, "Your kingdom come"!

The decision may not be conscious, but have you decided, in practice, to exclude the royal authority of Jesus from your social life, your thought life, your sexuality, your ministry, your future plans, your current schemes, or your past hurts? Caution! When you genuinely pray, "Your kingdom come," you are asking Jesus to be your everything. You are asking him to be the Lord of your life. You are asking him to take up residence in your inner being and to lead you in all things. "Your kingdom come" changes you; it molds you into his likeness for his glory.

If you don't want this, then *do not* pray, "Your kingdom come"! If you want to preserve your little, fleeting fiefdom, I strongly caution you not to pray the Lord's Prayer. If there is any part of your life, any earthly connection, any position, any dream or hope, any passion that is too valuable to entrust to God's loving sovereignty, then definitely do not pray, "Your kingdom come." If you do, the wrecking ball will swing, and the King will destroy the temporary, fading, and small idols in your kingdom and replace them with what is eternal, lasting, and invaluable in his kingdom.

In a letter to the Corinthians, the Apostle Paul gave us fair warning and legal notice of the destruction of all things belonging to the kingdom of this earth:

> But in fact Christ has been raised from the dead, the first-fruits of those who have fallen asleep. For as by a man came death, by a man has come also the resurrection of the dead. For as in Adam all die, so also in Christ shall all be made alive. But each in his own order: Christ the first-fruits, then at his coming those who belong to Christ. Then comes the end, when he delivers the kingdom to God the Father after destroying every rule and every authority and power. For he must reign until he has put all his enemies under his feet. The last enemy to be destroyed is death. For "God has put all things in subjection under his feet."
> **—1 Corinthians 15:20–27a**

Don't worry, though, because the Lord's Prayer is

perfectly harmless when not mixed with faith. In complete ease and comfort, you can repeat the prayer like a mantra or go through the motions. You can recite it like the alphabet if you aren't putting your faith in Jesus. The safety is on when your trusting confidence in the King is off. Or, better yet, just don't pray the Lord's Prayer at all if you don't truly want the Lord's kingdom to come in your life.

But what if you do want Jesus, the King of kings, to rule your life? What if you want to discover that the kingdom of heaven is like a treasure hidden in a field that's worth having a liquidation sale of all your worldly assets to purchase? Then, by all means, day and night, in urgent faith, pray, "Your kingdom come." Just wear a hard hat. Your life won't be safe, but it will be good.

CHAPTER TWO FIELD TRIP

Bird Watching

Warning: bird watching is *highly* addictive. Once you become a birder, there is no going back.

Jesus loved birds, and he told his disciples to pay careful attention to them. As they struggled to understand the really real kingdom Jesus was inaugurating, he encouraged them to "look at the birds" (Matthew 6:26). I believe that he actually meant what he said, so for this field trip, you are going to become a bird watcher. Birds are literally everywhere: your yard, parking lots, cities, forests, lakes, highways, high mountains, deserts, and oceans. They are hiding in plain sight, always and everywhere. Everywhere you go, you can find a huge variety of birds. My wife and I have seen 125 different birds in our backyard alone, just by paying attention.

Field Trip Details

Travel: Minimal to extensive

Cost: No cost to expensive

Time: Minimal to extensive

Physical Demands: Minimal to rigorous

Gear: Binoculars, bird identification book, birding apps for your phone

Key Scriptures to Guide Your Trip: Genesis 1:1–31; Job 12:7–12; Psalm 148:7–12; Psalm 50:1–11; Jeremiah 8:7; Matthew 6:25–34

Schedule this field trip now. Put it on your calendar!
Day: _____
Time: _____
People invited to join me: _____
_____
_____

With only a little attention, you'll soon see that birds are not "just birds." They are living, thriving, creative, intelligent, and hilarious. Birds are tremendously varied. There are tiny, flitting hummingbirds and massive, soaring eagles. Some are well camouflaged and elusive, like fox sparrows. Others are colorful and brazen, like rock pigeons.

A pair of binoculars is not essential but very helpful to successful birding. If you don't have them, then somebody you know probably does. Even a pair of low-end binoculars will prove useful. Soon after you get hooked on bird watching, you'll want to buy a decent pair that you'll never leave home without.

There are a number of mobile phone apps that will help you to identify the birds all around you. I've found these to be most useful:

- *Merlin Bird ID*: A free app by the Cornell Ornithology Laboratory. With only a few observations, such as size, color, and location, the app provides a list of likely birds to help you narrow down the choices for identification. This app includes pictures, bird sounds, and excellent descriptions.

- *Bird's Eye*: A free app that shows you in real time the birds that have been sighted around you based on GPS locations. Relatively inexpensive upgrades to the app add additional features, such as bird sounds, pictures, and more elaborate descriptions.

- *eBird*: Another free app by the Cornell Ornithology Lab that lets you record your bird observations and build life lists. Your observations are sent to the Lab as a part of the largest "citizen science" project on earth. Join hundreds of thousands of other birders whose observations and checklists create a massive global database that scientists use for critical research.

If you are trying to spend less time on a mobile phone, there are a number of excellent bird identification books. I recommend anything by David Allen Sibley, Roger Tory Peterson, Kenn Kaufman, or Stan Tekiela.

Seeing the Kingdom Connection

Bird watching slows you down. When you're looking for birds in a park, at a beach, or in a forest, you listen as much as look. Your pace drops. Every small sound becomes a clue in the hunt. As you grow more confident in bird watching, you will find that worries, cares, and distractions have less of a grip on your mind. Your breathing slows. Your heart settles. Your thoughts clear.

In his parable of the sower and the seed, Jesus taught

that the seed of "the word of the kingdom" can be strangled by thorns:

> Hear then the parable of the sower: When anyone hears **the word of the kingdom** and does not understand it, the evil one comes and snatches away what has been sown in his heart. This is what was sown along the path. As for what was sown on rocky ground, this is the one who hears the word and immediately receives it with joy, yet he has no root in himself, but endures for a while, and when tribulation or persecution arises on account of the word, immediately he falls away. **As for what was sown among thorns, this is the one who hears the word, but the cares of the world and the deceitfulness of riches choke the word, and it proves unfruitful.** As for what was sown on good soil, this is the one who hears the word and understands it. He indeed bears fruit and yields, in one case a hundredfold, in another sixty, and in another thirty.
>
> **—Matthew 13:18–23**

In order to see the really real kingdom of God, we need to ensure that "the word of the kingdom" is not being choked by "the cares of the world." Bird watching isn't just fun; it can also become a spiritual discipline that roots out the thorns by helping you to set aside the cares of the world, just for a bit. In that quiet and calm of seeing a Dark-eyed Junco or Spotted Towhee, you may also begin to see God's kingdom.

Finally, as another way to attune your sight, when you read the Bible, pay attention to how often birds pop up. I think that the Lord *loves* birds. He mentions birds six times in the first chapter of Genesis alone. You'll find a steady rhythm of birds in scripture if you pay attention.

Remember that the goal of your field trips isn't just to find birds, but to make connections with the kingdom. These trips are lessons in seeing and experiencing your real world to help you be intentional in seeing and experiencing God's really real kingdom.

At first, bird watching will be slow, clumsy, and a bit frustrating. But I remember the first *aha!* moment when I was able to identify my first bird: a Black-capped Chickadee. Then I was hooked. It was thrilling and worth the fumbling. When you start seeking God's kingdom, there will be an *aha!* moment when you stub your toe on the treasure hidden in the field. Once you see what you seek, you'll be hooked.

Questions for Reflection

1. What sticks out from this field trip or is a new idea for you?

2. What questions have come out of this field trip? What doesn't make sense to you?

3. How do you see Jesus and his kingdom in this experience?

4. How can you apply this to your life and take a next step?

5. What will you talk to God and other people about?

After this field trip, circle where you are right now in your journey to find God's kingdom as a hidden treasure.

| Blind | Aware | Ponder | Value | Trap of Inaction | Prioritize | Own/Sell |

Journal: Spend some time in your journal to record further thoughts.

SMALL GROUP GUIDE

Chapter Two Discussion Questions

Key Scripture
Parable of the Hidden Treasure
Matthew 13:44

1. *You can't see what you're not looking for.* Have you been blind to God's kingdom, or do you observe it all around you? Would you describe yourself as missing the treasure or as having started on the journey of pursuing it?

2. What are the greatest distractions that you face, whether from outside your control or self-imposed? In what contexts or situations do you find it difficult to ponder, and what is one practical way you can retrain your brain to focus?

3. If an outsider were to evaluate your life solely based on how you spend your time, money, energy, and attention, what would they conclude is your treasure in life? Describe a time when you determined to reorder your priorities, implement a new idea, or begin a new habit, only to become stuck in the Trap of Inaction.

4. Is your walk with God characterized by duty and drudgery or by joy and wonder? Do you think of Jesus himself as the treasure? How is knowing him better than anything you would give up to acquire the treasure?

5. If you had to sum up the story of your life in one sentence, what would it be? Does your personal story reflect the kingdom story? Why or why not?

6. Does your giving (both financial and of other resources) reflect a belief that God will supply all that you need?

7. Are you ready to pray, "Your kingdom come," over every area of your life? Be honest and realistic. Spend time in prayer and soul-searching about those areas where you are still holding on to your own kingdom and are not ready for the "wrecking ball" of Christ's kingdom to come in and disrupt your "safe" and controlled life.

8. Discuss your experience on the field trip. What did you learn? What surprised you? What challenged you?

Chapter Two Notes

CHAPTER THREE

The Hidden Kingdom

On November 16, 2014, my wife, Katie, and I celebrated our first wedding anniversary. At the Willows Inn on Lummi Island, we enjoyed what was by far the best meal of our lives. The food was so good, so well crafted, so much better than anything I'd eaten before. I felt like, for the first time, I had eaten *real* salmon because it was so good. Every piece of salmon I'd eaten prior seemed to be a cheap imitation knock-off of that small, delicious morsel. This was really real salmon—more real than the pale pink fish hermetically sealed in foil and shelved for years. And to think that all those years, I thought that the salmon I was eating was as good as it got. How wrong I was!

Most people have mislabeled the really real kingdom of God. They hold up history's millennia of empires and governments and say, "See! These are real kingdoms. These are as good as it gets."

To a degree, they are right. The kingdoms of this world have many elements of a kingdom, but they are all shadows and imitations of the really real kingdom of God. We ought to look to the really real kingdom of Jesus as the model for all earthly kingdoms, not the reverse. Yes, the kingdoms of the earth are real, but they only barely have enough ingredients to qualify them as kingdoms.

Like any other kingdom on earth, God's kingdom has real citizens, real territory, and real laws. The economy of God's kingdom is real and thriving. The Lord of the kingdom is really alive and really enthroned.

The kingdom of God has a story, a true story, that will utterly change yours when you start living out that true kingdom story. The Bible focuses on that story, each of its subplots and characters playing a supporting role. It's the story of God's kingdom coming on earth as it is in heaven.

What further separates the kingdom of God as *more real* is its permanence. It has an eternal quality that makes the kingdoms of this world seem like vapor. Often God's kingdom feels a dream, but there will come a day when all of the kingdoms of this world will seem like a dream, and there will be only one left standing. When you start to experience and live in God's kingdom, you'll find it to be more real than all the others.

But you've already experienced this in your life. You already know it deep down. Remember the times when you've dipped into behaviors or habits that you knew to be destructive, but you did it anyway? Yes, sin offers a real pleasure for a short time, but compared to the pleasure found with Jesus, sin's joy is a cheap knock-off. Sin's joy seems real in that moment, but it's a vapor. The joy that God gives is lasting! Remember David's words about true joy:

> *You make known to me the path of life; in your presence there is fullness of joy; at your right hand are pleasures forevermore.*
> **—Psalm 16:11**

We're only beginning to unpack why the really real

kingdom of God is like a treasure worth selling all to acquire. The big problem is that the treasure is hidden.

The Hidden Kingdom

We are faced with a massive challenge. The really real kingdom of God is often hidden—hidden because it's not looked for. God's kingdom is easily overlooked and far underestimated.

In parables, Jesus said that the kingdom is like a tiny mustard seed (Mark 4:30–32; Luke 13:18–19), a pearl clamped inside a clam (Matthew 13:45–46), and invisible leaven inside a lump of dough (Matthew 13:33). To his Jewish audience, even these parables had a double meaning that was hidden to many. Mustard shrubs were annoying weeds, a nuisance to farmers. Pearls were ceremonially filthy products of unclean creatures. Leaven violated sacred mold laws of the Jewish religion. So the Hebrew Messiah's message was that the kingdom of God, *his* kingdom, seemed to be not only insignificant, but also unexpected, perhaps even unwanted, annoying, or disgusting to his own people.[15]

On the eve of his crucifixion, Jesus insisted that his disciples look at the trees around them. Seeing those trees could help direct their attention to the kingdom:

> And [Jesus] told them a parable: "Look at the fig tree, and all the trees. As soon as they come out in leaf, you see for yourselves and know that the summer is already near. So also, when you see these things taking place, you know that the kingdom of God is near.
> **—Luke 21:29–31**

In all of these parables and stories, Jesus sent a clear message, if not a warning, about his kingdom. Though it is near, it can be overlooked. We can't see what we're not seeking.

In Plain Sight

How can something so obvious be hidden? A recent episode from my pastoral ministry is a glaring example.

To set up the story, you need to know that I have rocks. I'm a geologist, after all, so I have rocks. Lots of rocks. If we're being honest, I probably have too many rocks. But I'm still thrilled whenever a new rock is added to the collection. There are rocks in every room of my house. I collect rocks to mark significant events: my son's baptism, my wedding day, my dad's seventy-fifth birthday, my wife's brain surgery. A stone commemorates nearly every milestone in my life. Even my office has a rock on almost every surface, samples from all over the world. People who know me are tasked to collect a rock for me when they travel.

Recently I had a meeting with a church member in my office. After an hour of conversation, my former career came up, and I mentioned that I was a geologist, explaining why there were a few hundred rocks all around the office.

The church member gasped. Her eyes popped wide open, and she even let out a little shriek. "I didn't even see these rocks!" She was stunned, and, frankly, so was I. She had spent an hour in that room and even had to move one of the rocks on the coffee table to set down her coffee, but it never entered her mind that there were rocks everywhere around her. She couldn't see what she wasn't looking for. After all, why should she look for rocks in a pastor's office? I often ask myself this same question. But once I pointed out the rocks, they became obvious. They were hiding in plain sight. She felt a bit foolish, but we both laughed.

The kingdom is hidden in this same way. It's here in plain sight, but not everyone can see it because not everyone is looking for it.

Our brains have a phenomenal ability to filter out what enters through our senses, especially our sight and hearing. Our eyes and ears take in far more than our brains can process, so our brains only bring to consciousness what is a priority and what we've told it to pay attention to. Everything else vanishes from the world we experience.

This happened when I bought a Subaru Outback. Suddenly, it seemed as if everybody was driving an Outback. Was there sudden mass interest in this specific vehicle? No, Outbacks just popped up on my radar because I was paying attention to them now that I owned one.

Kingdoms of this world also have invisible qualities and become hidden. Think of your city government as a type of kingdom, with the mayor as a type of ruler. You can go through life fully unaware of the exercise of power, authority, law, civic order, and provision all around you. You drive on roads but don't see the hand of the Public Works Department with delegated authority from city government to do the work. Every inch of pavement and sidewalk is the result of the government allocating resources for the good of the citizens. Laws in the city exist, but they usually recede to the background until they are egregiously violated.

If you're living on a grid, then every drop of water from a faucet, spark of electricity from an outlet, or whiff of natural gas from the stove is delivered through a carefully designed government infrastructure. The waste from your toilet magically disappears into an underground network of sewers overseen by your city government. This "kingdom" of your city government is nearly always invisible, but it is hiding in plain sight. It will remain invisible until you start looking for it. It will evade your attention until you pay attention.

God's kingdom is no different. You need to pay attention to the elements of God's rule and reign in order to make the invisible kingdom appear from its hiding place in plain view.

The Invisible Homeless King

During my trip to Israel in 2018, I was with a group that visited Capernaum on the northern shore of the Sea of Galilee. Hundreds of thousands of people go to this location yearly. They stand where Jesus stood in the ruins of the synagogue where he taught. They gape over the unearthed ruins where Jesus healed Peter's mother-in-law.

I was shocked by my personal yearning and deep desire for physical proximity to the millennia-old events of this Jewish rabbi. But on the tour, nearly everybody missed one of the most important features of Capernaum—Jesus himself.

There's a small park at the entrance to Capernaum. Most of the masses of people rush past a bench with the bronze cast of a sleeping figure beneath a blanket. We've all walked by a myriad of people like this—homeless, destitute, invisible. We don't see them.

16

But for some reason, the figure caught my attention. I stopped and looked, and an important detail jumped out. There were a pair of feet poking out of the blanket of the sleeping statue. The feet had the nail wounds of a crucified man.

As people rushed by in hopes of touching a place where Jesus once lived and performed ministry, they nearly all missed the figure of Jesus himself. Jesus was hidden in plain view on a park bench.

The statue is a bronze cast by the sculptor Timothy Schmaltz, who has installed dozens of these "Homeless Jesus" statues around the world.[18] The power of this unusual statue of the King of kings rests in the obscure humility, not the opulent majesty. Apart from a meager 120 disciples gathered after his resurrection (Acts 1:15), Jesus was nearly overlooked and missed as the long-awaited Messiah, the coming king who would bring restoration to the world.

The Gospel of Luke encapsulates the essence of this King and kingdom hiding in plain sight:

*Being asked by the Pharisees when the kingdom of God
would come, [Jesus] answered them, "The kingdom of God
is not coming in ways that can be observed, nor will they
say, 'Look, here it is!' or 'There!' for behold, the kingdom of
God is in the midst of you."*

—Luke 17:20–21

Nobody was anticipating a kingdom ruled by a suffering King. Nobody was looking for a kingdom that would be inaugurated by a rejected Messiah.

The casual reader of this Luke account would be tempted to say, "Aha! The kingdom can't be seen! It must be some future heaven that has no place on earth here and now."

But the careful reader notices that Jesus was addressing *the Pharisees* in his response. There was a subtext implied as he addressed the religious rulers, who had murder in their hearts: "The kingdom is not coming in ways that can be observed *by you!*"

These Pharisees had been dogging Jesus throughout Luke's Gospel, and Jesus had accused them of being grumblers (Luke 15:2), hypocrites (Luke 12:1; 13:15), and wicked servants (Luke 12:41–48). Clearly the hardness and cruelty of their hearts would prevent them from seeing God's kingdom, even when it was standing in front of them.

The Pharisees and the other elite, greedy religious rulers could not see what was before their eyes. But the disciples and the ones who humbly bowed their knees before Jesus could see in an unraveling and marvelous process. Indeed, the disciples were *commanded* to seek the kingdom as lowly sheep (Luke 12:32–34). It is the humble flock of Jesus' followers who will not only see the kingdom, but also receive the kingdom as a gift from their Father in heaven. The one who has a heart inclined to be generous to the homeless person on a bench will be able to see the Homeless King and his kingdom come.

Why Are We Blind? The Seven Veils

At first, we all are blind to the kingdom. I've felt angry at times because it took almost twenty years of my Christian life for me to see that God's kingdom is really real. But there are powerful forces behind our blindness, both natural and supernatural.

Before the advent of our modern ubiquitous media, most citizens of a kingdom would never personally see the king. Why? Because the king spent most of his time enclosed in his palace or walled off in his throne room. To the average citizen, the king was invisible, yet the rule of that king would be undeniable and as certain as the light of the sun on the citizens.

His emissaries were always visible. His laws and decrees were carried out and upheld with reward or broken under punishment. Conflicts with other kingdoms were handled and addressed. The effects of rule and reign proved that there was someone ruling and reigning, even if the king was not seen outside of his palace. Citizens could see evidence of the king through the effective execution of his will. The more widespread and encompassing his will, the more glory and praise would be ascribed to the king, even though he was unseen.

We need to look for the effects of the reign of Jesus, the King of kings, so that we can see the kingdom. If Jesus the King personally chooses to be enthroned in his unseen heavenly throne room for a time, his kingdom can still be seen at work in the world.

Jesus addressed our blindness about his really real kingdom by directing our attention to the real world around us. By focusing on what the King made in creation, we can be trained to see the King's kingdom.

For me, the really real kingdom was hidden for the first twenty years of my Christian life, even after I received Jesus as my Lord (and King, ironically!). I had even been attending a church named "Christ the King," but the kingdom was invisible to me. I was blind to it. Why?

Jesus said that the kingdom is easily missed and often overlooked, like a seed, a pearl, leaven, a net in the water, a key, a secret, or a hidden treasure (Matthew 13:1–52). Jesus said that the kingdom requires eyes to see and ears to hear (Matthew 13:13–17). He told Nicodemus, a Jewish leader, that "unless one is born again he cannot see the kingdom of God" (John 3:3). On his way to Jerusalem prior to his crucifixion, Jesus' purpose as a suffering, sacrificial King was hidden from his followers (Luke 18:31–34). They couldn't see the big story of the kingdom, supposing instead that it would come immediately in full political might (Luke 19:11).

To a group of unbelieving Pharisees, Jesus said the kingdom was coming in ways that could not be observed by them even though it was happening in their midst (Luke 17:20–21). How is that even possible? It's possible because we cannot see what we are not looking for or expecting.

Now, an astute person would take 1 Timothy 1:17 and make this whole line of thinking crumble like a teetering deck of cards:

> To the King of the ages, immortal, invisible, the only God, be honor and glory forever and ever. Amen.

Aha! There! How can we see what's invisible? To press the point, this astute person would add in the numerous other scriptures that testify to God's invisibility (John 1:18; Colossians 1:15; Hebrews 11:27; 1 John 4:12).

Since the King is invisible, how can we possibly see the kingdom?

Side Trip: Wind

Invisible does not mean unnoticeable. Wind is invisible, but its effect and power are easily noticed if you are looking for the traces. Put the book down right now and go outside. At first glance, there may be no evidence of wind at all. But if you look closely enough, you'll see a grass blade quiver, a leaf shake, or even a tree sway slightly. When you wait and listen and seek long enough, you'll see the invisible wind.

Let's look at the reasons behind our blindness. There are seven old, heavy veils that keep us from seeing God's really real kingdom:

1. Greatness
2. An outsider's perspective
3. A language barrier
4. Familiarity
5. The kingdom of darkness
6. Our brokenness
7. God's own hand

We'll look at each to understand why we often overlook this treasure hidden in the field.

1. Blinded by Greatness

Often we miss seeing something because it's too grand, too big, too great. Greatness is a veil that can hide what's obvious in plain sight. Permit me an example from geology. When you look at satellite imagery of eastern Washington, Idaho, and Montana, a trained eye can see clear evidence of the Ice Age Floods, which resulted from the cataclysmic failure of a glacial dam that held back a full ocean of impounded water (2,000 feet deep!) stretching all the way into Montana. When the ice eventually melted and the dam broke, the full might of an ocean unleashed. It carved out massive gorges and falls and scoured the landscape on an epic scale. The foothills found in Camas Prairie in Montana are not just foothills; they are the ripple marks of this unimaginable torrent.[19]

All of this evidence of a cataclysm was completely missed and invisible to geologists. They had never seen erosion on such a scale anywhere on earth before. Most ripple marks that could be seen were in streams or ocean shores, and those little sand features stood only inches tall. The Camas Prairie hills are fifty feet high. These sedimentary features were too big to be noticed for what they were. Scientists were blind to what is now obvious.

Pioneering "rebel" geologist J. Harlen Bretz was ridiculed for decades and scorned by his colleagues for suggesting a theory of the Ice Age Floods. He could see what was then invisible because he looked at a different scale, through a wider lens.[20]

We often miss the kingdom of God because it looms too large, is too pervasive, and encompasses too much. We're accustomed to kingdoms that have borders and defined territories. Our eyes are trained to see only kingdoms that fit that scale. To see the entirety of God's realm, we need a lens wide enough and a viewpoint far away enough to see the whole cosmos at once! Or, barring that perspective, in order to see God's kingdom, we need to attune our eyes and realize that *everything* in our view and lives, at some level, is the signet of King Jesus, comes from his power, is held together by his hand, and was originally made by his design. Sometimes we are blinded to God's kingdom because it's too big and ubiquitous.

2. Blinded by an Outsider's Perspective

For years, I was completely stymied by an annual event that took over my Washington hometown. For no apparent reason, thousands of people ran through Bellingham, congregated at the high school, then completely vanished the next day. I was baffled.

Over and over, I saw an insignia, and I had no clue what it meant or what was happening. From time to time, a bumper sticker would show up on a car, or the logo would pop up on t-shirts or hats. Often I shook my head and muttered, "Whatever."

I was an outsider.

Later I found out that this was the Ragnar Relay Series, a 200(ish)-mile running race in my area that coursed from the Canadian border to the southern tip of Whidbey Island in a race called the Ragnar Northwest Passage.[21] Even though I saw thousands of runners, saw the hoopla, saw the logo everywhere, the whole event was essentially meaningless to me because I was an outsider. I was even annoyed that it clogged the roads and got in my way. Ragnar was cloaked from my perspective of looking in from without.

Then, one year, I was invited to drive a van in the race for a team of runners. My whole perspective changed, and my eyes opened. In a moment, I became aware of the fun, thrill, and challenge of Ragnar. What was meaningless to me as an outsider opened up a new world as an insider. Now I get it.

As I'm writing *The Kingdom Field Guide*, I'm still basking in the glow from my last Ragnar run just a few days ago. The adrenaline is still wearing off; my muscles are still sore. I'm still a bit rummy from sleep deprivation. I'm now an insider. I see Ragnar. Even seeing the Ragnar symbol on a hat or water bottle evokes a full rush of feelings, memories, and anticipation for the next race. I'm immediately connected to a community of other runners when I see them wearing the Ragnar swag. All of this was hidden from me until I entered the race—hidden in plain sight.

It's not strange that God's kingdom would be cloaked to those on the outside, citizens of the kingdom of darkness, but it is strange that many Christians are living as outsiders to God's kingdom. They are kingdom citizens (Ephesians 2:19; Philippians 3:20). They are adopted children of the King (John 1:12–13; Romans 8:14–17, 23; Galatians 4:4–5; Ephesians 1:5). They are seated on the throne (Ephesians 1:20) and are heirs to the kingdom (Luke 22:29–30; Ephesians 1:11–14). They are commissioned by the King (Matthew 28:16–20). But, staggeringly, they are living as outsiders. The kingdom is hidden even to many of its heirs. Kingdom citizens are blinded to the kingdom if they are living as outsiders.

3. Blinded by a Language Barrier

Confession: I'm not fluent in the Swahili language. Because of this, the full meaning of even the simplest Swahili book is hidden to me. I can see the text, but the narrative, characters, drama, and plot line are obscured, hidden in plain sight. Believers in Christ and non-believers alike don't recognize the kingdom language of the scriptures, so the kingdom remains hidden both in the passages of the Bible and in the passing of our lives. We need to become fluent in the language of the kingdom, familiar with the symbols, and educated in the plot line of the drama in order to see what is invisible even to most Christians, yet is obviously scripted in the Bible, our world, and our lives.

Nearly all of the most popular movie franchises are kingdom stories: *Star Wars*, *The Lord of the Rings*, *Harry Potter*, the Marvel universe, and *The Hunger Games*. From ticket sales alone, these movies have commanded over $35 billion in sales (never mind the endless spin-offs and merchandizing).[22] *Game of Thrones* absolutely shattered HBO ratings records.[23] How many hours have you logged in *Downton Abbey* binge-watching? All of these shows are saturated with kingdom language, themes, and elements. All of them are kingdom stories hidden in plain view.

The kingdom narrative is being replayed constantly, and people pay billions of dollars to consume the same storyline. The kingdom story is encoded in our DNA because we were designed to live eternally in God's kingdom. We are kingdom creatures, and that DNA drives us to make our own kingdoms, consume kingdom stories, and worship and serve a variety of kings. But this is all cloaked when we're illiterate in kingdom language, despite our constant consumption.

4. Blinded by Familiarity

The most common image disappears into the background if you see it often enough. The loudest noise becomes inaudible if you hear it too much. If you live in the country, there's a good chance that your first night in a city hotel will be sleepless because the background noise of cars, sirens, and yelling will be deafening. But when you live your whole life in the city, that deafening city clatter becomes inaudible white noise in the background.

In the Pacific Northwest, there are blankets of

evergreen trees on the west side of the Cascade Mountains. Everywhere you turn, there are majestic firs, cedars, and hemlocks. When I first moved from California to Washington, I was struck by how green the Evergreen State really is. I was accustomed to the brown rolling hills of the California Bay Area, so my system was initially shocked by the countless stands of forest in Washington. Now, twenty-eight years later, I often don't see what's all around me. The green has become too common and cloaked in familiarity. Because God's kingdom is always all around us, for some people it has become just white noise that they have tuned out. But, saddest of all, when the kingdom gets tuned out, so does the full goodness of the King.

5. Blinded by the Kingdom of Darkness

In World War II, the success of the Allied invasion of France on D-Day hinged largely on a massive deception campaign called "Operation Bodyguard."[24] For up to a year prior to the invasion, the Allies played hundreds of feints, set up dummy tanks and aircraft, fed false intelligence to double agents, and issued fake radio transmissions. In the end, this deception convinced the German military that an invasion would occur in Pas-de-Calais instead of Normandy. Hitler was entirely blinded by the brilliant ruse leading up to the invasion on June 6, 1944.

Deception is an integral art of war. Some of the blindness to God's kingdom of light comes from deception by the kingdom of darkness (2 Corinthians 2:10–11). Real kingdoms have real enemies. God's really real kingdom is no different.

...the god of this world has blinded the minds of the unbelievers, to keep them from seeing the light of the gospel of the glory of Christ, who is the image of God.

—2 Corinthians 4:4

Deception is the primary weapon of the enemy kingdom ruled by Satan, known as "the ruler of this world" (John 12:31; 14:30–31).

Jesus said that the native language of Satan is lies (John 8:44). He fluently speaks that twisted dialect. From the Garden of Eden (Genesis 3:1–5) to the Garden of Gethsemane, the serpent has been at work to deceive humanity and wage war against the kingdom of light (Ephesians 6:11–16). And he will continue to do so until the end of this age (Revelation 20:1–3).

Just how deep does the deception of darkness go? Recently a UCLA professor published *Satan: A Biography*,[25] arguing that Satan isn't really in opposition to God, and he isn't really evil.[26] I looked for evidence that this book was a spoof produced by a satirical source like "The Onion" or "The Babylon Bee," but no luck. Even world-class academics can be blinded.

Satan's deception is more than sleight of hand or parlor tricks. He has genuine power (Job 1:13–22; Revelation 13:1–10) with convincing false signs and wonders (Matthew 24:24; Mark 13:22). That worm has brought a fallen world under his dark cloak (2 Thessalonians 2:9–12; 2 John 1:7; Revelation 12:9). Sometimes that even includes God's own people (Matthew 24:24).

Not all of our blindness to God's kingdom is attributed to Satan. Let's not give that limp worm too much credit. But we fool ourselves if we think that God's enemy in darkness does not wage at least a decent propaganda campaign in his war against the light. The prince of darkness gets some credit for our blindness.

6. Blinded by Our Own Brokenness

Tragically, we are also blinded by our own brokenness. In the dramatic narrative of scripture, sin is more than a moral failing, more than an accidental "oops." Sin is rebellion and mutiny against the reign of God. Our own sin, ingrained in our DNA and manifest in our daily lives, is often a prime contributor to our ignorance of God's kingdom.

The Apostle Paul wrote to the church founded in the largely pagan city of Ephesus. He warned them not to live in a way that was futile, with hard-heartedness and callousness, saying that such people "are darkened in their understanding, alienated from the life of God" through their own folly (Ephesians 4:17–19).

This characterized large periods of my life, even parts of my life as a Christian when I claimed faith in Jesus but gave myself over to old practices of darkness. I was living as a Christian on Sunday (morning), but I often stumbled blindly Monday through Saturday.

The Apostle John wrote to his congregations, warning against the blinding power of sin:

> But whoever hates his brother is in the darkness and walks in the darkness, and does not know where he is going, because the darkness has blinded his eyes.
> **—1 John 2:11**

A life of habitual rebellion, of constant turning away from God's goodness and right order, can pull a heavy, thick veil over us.

7. Blinded by God's Own Hand

There are so many veils covering us, blinding us. Some are of our own making, some are from a dark enemy, and some come from God himself!

> *Therefore they could not believe. For again Isaiah said, "[God] has blinded their eyes and hardened their heart, lest they see with their eyes, and understand with their heart, and turn, and I would heal them."*
> **—John 12:39–40**

Is there any hope at all for seeing God's kingdom? If God himself can be the cause of our blindness, then what hope is there?

Fortunately, there is great hope.

> *But when one turns to the Lord, the veil is removed.*
> **—2 Corinthians 3:16**

As we turn to the Lord, we find that he takes away our blindness. In him, we can see. The Maker of our eyes can give us sight. Jesus can not only heal physical eyes and restore sight to the blind, but also help us to see the really real kingdom that's been hidden from us.

The Lost Kingdom

Recently I learned about an ancient example of a hidden kingdom. A 1,200-year-old city was discovered by an Australian research team in Cambodia near the Angkor Wat temple complex.[27] The team used lidar remote sensing, a laser technology that "sees" through vegetation. Lidar is advanced satellite technology, and from the lidar aerial images, archaeologists found an entire lost city of roads, aqueducts, and temples. All of it was completely overgrown by jungle and eons of earth's decay. It was undetectable to someone just walking on the ground, but poke-in-the-eyeball obvious from the lidar.

At first, I was intrigued by how an entire city can just vanish for a millennium. Then I realized that literally all it takes to lose a city is to stop mowing the lawn. Just let the weeds grow.

Those who live in the Pacific Northwest know this to be true. Turn your back for one minute on a blackberry bramble, and it will wrap its spiky tendrils around your neck and steal your wallet. Put the weed whacker in the shed, and just weeks later, your yard will be overgrown.

The kingdom of God can be rapidly overgrown and choked out of our lives by anxious worries, maddening desires, and deceitful sin (Matthew 13:1–23). It takes a few hundred years for the jungle to claim a civilization, a few years for weeds to consume a yard, but only days for the kingdom of God effectively to vanish from our lives.

Remember that Jesus said the kingdom is like treasure hidden in a field (Matthew 13:44). It's easily overlooked, quickly forgotten, and soon erased from memory. This world and our own sinful flesh are constantly trying to overrun God's kingdom and make it a lost city.

Side Trip: Seeds

In Matthew 13:18–23, Jesus said that "the word of the kingdom" is like a seed that is easily lost, abandoned, or choked if it is not heard and understood. Seeds are like that. If they are not used in the proper way, they are wasted.

For this Side Trip, find a small seed and carry it around with you for a week. Take it with you everywhere you go. Throughout the week, notice how easy it is to forget, misplace, or lose.

Incredibly, something as large and magnificent as God's kingdom can just as easily be lost or hidden—until we hear and understand the word of the kingdom. Then the kingdom takes root in good soil, bears phenomenal fruit, and multiplies far beyond its original state as a seed. God's kingdom is hidden and overlooked until it grows exceedingly great. If his kingdom is still small and invisible in your life, that's okay. It's just a signal that you need to pay closer attention. Use this seed exercise to remind yourself of the importance of hearing and understanding the word of the kingdom.

If you want a disturbing but highly relevant analogy, watch the Planet Earth video about deadly fungi that overrun ant colonies.[28] It is a disgusting but fantastic metaphor of life being choked by weeds. This fits our lives in so many ways.

How can we keep from being consumed by the world's toxic worries and our sin's twisted desires? How can we prevent the kingdom of God from being a lost empire in our lives? Jesus told his disciples to seek God's kingdom first (Matthew 6:33).

Understand and apply these three aspects of Jesus' instruction in order not to lose the kingdom:

1. *Seek*: Search earnestly, look passionately, scour frantically. Not as you would look for a book to read in a library, but as you would seek a lost child. Not as you would look for butter in a store because you're baking a cake, but as you would seek an emergency room because you've broken your leg. Seek and keep on seeking.

2. *God's kingdom*: God's kingdom is God's rule and reign. God's kingdom is God's provision and protection. God's kingdom is God's will on earth as it is in heaven

(Matthew 6:9–13). Live as if God is sovereign over every minute of your day and each dime in your bank account *because he is.*

3. *First*: Seek God's kingdom as your utmost priority, with the first of your energy. Placing God's kingdom number two or number three in your life is placing it last.

We won't lose God's kingdom if we seek it first.

CHAPTER THREE FIELD TRIP

Geocaching

Geocaching is the world's largest treasure hunt, in which millions of small boxes have been hidden all over the world, and anyone with the time and determination can uncover them. Here's your chance to discover what has been hidden under your nose for years.

First visit the Geocaching website (https://www.geocaching.com/play) to get specific details for instructions on finding a cache near you.

Field Trip Details

Travel: Ranges from minimal to extensive.

Cost: Minimal

Time: Ranges from a few minutes to all day.

Physical Demands: Minimal to rigorous

Gear: A GPS or a smart phone, helpful but not required

Key Scriptures to Guide Your Trip: Matthew 13:1–23; Matthew 13:44; Matthew 6:33; Matthew 6:9–15

Schedule this field trip now. Put it on your calendar!
Day: _____
Time: _____
People invited to join me: _____

_____

_____

Geocaches are virtually everywhere—the wilderness, cities, neighborhoods, parks, shopping malls, and public squares. Pick a setting that you'd like to explore, and then use the geocaching website to zero in on a few geocaches to hunt.

Finding a geocache can take just a few minutes, or it may require an all-day adventure. On the geocaching website, try typing in the area code of your town and don't be surprised if hundreds of geocaches are hidden within walking distance or a short drive.

You can use the basic Geocaching website and mobile app for free. Additionally, there are multiple other iPhone and Android mobile apps that can help you to find geocaches. If you want to upgrade, the premium membership costs about $30 per year. Having a mobile phone or GPS unit[29] greatly helps, but it isn't required to find many of the caches. The geocache treasures are usually little boxes that contain toys for kids. Good geocaching ethics suggest that if you take something, then leave something for somebody else.

Always bring clothing and shoes that fit the terrain and weather conditions. Wilderness geocaching requires appropriate wilderness gear. Many caches are found in convenient, easy-to-reach places, like a park bench or behind a tree in a shopping center parking lot. But some caches are quite technical and require climbing, scuba, or other specialized gear to reach.

The first time you look for a geocache, you will be stunned at the sheer number of treasure boxes hidden all around you. It's likely that many are within a short walk from your doorstep. They've just been invisible until now.

Seeing the Kingdom Connection

We can't see what we're not seeking. If Jesus were to do his public ministry in today's world, I'm convinced that he would tell kingdom parables using geocaches.

Geocaching gives you an experience of finding something that is invisible in everyday life. Once you attune your focus, suddenly the hidden boxes will become an obvious and easily seen element of the world around you. Sometimes as you search for a geocache, you'll literally stub your toe on a cleverly hidden box.

God's kingdom isn't even cleverly hidden. It's hiding in plain sight. When you begin to seek God's kingdom, eventually you will stub your toe on that treasure hidden in the field—probably sooner than you think.

Questions for Reflection

1. What sticks out from this field trip or is a new idea for you?

2. What questions have come out of this field trip? What doesn't make sense to you?

3. How do you see Jesus and his kingdom in this experience?

4. How can you apply this to your life and take a next step?

5. What will you talk to God and other people about?

After this field trip, circle where you are right now in your journey to find God's kingdom as a hidden treasure.

| Blind | Aware | Ponder | Value | Trap of Inaction | Prioritize | Own/Sell |

Journal: Spend some time in your journal to record further thoughts.

Chapter Three Discussion Questions

> **Key Scripture:**
> The Lord's Prayer for the Kingdom
> Matthew 6:9–15

1. What are some small, proactive ways you can begin to see (pay attention) to the reality of God's kingdom all around you? What habits do you need to build into your life in order to be able to observe the kingdom? How can you pray the Lord's Prayer within the routines of your life?

2. Look at the list of the seven veils that blind us to God's kingdom. Which one(s) have most obscured your vision of the King? Describe a time when you were able to get through one of these veils to obtain a clearer view of God. How can you set aside the veil that most blinds you now?

3. Describe something in your life that was originally hidden but then became visible once you started paying attention to it. Describe a time when you chose sin's pleasures over God's joy. What was the difference

between the two pursuits, both short-term and long-term?

4. What are some specific weeds in your life—toxic worries of this world or your sin's twisted desires—that have tried to overgrow God's kingdom and obscure it from your sight? How will you begin actively and practically to seek God's kingdom first in your daily life?

5. Discuss your experience on the field trip. What did you learn? What surprised you? What challenged you?

Chapter Three Notes

CHAPTER FOUR

Really Real

I am in (partial) recovery from a *Downton Abbey* addiction.

During the Christmas of 2018, my wife and I were surfing Amazon Video, hoping to zone out. We had heard about the show but knew nothing about it, so we decided to give it a try. From the opening scene, I was hooked.

Downton Abbey is a soap opera set at the royal estate of Lord Robert Crawley, the Earl of Grantham. All of the typical soap opera clichés drive the storyline: murder, marriage, pregnancies, infidelity, war, power, money, and politics. The villains are villainous, but with charm. The heroes are heroic, but with heart-breaking weaknesses. The show leaps from one dramatic turn to the next, but more than anything else, *Downton Abbey* is a kingdom story. I became engrossed with this portrayal of British nobility.

It's hard to miss the kingdom themes when you watch the show. The family of nobles lives in an opulent estate with a turreted mansion. The family crest adorns ornate furnishings. The busy staff of maids, footmen, and servants are at the beck and call of his Lordship and her Ladyship. The Kingdom of Great Britain is unmistakable in the way people talk, dress, and act. The power of the nobility is easily marked by the snap to attention when Lord Crawley walks into the room of attendants. The grounds of the estate are meticulously kept in prime condition. The silver is never tarnished. Every job is done with excellence in order to magnify and uphold the honor of the family name. A small torn seam in the footman's livery jacket is met with scorn because it does not meet the impeccable standards of a noble house. Everything screams, "Kingdom!" in the *Downton Abbey* show.

But what about God's kingdom? We've identified some of the reasons why we can live in God's kingdom but not recognize it. We've shown how the seven veils are quite effective at hiding God's kingdom in plain sight. Now let's unpack how to see the kingdom that's right in front of you. In doing so, you'll find the treasure hidden in the field.

There are three main ways we can see God's kingdom on earth even though Jesus is enthroned in heaven:

1. The King's *body* on earth

2. The King's *work* on earth

3. The King's *residence* on earth.

Yes, Jesus is in heaven, but his *body*, *work*, and *residence* are visible on earth—that is, if you train yourself to look.

1. The King's Body

If you've ever encountered somebody very important, you've probably noticed your heart racing, your hands sweating, and your breath accelerating. During the 2004 election, I was near the presidential motorcade of George W. Bush during one of his campaign stops in Washington state. I had a sense of thrill because he was, arguably, one of the most powerful people on earth. He embodied the full might and power of the government of the United States. When I saw the President, I was seeing the whole executive branch of the government in person.

The same is true for seeing the kingdom of God. When you see the King, you are seeing the kingdom embodied because the power, resources, majesty, and authority of the kingdom are wrapped up in the body of the King.

The Bible is quite clear that Jesus is no longer on earth. Two times Luke gives eyewitness testimony that Jesus was carried up to heaven after his resurrection (Luke 24:50–53; Acts 1:6–11). So aren't we dead in the water if we're trying to see the King on earth? Isn't it impossible since he is in heaven, some invisible realm way up there?

While Jesus is in heaven, the body of Christ is on earth. Look at the clear teaching of Paul in his first letter to the church at Corinth:

> *For just as the body is one and has many members, and all the members of the body, though many, are one body, so it is with Christ. For in one Spirit we were all baptized into one body....* **Now you are the body of Christ and individually members of it.**
> **—1 Corinthians 12:12–13, 27**

Paul taught that baptism is much more than a dunk in the river. Our baptism is an immersion into the body of Christ. We become members of Christ's body on earth, with each part having a unique function and form. In his letter to the church at Ephesus, Paul reinforced this. He made another connection to our baptism into the body of Christ. Then he developed the idea even further, saying that since there is now in Christ "one body and one Spirit" in the church (Ephesians 4:4), we are to work at "building up the body of Christ" (Ephesians 4:12). Christian maturity is fully expressed with Christ's love embodied in us (Ephesians 4:15–16).

We are the body of Christ, and Jesus is the head. He is the one who gives unity and purpose. As our heads direct our bodies, so Christ directs his body, the church. This was a common theme in Paul's writing. He described each believer as having a unique role in the church, just as each limb, organ, and cell has a unique contribution to the health and wholeness of a body (Romans 12:3–5). When he wrote to the church in Colossae, Paul continued to bang the drum that believers are the body of Christ (Colossians 1:24–29).

The church is the body of Christ. Christ is in the church as much as you are in your own body. When we see the church, the body of Christ, we are seeing Christ embodied! We are in Christ, and Christ is in us.

Why was Paul so clear and adamant about this? Perhaps his passion about the body of Christ can be traced back to his former life as "Saul" before he personally encountered Jesus. Saul was a Jewish Pharisee who felt threatened by the new growing church of Christian believers. He persecuted them, arrested them, and even pursued them to death. Then one day, on the road to Damascus, Saul was stopped dead in his tracks. Jesus knocked him off his horse.

> And falling to the ground, he heard a voice saying to him, "Saul, Saul, why are you persecuting me?" And he said, "Who are you, Lord?" And he said, "I am Jesus, whom you are persecuting."
> —*Acts 9:4–5*

The Apostle Paul didn't invent some clever way of describing the church as the body of Christ. He learned this directly from Jesus himself. When Saul was persecuting Christian disciples, Jesus himself said, "Why are you persecuting *me*?" When Saul asked for the speaker to identify himself, the voice from heaven said, "I am Jesus, whom you are persecuting." Saul learned from Jesus that the believers were, in fact, Jesus embodied on earth. If you persecute a person's body, you are persecuting that person. Because Saul was persecuting the body of Christ, Jesus could say that he himself was being persecuted.

Where does that leave us in terms of seeing God's kingdom? Because the church is the body of Christ, the King, when we see the church, we are seeing the King. And when we see the King, we are seeing the kingdom.

It's hard to remember that the church is a "who," not a "what." The church is the body of Jesus, not a building or a worship service. Any time we see a gathering of believers, we are seeing an expression of the body of Christ, the King. We can use the physical structures as markers of Christ's body on earth, but his body is the people within. When you see an individual disciple of Jesus, you are seeing a member, or body part, of the King, which means that you are seeing the really real kingdom.

2. The King's Work

In his book *Fearfully and Wonderfully Made*, Dr. Paul Brand claims that he can prove the existence of God from a thumb.[30] Springboarding off that, you can also prove the existence of God's kingdom from your hand. So take a moment really to look at your hand.

- Your hand was designed by the King.
- Your hand is a work produced by the King.
- Your hand is attached to you, and you are a member of the body of Christ, the King.

- Your hand can create work and bring good that gives glory to the King.

- Your hand is attached to you, and you are an ambassador representing the King's authority on earth.

When you see the works of a king, you are seeing evidence of a king. And when you see a king, you are seeing a kingdom. When you start seeing the world as a work produced by King Jesus, then God's kingdom becomes supremely visible because God's work is supremely present. Everywhere. Always. The dirt beneath your feet is his work. The air in your lungs is his work. The red blood cell racing in your vein is his work—every atom, every molecule. All of it is a work of the King, and where you are seeing the work of a king, you are seeing his rule and reign. You are seeing his kingdom.

The Apostle Paul said that "we are [God's] workmanship, *created in Christ Jesus for good works*, which God prepared beforehand, that we should walk in them" (Ephesians 2:10). People are the workmanship of the King, evidence of his rule and reign. People are a product of his kingdom, so when you see people, you are seeing the kingdom, the result of the rule of the King. By extension, whenever you see the works of the people of Christ, you are seeing the reign of Christ in action. The "good works" prepared for us in Christ, using Paul's language, are evidence of the kingdom of Christ.

Throughout history, Christians have been pioneers of hospitals, public education, democratic governments, the creative arts, civil rights, and groundbreaking science. These are all good works reflecting the goodness of the King through his people. To one degree or another, when you see a hospital, you are seeing a good work that stems from the good rule of King Jesus.

The kingdom became invisible to us when we stopped recognizing the work of the King. We stopped seeing the result of his rule, and we disconnected goodness from the good reign of Jesus. So, again, look at your hand. The kingdom of God is, literally, at hand.

2. The King's Residence

If you want to see a king, you often will look for his residence. The palace of a king is a reflection of the glory of his rule and reign. His residence isn't just where he sleeps and eats; it's the center of his rule. It is the functional base from which his authority emanates to the rest of his realm. The grandeur of the monarch's reputation is captured by the splendor of his home, his palace.

Alexander the Great spent most of his career on the move, constantly pressing eastward as he pursued the most successful military campaign of history. He left his palace behind for the adventure of unknown lands and cultures. But don't be fooled. He was still king! One way that he projected his power was through his royal tent. This was no simple cloth shelter. The tent declared his strength, majesty, and power:[31]

When deciding cases among the Bactrians, Hyrcanians, and Indians, [Alexander the Great] had a tent made as follows: the tent was large enough for 100 couches; fifty gold pillars supported it; embroidered gold canopies, stretched out above, covered the place. Inside the tent 500 Persian Apple Bearers [elite soldiers] stood first, dressed in purple and yellow clothing. After the Apple Bearers stood an equal number of archers in different clothing, for some wore flame-colored, some dark blue, and some scarlet. In front of these stood Macedonian Silver Shields, 500 of the tallest men. In the middle of the room stood the gold throne, on which Alexander sat to give audiences.

The greatness of this pavilion represented and projected the awesome power of Alexander the Great.

Alexander wasn't alone in this practice. When kings of antiquity traveled, they didn't stay in a Four Seasons resort. They used tents as mobile palaces that displayed some of their riches and grandeur, but on a portable scale. The tent was the king's traveling locus of power and authority. It served as both a functional center from which the king's agenda advanced and a symbol for the rule and reign of the king. The range of the tent's travel encompassed the range of the king's realm. The reach of the tent in the world measured the long arm of the king's rule. The greatness of the tent fit the greatness of the king.

With that backdrop, now look at the "tent" of our God, the King of kings. The scriptures say many times that the *heavens* are the tent of God (Psalm 104:1–2; Isaiah 40:21–22). Modern readers are disadvantaged when we read the word *tent* in these scriptures. Through the lens of our Western world view, the word *tent* summons an image of either a camping tent or a circus big top. But the original readers of these scriptures would immediately have had in mind the image of the mobile palace and dwelling of King YHWH. Associations with the desert tabernacle following the Egyptian exodus would be the default image (Exodus 26), not YHWH's yurt when he went camping.

If we marvel at the roving palace of Alexander the Great, how much more should we be in awe of the tent of our God. Look at the heavens! Relive the feeling of being punched in the gut when you gazed at the Milky Way on a dark night. Think about being stunned speechless with the beauty of an ocean sunset. If you witnessed the 2017 total solar eclipse, recall the staggeringly strange experience of two minutes in totality when the sun was as black as ink and emblazoned with a radiant corona. This is the tent of the King of kings. The greatness of the tent of the heavens fits the greatness of the King who rules there.

We commend Alexander the Great for creating his awe-inspiring tent. How much more should we worship and give glory to the one who created the heavens for his dwelling (Isaiah 42:5; Jeremiah 10:12)!

The heavens are YHWH's center for his rule and reign. They are evidence of his majestic dwelling and emblematic of his majestic kingdom. But in order to be more tangibly present with his people, God traveled with the Israelites in a tent called "the tabernacle" after the Egyptian exodus. As you read the detailed blueprints of YHWH's mobile palace, you'll soon realize that his tent far exceeded Alexander the Great's tent as a show of power and rule among the people of Israel (Exodus 25–30). The gold overlays, the cherubim statues, the coverings, the priestly attendants, the military officers, the towering columns, and the heaven-inspired tapestries all spoke of the glory of God as the Israelites traveled to the promised land of Canaan. But the tabernacle was still just a shadow of the whole canopy of the heavens, which is God's "tent."

When you look at creation, you are seeing the dwelling of the King. It's evidence of his really real kingdom. Don't miss this. A thunder-clouded horizon is not just symbolic of God's reign; it's really his dwelling from which his kingdom's agenda is advanced.

Even more strangely, this mighty God, the all-powerful King who defeated the Egyptian Pharaoh, humbled Babylonian King Nebuchadnezzar, and moved the Persian King Cyrus like a chess piece—this God named YHWH—took up a human body like a tent, like a tabernacle.

In the beginning was the Word, and the Word was with God, and the Word was God. ... And the Word became flesh and dwelt [tabernacled!] among us, and we have seen his

*glory, glory as of the only Son from the Father, full of grace
and truth.*

—John 1:1, 14

Jesus, who claimed to be YHWH himself (John 5:18; 8:56–58), inhabited a human body as his tabernacle, his mobile tent, his embodied dwelling from which he will rule and reign for eternity. And lest you belittle the human flesh as some scrappy pup tent, remember that we are beautifully crafted by a master artisan (Psalm 139:13–15). From Jesus' physical body—his tabernacle, his tent—he exercised his rule and reign in the world.

Then, after his ascension, the church became the temple of Christ (1 Corinthians 3:16–17; Ephesians 2:19–22; Ephesians 3:17; 1 Peter 2:5). We are his "tent," his mobile palace from which the rule of the King goes out to the world. The glory of the King's tent reflects the glory of the King.

The Really Real Kingdom

We need to be crystal clear why God's kingdom is really real, not just real, and why Jesus is a really real king, not just a real one. To do so, we need to go to the moon.

In the 1960s, the race to the moon was at a fevered pitch. The entire world was enthralled by a competition between superpowers to be the first to land on the moon. Hundreds of millions of people watched the footage of Apollo 11 and the unearthly daring of astronauts Neil Armstrong, Buzz Aldrin, and Michael Collins make it there and back. To those who were spectators in one of mankind's most daring, dangerous, and ingenious endeavors, the moon landing was real. Ask people from the 60s generation, and they will tell you where they were when the first boot print was made in moon dust. The program was on their minds, but they also had lives that consumed most of their energy and resources.

But to 400,000 engineers, scientists, contractors, administrators, astronauts, and families, the moon mission wasn't just real; it was *really real*. They invested all of their energy into it and devoted all of their ingenuity to it. All of their blood, sweat, and tears were poured into that mission. Everybody made tremendous sacrifices. Some gave their very lives. Every minute of their waking day, every spare ounce of their mindshare, every priority list was claimed by the Apollo program. They were *seeking first* to go to the moon. Everything else was a distant and far second.

When you seek something first, it becomes *really real*. Endeavors that are really real aren't just in your mind, but are also embodied in every corner of your life. When Neil Armstrong stepped on the moon, that was the collective footprint of nearly half a million people on the NASA team. To these people, the program was at the top of their minds, and all of their energy and resources were devoted to one end.

Shockingly, there are some people who still, to this day, do not think that we landed on the moon. They believe that the whole mission was a clever hoax. They suspect a conspiracy to pull the wool over the eyes of the world. To these people, the moon program was *out of mind*, and they had no devotion of energy and resources to the aim of the moon mission.

To most of the world's spectators, the moon mission was real. To the 400,000 people working on the project, the moon mission was really real and was embodied in every aspect of their lives. To a tiny fraction of conspiracy adherents, the moon mission was not real at all. This spectrum can be summed up in the simple chart below.

Really Real
Top-of-mind attention to a
mission embodied in life

━ ━ ━ ━ ━ ━ ━ ━ ━ ━ ┃

Real
Bottom-of-mind attention to a
mission marginal to life

━ ━ ━ ━ ━ ━ ━ ━ ━ ━ ┃

Unreal
Out of mind, no attention to a
mission absent in life

Where are you on that spectrum regarding God's king-dom? Are you a spectator? Maybe you think that God's kingdom is real, but it doesn't have much impact on your life apart from an occasional interest when something spectacular happens. Or perhaps you think that the king-dom is real, but it's something far away or far off. Either way, the mission of the kingdom doesn't have much bear-ing on your day-to-day life.

Or are you living functionally as if God's kingdom is unreal? Sure, you've seen some flannelgraphs, and you've heard some stories. But are you living as if the kingdom has no bearing in reality and certainly not in your own life? Do you spend your time, money, energy, and atten-tion as if the kingdom of Jesus were a fairy tale or conspiracy theory?

Or is God's kingdom really real to you because you are living the Great Co-Mission (Matthew 28:16–20)? Is God's mission your mission for his kingdom to come? Does the footprint of King Jesus on earth include your foot in the boot?

This means that every hour, dime, and talent is devoted to the mission of the King and his kingdom. Every thought is dominated by the agenda of seeking first the rule and reign of Jesus. Not only has your mind been captured by what's on Jesus' mind, but your life embodies the life of Christ on earth to bring his really real kingdom.

CHAPTER FOUR FIELD TRIP

People-Watching

I love airports. Well, I love the part of airports that exists *after* security! Airports are the best people-watching spots in the world. Thousands of people from countless walks of life converge on a tiny hub. The variety is infinite. There's an endless parade of stories walking by. There are so many sizes, shapes, colors, emotions, ages, and stages. Airports are people on parade.

For this field trip, you are going to a prime people-watching location. This could be an airport (if you have a ticket), a mall, a downtown hub, or a sports arena. Grab a comfortable spot and start looking at the variety of people. Notice faces. Pay attention to small details. Try to read emotions. See people as individuals with individual stories.

Some of these people may be part of the body of Christ. When you see Christ's body, you are seeing the King. And when you see the King you are seeing the kingdom.

Field Trip Details

Travel: Go to a prime people-watching location, such as an airport, a bus station, a mall, a church, or a busy street downtown.

Cost: Zero

Time: Spend at least an hour people-watching.

Physical Demands: None

Gear: Bible and journal

Key Scriptures to Guide Your Trip: Romans 12:5; 1 Corinthians 12:12–27; Ephesians 3:6; Ephesians 5:23; Colossians 1:18, 24

Schedule this field trip now. Put it on your calendar!
Day: _____
Time: _____
People invited to join me: _____
_____
_____

Seeing the Kingdom Connection

For this field trip, you are seeing people as the body of Christ. Mind you, some of them won't actually be Christians. That's okay. They are still made in God's image and bear his likeness.

But some of these people *will* be Christian. When you see Christians, you are really seeing the body of Christ. You are seeing Christ incarnated on earth in his body. When you see the body of the King, you are seeing the King. And when you see the King, you are seeing his kingdom. You're seeing the treasure.

Questions for Reflection

1. What sticks out from this field trip or is a new idea for you?
2. What questions have come out of this field trip? What doesn't make sense to you?
3. How do you see Jesus and his kingdom in this experience?
4. How can you apply this to your life and take a next step?
5. What will you talk to God and other people about?

After this field trip, circle where you are right now in your journey to find God's kingdom as a hidden treasure.

Journal: Spend some time in your journal to record further thoughts.

Chapter Four Discussion Questions

> **Key Scripture:**
> The Body of Christ
> 1 Corinthians 12:12–31

1. Describe a time when you directly saw the work of somebody famous. It could be a painting, a sculpture, a theater performance, a building, etc. How did the close proximity to that work help you to feel somehow connected to the person? What was your reaction to being close to the work of somebody so great?

2. *The church is the body of Christ. Christ is in the church as much as you are in your own body.* How does this statement line up with the currently popular notion that you can love Christ but hate the church? Is that idea biblical? How should believers respond when the church does un-Christlike things?

3. What are some of the amazing works of the King in creation that cause you to see his kingdom? What are some of the good works of his body, the church, that have enabled you to see the kingdom of God?

4. How real is the kingdom of God to you—really real, real, or unreal? As you consider this, think about your life and how the kingdom influences your actions throughout each day. Using the analogy of the Apollo 11 space program, what would it take for you to join the mission and have God's kingdom become really real for you?

5. How does Jesus coming to "tabernacle" in a human body give greater dignity to all human flesh (John 1:14)? How should Christians view their own bodies and the value of human life in light of Christ's taking on a human body for himself?

6. Where are you growing in how you see God's kingdom? What challenges do you still have?

7. Discuss your experience on the field trip. What did you learn? What surprised you? What challenged you?

Chapter Four Notes

CHAPTER FIVE

God's Kingdom Is Not...

Michelangelo sculpted the magnificent statue of David out of stone. I am not a sculptor, but I imagine that Michelangelo had to do a fair amount of chiseling in order to reveal the shape that would ultimately become the famous David statue. He had to keep chipping away everything that didn't belong to David, everything that wouldn't be part of the finished work of art.

When we embark to understand, see, and live in the kingdom, there is much in our minds that needs to be removed. As the beauty of the grand David statue was released from hard layers of useless stone, the kingdom of God must be unearthed from a crust of misconceptions. Take out your hammer and chisel. There's work to do.

Not a Metaphor

God's kingdom is not a metaphor. It's not a symbol. Jesus used parables to explain the kingdom, but this did not banish his really real kingdom to an unreal realm of imagery.

In the opening statement of his public ministry, Jesus didn't announce a clever allegory of an imagined rule, but declared in truth that "the kingdom of God is at hand" as he inaugurated his reign as the King of kings (Mark 1:15). If the kingdom of Jesus is merely a symbol, then Jesus is not a real king.

When Jesus cast out demons, healed the sick, and gave sight to the blind, he wasn't hinting at some vague sentiment like a performance artist, but was demonstrating the truth of his reign in real space and time. As a real king, Jesus established a new law (John 13:34), created a new covenant (Luke 22:19–20), and commissioned ambassadors to carry out his agenda (Matthew 28:16–20).

In perhaps the greatest irony of all time, Jesus really was crowned king by his Roman executioners (John 19:2–3), who also publicly announced this King to the world (John 19:14, 19–22). While they were acting in cruel jest, God used this pagan joke to proclaim his real intention to restore this world.

After he rose from the dead, Jesus didn't spend the forty precious days prior to his ascension further explaining a metaphor but, rather, taught his disciples about the real kingdom that had come and was coming (Acts 1:3). When he ascended, Jesus didn't just vanish into some ethereal land of clouds and harps; he was seated on a real throne at his Father's right hand (Acts 2:29–35).

Paul didn't spend two years in Rome giving ever more elaborate details of a symbolic kingdom. Rather, he explained to the church just what the rule and reign of Jesus among them was (Acts 28:23, 30–31) and how, in practical terms, they ought to arrange their lives in that kingdom.

The persecution that haunted the early church wasn't a figure of speech to train the disciples. It was a reality that announced the really real kingdom of God as being at odds with the kingdoms of Caesar, Herod, and Satan.

The parable of the hidden treasure makes no sense if the kingdom is merely an allegory. Who would trade everything real in his or her life for a symbol that has no substance or reality in the world? Are you living as if God's kingdom were a symbol, representation, or metaphor? If so, take your hammer and chisel and start chipping away those layers. The really real kingdom is to be found beneath your hardened mindset of symbolism. Like Michelangelo, let's remove those calcified veins that hide the best life possible under the good rule and reign of King Jesus.

Not a Tyranny of Tasks

The good, abundant life in God's kingdom is not a tyranny of religious tasks. God's throne is not a leather chair in a corporate corner office from which flow the dictates of a tedious micromanager. God doesn't intend our lives to be burdened by a jam-packed Google calendar of spiritual events. King Jesus is not a taskmaster like the Egyptian Pharaoh, who loaded Israel down with cruel labor and demanded that they make bricks and collect straw (Exodus 5). We need to recognize this and then chip away at this false belief.

Does your life of faith feel crushing? Are your religious works driven by the sting of a slave master's whip? The Exodus story illustrates what God's kingdom is not. We are not on some hamster wheel spinning with accusations of laziness and a barrage of impossible orders (Exodus 5:6–14), yet so many of us feel the oppression of a taskmaster breathing down our necks, dictating what our faith should and shouldn't be. If you've ever felt driven to endless toil without enjoying the fruit of your spiritual work, that's not the life of God's kingdom. That's the life of a slave.

God didn't deliver Israel from one slavery into another. He set them free in order to be a thriving, flourishing kingdom with an expansive life so filled with God's goodness that it would overflow to the rest of the world. In the same way, he didn't deliver Christian believers from one slavery into another.

New Testament authors did sometimes use the language of servants and slaves to describe our place in God's kingdom (Romans 1:1; 1 Corinthians 4:1; James 1:1; 2 Peter 1:1), but that language of service or slavery is not set within the context of oppressive tyranny or despotism. Our "slavery" is always within the framework of a covenantal, loving relationship, as a Father with his adored child or a groom with his beloved wife. Service under tyranny is true slavery, but service under love is true freedom.

I spent a few years inside a spiritually abusive church (AKA cult). The life of the church members in that group was akin to confined, exhaustive religious captivity. We were constantly driven by the taskmasters to attend more meetings, pray more, read more of the Bible, knock on more doors, preach on more corners, hand out more tracks, repent more, and confess more. All the while, when somebody asked, "Are you rejoicing, brother?" the answer had better be "Absolutely, brother." Or else.

If you are wearing a spiritual yoke that is difficult and are carrying a heavy burden, then you are not experiencing God's kingdom. That yoke is not the yoke of King Jesus (Matthew 11:28–30).

The parable of the hidden treasure does not make sense if the contents of that treasure box are shackles of religious duties. Who would sell all for that?

Bible Trip: No Longer a Slave

God's kingdom is not a tyranny of religious tasks. In your life of faith, do you seem to be running on a treadmill? Are you giving lots of effort but not getting very far? Are you driven from one task to another—Bible study, prayer, church services, small group, mission trips, and service projects? There's life in spiritual disciplines, but that life can be sucked out by guilt, shame, and feelings of inadequacy. We live in a self-imposed slavery, but let's look at the clear declaration of our freedom in the scriptures. Read these passages and claim them for your very own: Romans 8:14–15; Romans 14:17; Galatians 5:1; Matthew 11:28–30.

Small Group Guide

Read these scriptures together. Discuss your experience with journeys from slavery to freedom. Where have you been trapped in the past? Where are you trapped now? How have you been set free? Where are you being set free?

Not Far or Future

You may not believe that God's kingdom is merely a metaphor, but perhaps you think that it's very far away or a long time off. There's some good reason to think this. Take a quick look at a newspaper front page or your social media feed, and wreckage will jump out. How can God's kingdom be here and now when chaos, evil, and calamity seem to rule the day? Can Jesus really be King when the world is shut down by the coronavirus? Is Jesus really King when racial tensions and unjust civil systems bring terrible wreckage? If we're being honest, we don't even need to look at the news. We can just look at our own homes and hearts to wonder if or when God's reign might fully take hold.

Those who have watched cheesy 1970s "end times" movies or read popular apocalyptic novels may imagine that God's kingdom only follows worldwide catastrophes, global antichrist 666 tattoo campaigns, and Orwellian control by a dragon emerging from the sea. Before we live in the kingdom, do we first need to decipher headlines through enigmatic Revelation and Daniel codes? Should we be praying fervently that when we get raptured, we don't leave the oven on?

If we think that the kingdom of God is either far away or far off in time, we'll completely miss the kingdom that is here and now. Yes, the fullness and consummation of the kingdom may be distant, but that doesn't negate the reality that his kingdom is accessible to us at this very moment.

The biblical study of eschatology comes from the two Greek words *eschatos*, meaning "last,"[32] and *logia*, meaning "collection, gathering (study)."[33] Eschatology looks at both what's already come to pass and what has not yet fully arrived—the "already/not yet." People who relegate God's kingdom entirely to the "not yet" are blind to what's already present.

Many biblical passages and sources demonstrate that the reign of Jesus is presently active, not just a future hope. The testimony is unassailable that the really real kingdom is here and now. Both John the Baptist and Jesus declared that "the kingdom of heaven is at hand" (Matthew 3:1–2; 4:17). In his public ministry, Jesus didn't say that someday he would have authority on earth to forgive sins but that he "*has* authority on earth to forgive sins" (Matthew 9:6–8). Present tense, not future.

What did Jesus do with that present-tense authority? He gave his disciples present-tense authority so that they could act on behalf of the King right then and there (Matthew 10:1). Why? Because the kingdom is not far or future. It is here and now.

The parable of the hidden treasure is not about some far-distant land hidden by the mists of eternity. We can enjoy the treasures of God's rule right now. We won't experience the fullness of that treasure here and now, but our lives will be incomplete if we miss his good reign today, in this moment.

Side Trip: Resources

Kings entrust resources to others, enlisting their help to rule the kingdom. Walk around the home where you live. What resources has King Jesus entrusted to you? Pay attention to physical and financial resources at your disposal that you can use for good. For example, do you have a kitchen table? Can that be a place where you invite others to share a meal with loving hospitality? Do you have a car that might serve somebody else who needs transportation? Flip through your checkbook or bank statements to see how your money is being spent. Is there evidence of generosity in the name of Jesus to show other people kindness? Record in your journal all of the "here and now" resources of God's kingdom that he has entrusted to your management in his name.

Not Divorced from the World

God's kingdom is not a disembodied existence with harps and clouds. We don't leave this earth to go to some distant heaven separate from creation. The kingdom isn't a Platonic spiritual existence in which you are finally freed from the constraints of the material world. God's kingdom is on earth now and will be on earth for eternity.[34]

This is why Jesus wanted to focus our intercession on making what's real in God's realm become real in our realm on this planet:

*Pray then like this: "Our Father in heaven, hallowed be your name. Your kingdom come, your will be done, **on earth as it is in heaven.** Give us this day our daily bread, and forgive us our debts, as we also have forgiven our debtors. And lead us not into temptation, but deliver us from evil."*

—Matthew 6:9–13

The imagery of the final eternal kingdom is not an "adios" to this world, but a renewal of the earth, restored and refreshed:

Then I saw a new heaven and a new earth, for the first heaven and the first earth had passed away, and the sea was no more. And I saw the holy city, new Jerusalem, coming down out of heaven from God, prepared as a bride adorned for her husband. And I heard a loud voice from the throne saying, "Behold, the dwelling place of God is with man. He will dwell with them, and they will be his people, and God himself will be with them as their God. He will wipe away every tear from their eyes, and death shall be no more, neither shall there be mourning, nor crying, nor pain anymore, for the former things have passed away."

—Revelation 21:1–4

Notice a few things from this passage. First, there is a new earth in the eternal age, not just a new heaven. Second, there is a new Jerusalem, God's royal capital city. Third, that capital city is coming *down* to earth. Finally, not only is God's capital city coming down to earth, but God himself will come down and dwell with us, among the people.

Rather than some foggy cloud-land in the skies, God's kingdom has gates, roads, walls, and foundations (Revelation 21:9–26). Furthermore, when Jesus taught us to advance his kingdom, he didn't separate the spiritual from the physical. He didn't create a false dichotomy of spiritual stuff as good and material stuff as bad. In fact, he often taught his disciples that their actions in the physical world matter to his kingdom reign.

Consider his parable of the sheep and the goats as a warning not to neglect the importance of earthly action as a part of his good order (Matthew 25:31–46). In that punch-in-the-gut teaching, Jesus talked about his moment of judgment when he will sit on his glorious throne with the whole world assembled at his feet. Those "sheep" who provided physical aid and comfort to "the least of these" are welcomed to receive the kingdom ready and waiting for them (Matthew 25:34–40). But the "goats" are commanded to depart from the throne because they neglected physical aid and comfort to those in need (Matthew 25:41–46).

If your life of faith is divorced from these workings of this world, then you are not fully living the good life of God's kingdom. Giving others food, water, housing, and clothing is the stuff of spiritual life as much as church attendance. The parable of the hidden treasure makes no sense if the only valuables inside are "spiritual" practices of worship songs and prayer. Tilling a garden, walking the woods, surfing a wave, or preparing a meal can have as much spiritual substance as fasting or reading the Bible.

Bible Trip: Here and Now

Dig into some scriptures that bang the "here and now" drum for God's kingdom. Look at the present, active, and current language that describes the rule of Jesus as King. These passages show the actions of one who *is* King, not one who will someday be King. As you read, search carefully to pick out the kingdom themes. Pay attention to the details about Jesus' authority, titles, claim, throne, and power. Also look for what others say about Jesus. Why? Finding the kingdom in scripture helps you to find the kingdom in your life. Keep in mind as you read these scriptures that "the right hand of God" is the place of royalty, rule, and authority in God's kingdom.

Matthew 10:1; Matthew 12:28; Matthew 28:18–20; Mark 15:1–2; Mark 16:19; Luke 4:33–36; Luke 19:37–40; Ephesians 1:20–23; Revelation 1:4–6

Small Group Guide

What are the challenges of reading the Bible with a kingdom perspective? How do scriptures change when you pay attention to kingdom themes? How can these themes start to spill over from the pages of the Bible into the actions of your life?

Not Dependent on the World

One modern strand of kingdom theology insists that God's rule and reign requires the institutions of this world to become explicitly Christian. So-called "Dominionism" and "Kingdom Now" adherents strive for Christian control of important sectors of society, such as media, healthcare, education, government, law, and business.[35]

This theology contends that God's kingdom requires these secular institutions to become controlled by Christian believers. If this doesn't happen, the world will remain under Satan's dominion. In effect, Kingdom Now theology requires sectors of earthly power to advance the power of the heavens. God's kingdom *can't* come without Christians in control. The rule of Jesus *won't* be advanced without a Christian in the Oval Office and a Christian Supreme Court. Without Christian teachers in universities, God's kingdom will be restrained.

But the clear teaching of Jesus was that his kingdom is not dependent on earthly powers and institutions.

Jesus answered, "My kingdom is not of this world. If my kingdom were of this world, my servants would have been fighting, that I might not be delivered over to the Jews. But my kingdom is not from the world."

—*John 18:36*

Yes, there are spheres or arenas where Christ followers ought to live out their faith, but only for the sake of being light in the darkness (Matthew 5:16). Not for the sake of programming the 5 o'clock news hour, but for the sake of loving people in every stratum of society.

The government of heaven under Christ does not depend on the government of China becoming Christian. In fact, an argument from history proves precisely the opposite of Dominionist or Kingdom Now theology. The church has thrived and "gone viral" when the governments and institutions of secular society were hostile to God's people, not controlled by God's people.

The explosion of the gospel recorded in Acts resulted from persecution of the fledgling church. Paul's missionary journeys were spread along the roads of Roman civil infrastructure built by pagan emperors who literally torched Christians. The gospel of King Jesus has flourished within millions of underground house churches hiding from oppressive rule. During the COVID-19 crisis of 2020, the infrastructure of the "evil internet" became the highway for God's good news to travel through online streaming of worship services and small groups that met over Zoom video conferences.

God wants Christians in the healthcare sector, but he doesn't need them there more than he needs Christians in factories, at construction sites, and playing professional baseball. Jesus does not need a gavel, a news camera, a microphone, a chalkboard, or votes to advance his kingdom. Jesus is not gathering infrastructure for citizens of his kingdom. He is gathering citizens. He wants followers in every sector and sphere of society, not because he wants the equipment or needs the brass plaques but because his commission is to go into all the world (Matthew 28:16–20).

The treasure in the field does not require an external kingdom support system for it to be any more relevant or effective than it already is. God's kingdom is present and advancing with or without our participation.

Not Divorced from Humanity

Jesus, the King of kings, is not looking for a one-sided relationship. He doesn't want an army of robots, mindlessly carrying out his orders. If he were a business manager, for example, his leadership would welcome diverse personalities, creative input, risk-taking, and trial and error from his employees.

Real kings rule real kingdoms through the citizens of those kingdoms. No king does all the work himself but, rather, enlists others to accomplish his sovereign will. Because Jesus is the King of his really real kingdom, he enlists people to do the work and advance the agenda of his realm.

God's kingdom advances through people who are entrusted with God's resources and then act in alignment with God's character. He does not make every decision for us, but he has given us creative minds to bring out the goodness embedded in his creation. *We are co-creators.*

In God's kingdom, he has adopted us as sons and daughters and made us the heirs of all things. As his children, we shall inherit the kingdom and rule for eternity with Christ. *We are co-heirs.*

In God's kingdom, he has delegated power and authority to us. We are sent into the world as ambassadors to act in the name of Jesus. We are his agents sent to bring his blessing to the nations in love, truth, justice, and peace.

We are vice-regents.

God's sovereign rule does not exclude our free will and independent decisions. Rather, in a greater order of sovereignty, his providential rule is accomplished through our free will submitted to his good designs. People are not incidental to the active rule in the kingdom; they are a primary means of that rule. *God's kingdom comes when your deepest joy meets a most desperate need and brings the greatest good in the world around you.*

This is the clear story of scripture repeated over and over from Genesis to Revelation. Moses is an excellent Old Testament example of a human being called to be God's representative. God could have popped into Pharaoh's throne room himself, zapped the evil tyrant, and then led Israel out of Egypt in a blaze of glory. Instead, he commissioned Moses to be his representative. Through Moses, God performed miracles, passed judgments, and delivered his people. In his rule as King, God chose Moses to be his right-hand man, who would carry out the work and speak on his behalf.

In the Exodus narrative, God said, "The Egyptians shall know that I am the LORD, when *I stretch out my hand* against Egypt and bring out the people of Israel from among them" (Exodus 7:5). Shortly thereafter, God again said, "By this you shall know that I am the LORD: behold, *with the staff that is in my hand* I will strike the water that is in the Nile, and it shall turn into blood" (Exodus 7:17). But as the story unfolded, it was the hand of Moses (and Aaron) that struck the Nile (Exodus 7:19–20). God's hand acted through human hands.

In the New Testament, it is made clear that the church body is the body of Christ, and it is through the church that God's rule extends to the ends of the earth. However, this passage in Exodus is an Old Testament version of a human being the body of God. God could have appeared himself and done the work without a human mediator, but he chose people to be his body on earth.

Many times, God chooses *broken* people to bring his rule to a broken world. Messy people are selected to offer goodness to a messy world. Rebels are adopted into the royal family so that they can reach the rebels outside of the family. Idol worshippers are placed in seats of authority to establish the proper worship of the King amidst an idolatrous world. These broken, messy, rebellious, and idolatrous people have a real role establishing God's really real kingdom on earth.

We sometimes think that since God doesn't technically need us, there is no reason to enter into a deeper relationship with him. But make no mistake about it! God placed the treasure in the field because he desperately wants us to find it and interact with it. He wants us to be part of what he is doing, and he has a role for you and me. This is worth repeating: *God's kingdom comes when your deepest joy meets a most desperate need and brings the greatest good in the world around you.*

Side Trip: Deep Joy

Carry a journal with you for the next week. Any time you sense deep joy or satisfaction, record precisely what you were doing at the time. Were you crafting something with your hands? Offering a sympathetic ear to a friend? Cooking a meal? At the end of the week, look for patterns in your joy. These fulfilled desires are clues to who you were made to be. They point toward your personal role in God's kingdom. God handcrafted you with a unique set of talents, passions, and gifts. The more you understand these one-of-a-kind abilities, the more you'll discover your distinct purpose in bringing the kingdom on earth as it is in heaven.

Not Entirely Human

While the rule of God's kingdom is not divorced from humanity, it's not merely a human endeavor, either. We're not left alone to figure it out down below while God hovers over the smite button on his computer up above, waiting for us to mess up.

The ancient philosopher Epicurus believed that the gods, if they existed at all, were far off and never meddled in the affairs of this world. The Epicurean life is ruled by the random interactions of atoms, so human beings may as well enjoy the ride free from worry about any so-called deity. Theologian N. T. Wright argues that the world view of today's Western civilization is dominated by this third-century BC philosopher.[36] Our modern culture is Epicurean through and through. God has been banished to the attic and has no interest, ability, or business interfering with our enlightened world.

But ultimately, God's kingdom on earth is *God's* kingdom on earth. All earthly power is derived from his power. All goodness and love emanate from his goodness and love. All creativity can be traced to God's creativity as the source. The design of all creation comes from his mind. The deepest desire of every human heart finds satisfaction in God alone.

[Jesus] is the image of the invisible God, the firstborn of all creation. For by him all things were created, in heaven and on earth, visible and invisible, whether thrones or dominions or rulers or authorities—all things were created through him and for him. And he is before all things, and in him all things hold together. And he is the head of the body, the church. He is the beginning, the firstborn from the dead, that in everything he might be preeminent. For in him all the fullness of God was pleased to dwell, and

through him to reconcile to himself all things, whether on earth or in heaven, making peace by the blood of his cross.
—*Colossians 1:15–20*

All things are held together by the word of his power. God fills the church with his Holy Spirit as a guide, teacher, and comforter. Yes, God reigns through people, but his people are not cut off from God's resources, inspiration, and direction. At the end of this age, all worship and honor will be directed to Jesus the King. History will conclude with abundant clarity of what *he has accomplished* through our wobbly stewardship of the gifts, authority, and resources entrusted to us.

As we chip away at the various misconceptions that surround God and his kingdom, we are left with truth. That truth is that God's kingdom is really real and active today. Following Jesus brings freedom and partnership. This is a lifelong pursuit and an ongoing endeavor that will bring the best out of you and me, offering a life of abundance and fulfillment far beyond what we can imagine or achieve for ourselves.

CHAPTER FIVE FIELD TRIP

Creating Order

G. K. Chesterton said, "And the more I considered Christianity, the more I found that while it had established a rule and order, the chief aim of that order was to give room for good things to run wild."[37]

For this field trip, you will find an area of chaos in your life and bring some order. What is being wasted or has fallen into disrepair? Where is there something ruined that can be restored? When you create order from chaos, you are acting in God's image in making room for good things to run wild. That's how God's kingdom comes. God's kingdom brings goodness. His rule increases beauty. His reign results in an order that leads to flourishing.

When my wife and I bought our house, the one drawback was a terrible backyard. A weed-covered slope with a gravel pit rendered the space useless. The yard was a chaotic waste that required constant weeding and would get overgrown if we turned our backs for a moment. But from that chaos, we created a dream backyard. We hauled in forty dump trucks of sand to fill in the pit. Then we brought in ten dump trucks of huge boulders to create terraces, patios, and a firepit amphitheater. The work was back-breaking (and expensive!), but in the end, we have a space that is beautiful, peaceful, and amazing for entertaining people we love. We created order from chaos to bring out great good.

Find something that is chaotic and bring it into order. This can be something small or big. The chaos may be lurking in that disheveled closet, a broken car, or an unfinished project at work. The chaos could be a neglected relationship, your crazy calendar, or out-of-control finances. Perhaps a bad habit needs to come under God's good rule. Is it time to tackle your out-of-control social media? Drinking? Approval seeking and people pleasing?

Beware. The Trap of Inaction is crouching and lurking. It seeks to devour this field trip. You will be strongly tempted to do nothing about the chaos in your life. This may be the most difficult trip in *The Kingdom Field Guide*. Creating order from chaos can be supremely difficult. But if you want God's kingdom to come in your life, you will partner with him to create order and make room for good things to run wild.

Field Trip Details

Travel: None

Cost: Costs vary depending on your project. Creating order is often less expensive than allowing the chaos to continue.

Time: Varies, but be sure to schedule the time for this field trip. It may take a few hours or a few weeks. Put it on your calendar. Don't let the Trap of Inaction keep you stuck in your chaos.

Physical Demands: Vary depending on the project. Ask your small group to help if needed.

Gear: If you don't have the tools to do the job, borrow what you need from a friend, your family, or your small group.

Key Scriptures to Guide Your Trip: Genesis 1–2; Proverbs 25:28; Isaiah 32:17–18; Ephesians 2:14; Galatians 5:22–23; 2 Timothy 1:7

*Schedule this field trip now. Put it on your calendar!
Day: _____
Time: _____
People invited to join me: _____
_____
_____

Seeing the Kingdom Connection

When a kingdom captures territory, the king extends his order to that people and place. The chaos of the old realm is brought under the ruling order of the new. The creation account in Genesis 1–2 is presented in this context. From the chaos of the deep darkness, God was the King creating order. He separated dark from light (Genesis 1:3–5), heaven from earth (1:6–8), and sea from land (1:9–10), and day from night (1:14–19). From that order, life sprang out with overflowing flourishing (1:11–13, 20–25). And every step of the way, God the King pronounced the ordering of his creation "good."

This is a very basic definition of a kingdom: a king creates order from chaos to bring goodness to his people and land. That is what God was doing in Genesis. That is what God has been doing in all of history. That is love. That is what God is doing in your life right now. God wants you to partner with him to create order from chaos so good things can run wild.

Questions for Reflection

1. What sticks out from this field trip or is a new idea for you?

2. What questions have come out of this field trip? What doesn't make sense to you?

3. How do you see Jesus and his kingdom in this experience?

4. How can you apply this to your life and take a next step?

5. What will you talk to God and other people about?

After this field trip, circle where you are right now in your journey to find God's kingdom as a hidden treasure.

Blind   Aware   Ponder   Value   Trap of   Prioritize   Own/Sell
Inaction

Journal: Spend some time in your journal to record further thoughts.

Chapter Five Discussion Questions

Key Scripture:
Creating Order from Chaos
Genesis 1:1–2:25

1. Read Genesis chapters 1–2 through the lens of a king ordering his kingdom. How does this perspective change your view of the creation account? Do you believe that Christ's kingdom is literal or figurative? How is this belief manifested in your life?

2. Describe a time when you became pulled into religious "slavery," seeing God's kingdom as tasks, rules, and burdens. Why is this an easy trap to fall into? How can believers resist and refute well-meaning Christians (including leaders) who try to foist this view of the kingdom upon others?

3. Which parts of God's kingdom are "not yet"? Which parts are "already"? Which do you focus on more?

4. What are some distinctions that you tend to draw between "spiritual" activities and "regular" activities? How would it change your life if you were to view all

of your work and leisure as part of God's kingdom?

5. What are some of the dangers that can come with believers looking to Christian political or cultural leaders to build the kingdom? Give examples that you have observed. How can believers support and encourage Christians in the public eye without confusing these positions of earthly influence as the reign of God's kingdom?

6. *He does not make every decision for us, but he has given us creative minds to bring out the goodness embedded in his creation. We are co-creators.* What does it mean to you personally to be a co-creator with God? What are some practical ways you enjoy expressing your creativity? How can these activities bring glory to God?

7. What are some examples of when you have brought order out of chaos and seen goodness as a result? What is something chaotic in your life right now that needs to come under God's good ruling order? What would be a first step toward making that happen?

8. Discuss your experience on the field trip. What did you learn? What surprised you? What challenged you?

Chapter Five Notes

CHAPTER SIX

The Need for a New Narrative

A popular illustration is often used in evangelism and on mission trips to illustrate the gospel message. The image does show some truth of the gospel, but it more loudly proclaims what theologian David Bryant has termed the "Crisis of Christology."[38]

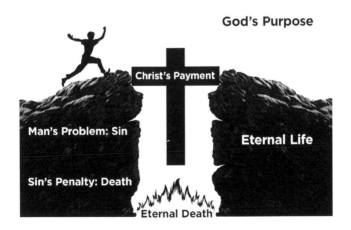

A solitary person is about to make "a leap of faith" over the gap between God and man. The poor soul's sin carries a death penalty, and the flames of hell perilously await below. In using a version of this comic, the evangelist typically points out to a lost sinner the good news that Christ's payment on the cross bridges the chasm so the soul can reach eternal life with God.

This carries some truth but raises many questions. Does this evangelistic tool indicate the full life that is available to us once we discover the treasure in the field (Matthew 13:44)? Is this how Jesus instructed his disciples to preach the gospel of the kingdom (Matthew 24:14)?

Jesus—The Bridge Girder?

If that image communicates the fullness of the gospel, then Christ is little more than a bridge girder, a metal truss with the sole function of spanning a fiery chasm so people can walk over him. That is a crisis of Christology.

In a church desperately needing an awakening to who Christ is, the gospel often gets reduced to some version of "Jesus died for you, so believe in him, escape hell, and go to heaven." But that's not the gospel of the kingdom. Why? Because it doesn't address God's kingdom or the exalted King. An evangelist who avoids the news of the kingdom undercuts the reality that there is now a new King ruling.

To be fair, the gospel of the kingdom is difficult to preach to people who don't have ready images for kingdoms in mind.[39] If I'm really being honest, in full disclosure, I even led a missionary effort in Honduras in which we used this very same visual to share the gospel in a mountainside village. One of our projects was to paint a water tank.

Please, hear me carefully on this. The cross of Jesus *does* bridge the gap between us and God. We *are* delivered from the eternal consequences of our sin by the sacrifice of Jesus. But we contribute to the crisis of Christology if we avoid preaching, teaching, and sharing about the kingdom.

A typical pushback in American churches is that people don't understand kingdoms since we live in a country that rebelled against a king. But shouldn't that same logic prevent teaching about justification, sanctification, substitutionary atonement, and eternal punishment for sins? Aren't these ideas even stranger than the concept of a kingdom? If that line of reasoning is true, shouldn't the math teacher avoid instruction on differential equations since the students don't understand calculus? Shouldn't the foreign language teacher avoid using Spanish since the students speak English?

The position of "we don't understand kingdoms" falls apart when you look at the entertainment we consume. Our movies, TV shows, and video games are absolutely dominated by kingdom narratives. Billions of dollars per year are spent on kingdom stories. *Star Wars*, *The Lord of the Rings*, *Harry Potter*, *Game of Thrones*, *Downton Abbey*, Marvel, Disney—all of them are kingdom stories. We are enthralled by kingdom narratives. Why? Because we were made and designed to live in an eternal kingdom.

The church's problem is not that people don't understand kingdoms. The problem is that we *only* understand kingdoms but have stripped the kingdom from the gospel. In modern Western culture, it seems that the only place you can go and not see a really good kingdom story is in most churches, the body of King Jesus. Communion gets offered without connecting that sacrament to God's kingdom, even though Jesus made this connection five times in four Gospel accounts. Baptism is divorced from the baptism story of Israel's deliverance from slavery to become a kingdom in the promised land. We preach about our deliverance from hell to heaven, but there is little mention of a real citizenship transferred from the kingdom of darkness to the kingdom of light. People go to church and take the name "Christian" but don't live in the royalty that Christ offers through his kingly name.

The Zoom Problem

Somehow in our gospel presentations, we zoom in very tightly on atonement theology and often completely miss the larger picture of the kingdom that atonement secures for us. In our Christian world view, we focus almost entirely on the wounds of the sacrificial Lamb hanging on the cross, and we miss the sign hanging above the Lamb that reads, "Jesus of Nazareth, the King of the Jews" (John 19:19).

Ironically, when Pilate wrote the inscription above Jesus on the cross, he used three languages—Aramaic, Latin, and Greek—so that the widest possible audience would understand that Jesus' claim to be king had landed him on the cross (John 19:20). But our modern gospel too often doesn't bring that same message to its audience. Yes, Jesus was crucified and rose from the dead, *but don't stop there.* He is the crucified and risen King who is bringing his kingdom to earth as it is in heaven. The marks inscribed on the sign above the crucified King are at least as important as the marks of the nails in his hands and feet. This is getting at the gospel of the kingdom.

When the Apostle Paul met with the elders of the church in Ephesus, he had a very instructional conversation with them. He insisted that he didn't hold anything back but declared to them "the whole counsel of God" (Acts 20:27). What was the dominant theme and primary content of that whole counsel? Paul said that he testified "to the gospel of the grace of God" and that he had "gone about proclaiming the kingdom" (Acts 20:24–25).

Paul was very concerned that the leaders of the Ephesian church should know the complete and full account of the gospel. He didn't withhold anything for their benefit. He taught repentance, faith, the lordship of Jesus, and the gospel of grace.

Those four things are captured in our comic strip of the poor soul looking to cross the chasm of eternal fire, but there's something else. Paul went about "proclaiming the kingdom" (Acts 20:25). He called people to faith not just in Jesus, but in the Lord Jesus Christ (Acts 20:21). His call wasn't just to prompt people to believe that Jesus existed but, rather, to prompt people to give their loyalty, obedience, and trust to Jesus as the Christ and the King. His gospel was entirely immersed in God's work to establish his kingdom. Matthew W. Bates' book *Salvation by Allegiance Alone* brilliantly explains why our faith is fully expressed as life-long allegiance to King Jesus, rather than mere mental agreement with a list of statements about Jesus.[41]

As Paul was about to depart from these beloved friends

at Ephesus, his final statement to them was secured with a lynchpin: "I did not shrink from declaring to you the whole counsel of God" (Acts 20:27). He insisted that the whole counsel of God includes the proclamation of the kingdom of God. It cannot be otherwise. The whole counsel of God without the kingdom of God is not the whole counsel of God, just as the gospel of the kingdom without the kingdom is not the gospel of the kingdom. The gospel *must* include the kingdom. Sharing the gospel without the kingdom is like selling a new car without the engine.

Was it only in Ephesus that, for some reason, Paul spoke about the kingdom? Was there some cultural reason for him to put the gospel in a kingdom frame that was not needed elsewhere? Not at all. The kingdom was a universal and constant theme as Paul shared the gospel of the kingdom in all of his writings, in all of the places he visited, to all audiences, both Jewish and Greek.

There's no coincidence that the book of Acts is bookended with kingdom proclamations. Acts begins with Jesus in Jerusalem, "appearing to them during forty days and speaking about the kingdom of God" (Acts 1:1–3). The book of Acts ends with Paul in Rome, "testifying to the kingdom of God" from morning to evening (Acts 28:23). Paul "lived there two whole years…, proclaiming the kingdom of God and teaching about the Lord Jesus Christ" (Acts 28:30–31).

The author Luke bookended his account with Jesus and Paul teaching about the kingdom to let us know that it is through the kingdom narrative that we can understand everything in between. That narrative requires us to proclaim and explain that Jesus is King and the present coming of his kingdom is really real.

A New Comic Strip

Perhaps we can hijack that popular comic strip and bend it toward a gospel that includes the kingdom, something like my own crude version below:

Jesus left his throne in heaven to bring the good reign of his kingdom to earth, making the way and securing his victory by suffering on the cross. Why? To bring the blessing of God to everyone and every nation on earth. It is a campaign of conquest, not to enslave but to set free.

The restoration of our royalty is a major part of the restoration of humanity. Just recently, Prince Harry and Meghan Markle quit their posts as senior members of the royal family in Great Britain. In a sense, they laid aside their crowns in the kingdom to move to Los Angeles. Imagine Queen Elizabeth crossing the chasm of oceans and continents and knocking on the door of their home in exile. When they open the door, Her Majesty holds out their rightful crowns with an invitation to resume their place as Duke and Duchess of Sussex. This restoration includes the renewal of the privileges and responsibilities of their true nobility.

Jesus is knocking on our doors in exile. He waits outside with not just forgiveness of sins, but also crowns in hand. He came to restore our rightful place of ruling with him for eternity, beginning right here and now. Then, as in the grand summary of the whole Bible story, "the kingdom of the world has become the kingdom of our Lord and of his Christ, and he shall reign forever and ever" (Revelation 11:15). This is the good news of the kingdom.

Resurfacing the Roman Road

Often the "kingdom-less" gospel shared with people draws a few passages from Paul's letter to the Romans. We call this the "Roman Road to Salvation." The typical Roman Road message leaves out Paul's emphasis on God's kingdom and instead has a narrow focus on faith, sin, and forgiveness. The hearer is left with only a leap across the gulf of flames by the cross of Jesus, the bridge girder. But if we must go down a Roman Road, can we at least always include the kingdom context in which Paul's theology was immersed? To get this context set in our minds, let's look at Romans 5:17–19:

For if, because of one man's trespass, death reigned through that one man, much more will those who receive the abundance of grace and the free gift of righteousness reign in life through the one man Jesus Christ.

Therefore, as one trespass led to condemnation for all men, so one act of righteousness leads to justification and life for all men. For as by the one man's disobedience the many were made sinners, so by the one man's obedience the many will be made righteous.

When Paul said that righteousness and grace *reign* through Jesus Christ, he was addressing the real rule of Jesus as a real King. If we must draw comics of this cosmic story, let's at least reflect the resounding heartbeat of that story. Doesn't this updated gospel comic better reflect the core message these Bible passages present as the gospel of the kingdom?

We need to take instruction from Jesus' parable of the four soils (Matthew 13:1–23). Read that parable closely. The seed is "the word of the kingdom" (Matthew 13:19). The good soil is those who hear and understand the word of the kingdom (Matthew 13:23). If that's true, we need pastors, parents, business owners, community leaders, and other influencers who speak and teach the word of the kingdom so that people can hear and understand it, yielding a crop of thirtyfold, sixtyfold, or a hundredfold.

It may seem silly to spend so much time considering comic strips, but there is something extremely powerful in those simple drawings. They represent the stories in our heads. Stories are powerful; they shape our world view. Personal stories literally control what we can see in the world. The stories in our heads drive our lives in the world.

God's kingdom is really real. Jesus Christ is the really real King. The stories in our heads must align with the reality of the world. If our personal narratives do not include God's kingdom, then we aren't living as if Jesus is King. And if we are not living as if Jesus is King, we have a true crisis.

Bible Trip: Theirs Is the Kingdom

With Jesus' parable of the hidden treasure, it's a fair question to ask, "What's in the treasure box?" If we are supposed to sell all to acquire that treasure, shouldn't we have full disclosure of the contents of the box? For this Bible Trip, you're going to lift the lid and peek inside.

Spend some time pondering. This is the pursuit of a lifetime, but your heart and mind must be captured before you're willing to trade all you have for all God has. Read these Bible passages as a meditation on what's waiting for you, hidden in the field:

Daniel 7:27; Matthew 5:3, 10; Luke 12:32; Ephesians 1:1–23; Colossians 1:13–20; Hebrews 12:25–29.

The Power of Story

The human brain is a story machine. Our minds generate stories with lightning speed. We are constantly engaged in creating narratives to make sense of the world around us. We can't live without stories. Every scrap of data our brains collect is instantly shaped into a story.

This happens in the packed aisles of Costco when somebody bumps your shopping cart as he angles in for the free sample of turkey pot pie, fresh from the toaster. You don't just get mad. Your brain generates a story, and the story makes you mad.

At Thanksgiving dinner, when your Uncle Wilmer tells another lame joke, your brain works it into a narrative about his pathetic life.

When your neighbors allow their lawn to become overrun with weeds, a story is generated about their lazy indifference to the market value of your house.

Social scientist and leadership guru Joseph Grenny

describes the process of story in his book *Crucial Conversations*.[42] Our brains whip through this process hundreds of times a day:

1. You see or hear an event. This data enters your brain.

2. Within a microsecond, your brain forms the data into a story.

3. The story generates an emotion.

4. The emotion motivates you to action.

Data never floats around loose in our minds. All of it is captured and crammed into stories. Then, right or wrong, those stories drive the actions of our lives. We have personal narratives in our homes, workplaces, schools, churches, and neighborhoods. Every relationship is driven by a story. And the stories we make have tremendous power over our lives. They drive our lives in the world.

N. T. Wright describes the power of story as follows:[43]

That, I believe, is one of the reasons why God has given us so much story, so much narrative in scripture. **Story authority, as Jesus knew only too well, is the authority that really works.** Throw a rulebook at people's heads, or offer them a list of doctrines, and they can duck or avoid it, or simply disagree and go away. **Tell them a story, though, and you invite them to come into a different world; you invite them to share a worldview or better still, a 'God-view'.** That, actually, is what the parables are all about. They offer, as all genuine Christian story-telling does, a worldview which, as someone comes into it and finds how compelling it is, quietly shatters the worldview they were in already. **Stories determine how people see themselves and how they see the world. Stories determine how they experience God, and the world, and themselves, and others.**

Great revolutionary movements have told stories about the past and present and future. They have invited people to see themselves in that light, and people's lives have been changed. If that happens at a merely human level, how much more when it is God himself, the creator, breathing through his word.

You have stories in your head, thousands of them, always. If you're not aware of them now, you need to be, because the stories you create for yourself determine who you are and where you are going, whether you know it or not.

Because God's kingdom is really real, we need the narratives in our heads to be aligned with reality. We are, in reality, kingdom citizens. We are, in reality, adopted by the King. We are, in reality, ambassadors of that King. We are, in reality, entrusted with authority from that King.

We need to get our stories straight. Why? Because when somebody is living a story that doesn't align with reality, that *always* creates wreckage.

The story in our heads must come into alignment with the reality of all creation, and everything in all creation is ultimately a kingdom under God's rule. We need a kingdom narrative that drives and integrates our whole being: mental, emotional, physical, spiritual, and social. In the biblical language of baptism, we are to be immersed in that narrative because our baptism is a full submersion into Jesus, and Jesus is still fully living a kingdom story.

Assume that your job defines your full identity. Could you work for Jeff Bezos and not have Amazon be the backbone of your story? Could you be employed by Bill Gates and not have Microsoft shape the narrative of your life?

Adopting a personal kingdom narrative is essential to having what biblical authors called "the mind of Christ" and "abiding in Christ." The Apostle Paul instructed the church in Philippi to be "of the same mind, having the same love, being in full accord and of one mind" (Philippians 2:2). What mind were they to have? None other than the mind of Christ (Philippians 2:5).

This is no robotic reprogramming or cultic indoctrination. Being of the same mind doesn't jeopardize your unique personality, wiring, or experiences. But when your story gets woven into the story of Jesus, then you can grow into the person God uniquely designed you to be. The Jesus way of thinking brings out the best of who you are. The Jesus way of being mindful enhances your personality without compromising it. The Jesus way of seeing and interpreting the world helps you to live fully in that world. Anything short of having the Jesus way of walking through this world is a crippling crawl.

Paul told the church in Corinth that we "have the mind of Christ" (1 Corinthians 2:16) and "take every thought captive to obey Christ" (2 Corinthians 10:5). To the church in Colossae, he wrote, "Set your minds on things that are above" (Colossians 3:2). He urged the church in Rome, "Do not be conformed to this world, but be transformed by the renewal of your mind" (Romans 12:2).

Jesus himself told his disciples that if his words lived vibrantly in their minds, they would be like thriving branches that bear fruit (John 15:1–8). Abiding in the vine of Jesus means allowing your whole self to be invigorated by him. This begins when the story in your head is shaped by the narrative that you are an heir of the kingdom, co-heir with Christ, created to receive the fullness of all the kingdom. That is the reality.

Bible Trip: The Story in Your Head

Reflect on these passages and take an honest assessment of your personal narrative. Does the story in your head

> align with the reality of your royal identity?
>
> • Daniel 7:13–14, 27
> • Matthew 5:3
> • Galatians 3:25–29
> • Galatians 4:1–7
> • Romans 8:14–18
>
> **Small Group Guide**
>
> Read these passages together. How much of your mental energy is spent on God's kingdom? How much attention is given to the reign of Jesus at home, at work, at school, or in your neighborhood? Wrestle together with the questions and challenges these Bible passages pose. Agree together to memorize one of these scriptures.

The verses from Daniel 7 provide one of the best pictures of what's inside that treasure box hidden in the field. If I may be blunt, we are fools if we don't align our lives with the truth that we were created to receive "the greatness of the kingdoms under the whole heaven" (Daniel 7:27). I say this in love.

Dr. David Reimer spells it out:[44]

[Wisdom is] that orientation which allows one to live in harmonious accord with God's ordering of the world.

God orders the world as a kingdom, his kingdom, and he has placed us in that world as heirs and stewards of that kingdom. God wants us to rule and reign in the really real kingdom with him. A life misaligned with this orientation lacks wisdom. We are somewhat crazy any time the story in our heads doesn't align with reality. The story in your head matters more than you know.

Side Trip: Six-Word Story

Grab your journal and go outside. Clear your thoughts and take some deep breaths. Now, in thirty seconds, write a six-word story that captures the narrative in your head right now about your life. Here are some examples: (A) Working hard, tired to the bone. (B) Lost, can't find my way home. (C) Can't wait for the long weekend. Don't worry about making it pretty. Just make it honest. What would it take for the story in your head to align with God's really real kingdom? Journal some of your thoughts. Write one action step you can prioritize today that would help to reshape the story in your head so that it aligns with God's kingdom.

Small Group Guide

Do this exercise in your small group. Share your six-word stories with each other. Why does that narrative capture your life right now? Don't try to fix one another. Be good listeners as others share their stories. Talk about how the story in your head can be more aligned with the story of God's really real kingdom.

Story Editing

How do you change the story in your head? First, know that it is difficult work. Very difficult. When a story gets planted, the roots often go deep. Brain scientists believe that stories get hardwired into the physical structures of our brains. Neural pathways develop to channel our thought processes in alignment with stories that guide our lives.

Want proof? Try this simple experiment. Think of a moment in your life when you got really angry. As you think of this incident, notice what story accompanies it. Who are the heroes and villains? Now notice your heart rate. What's happening to your breathing? Pay attention to your sweat glands. This is the wiring of your brain being triggered by a story to go into fight-or-flight mode. Now, depending on how emotionally flooded you are, put down the book and go do something else for at least twenty minutes. Don't rehearse the story while you do these things. Our brains need at least twenty minutes to switch out of fight-or-flight mode.

This is what we are up against to change the story in our heads, but it can and must be done. Changing your personal narrative begins with noticing that your brain is a storytelling machine and then paying attention to the stories you create. The good news is that the story of your life can be edited!

I recommend some other resources for a much more detailed treatment of story-changing techniques. *Redirect* by Timothy Wilson,[45] *The Power of Story* by Jim Loehr,[46] *Anatomy of the Soul* by Dr. Curt Thompson,[47] and the *Self Authoring Suite* by Dr. Jordan Peterson[48] are excellent. But for the purposes of *The Kingdom Field Guide*, you need to know that rewriting a personal narrative is not new. The biblical accounts are filled with God instilling a new narrative into our lives—the kingdom narrative.

During the early church period, there was a group of gentile pagans living in Asia Minor. They became disciples of Jesus and formed many churches in what's now modern-day Turkey. The Apostle Peter wrote to these formerly pagan Christians, urging them to adopt a new identity and a new narrative for their lives:

> But you are a chosen race, a royal priesthood, a holy nation, a people for his own possession, that you may proclaim the excellencies of him who called you out of darkness into his marvelous light. Once you were not a

people, but now you are God's people; once you had not re-
ceived mercy, but now you have received mercy.

—1 Peter 2:9–10

When Peter coached the believers, he reinforced how they were part of YHWH's story as God's people, his chosen ones, directly connected to the Exodus story. Peter made a direct reference to the story of the Jewish people at Mount Sinai. He connected to a time when the Jews needed to change their story from Egyptian slaves to a chosen and royal people, "a holy nation" (Exodus 19:6). Peter encouraged the pagan Christians of his day to make the story edits in their minds. Though once they had lived in the darkness of idolatry, they were now to live as royal citizens in God's kingdom. Their story had to change.

For us fully to enjoy the rich goodness of God's really real kingdom available to us, we must change the story in our heads.

Bible Trip: Gaps and Ambiguities

One way to adopt a kingdom story in our lives is to step into the kingdom story of the scriptures. Fortunately, the biblical authors were genius in creating narrative spaces for us to step into and explore. Old Testament scholar Jerome T. Walsh describes how biblical narrative intentionally creates gaps and ambiguities so that the reader is drawn to enter the story.[49]

One of the ancient Christian techniques of engaging the bible is called "Entering the Narrative" or "The Ignatian Method." I urge you to practice this simple exercise often. The more you inhabit the story of the kingdom, the more the story of the kingdom will live in you. For this Bible Trip, carve out half an hour in your week to try the Ignatian Method of entering a scriptural narrative.[50]

1. Choose a passage in scripture that narrates a story or a parable, ideally one in which God or Jesus encountered an individual or a group of people.

2. Read the passage at least two times to become familiar with it.

3. Bring the scene to life in your imagination with yourself as a participant. Use all of your senses to experience the scene around you. What do you see? What do you hear? What do you smell? What do you sense or feel? Can you taste anything? Take all the time you need to be in the scene as if you were actually there.

4. Consider all of the human characters. Is there one with whom you identify? Can you envision yourself as this person? Take time to imagine what you would be thinking and feeling in that person's shoes. What would you say or do?

5. Is Jesus in this scene? Is God the Father or the Holy Spirit in this scene? What is he doing? What is he saying to you?

6. Allow the scene to unfold. Don't try to control the story; let it happen. Allow yourself to be affected by the words and actions of the story.

7. Talk to God about what you've experienced. Ask him what the feelings mean. Receive the gift or invitation God is giving you through this experience. Is there anything you want to ask God for or about?

8. What is your response to God? Is there something you will do differently in your life in light of this? Give thanks to God for meeting you.

As you explore the space of biblical narratives, pay close attention to kingdom themes. You'll be shocked at how many details are shaped by royalty. Look for crowns, thrones, authority, kingdoms, rulers, kings, scepters, armies, territories, economies, laws, and covenants. Look for these details in the stories of scripture; they are also the details of the real story of your life.

These passages are great for this exercise: Matthew 8:23–27; Luke 5:17–39; Luke 1:26–38; Genesis 3:1–13; and 2 Samuel 9:1–13.

Small Group Guide

This is a great exercise to do with your small group! First, go through the Ignatian exercise on your own. Then share your experience with others in a small group discussion.

Israel's Baptism

The Bible can't be understood apart from the Exodus story of Israel escaping Egypt, and the Exodus story can't be understood apart from baptism. The miraculous crossing through the waters of the Red Sea is described as a baptism—an immersion not just into water, but into a whole new life (1 Corinthians 10:1–5; Romans 6:1–11). The moment Israel walked through those parted waters, the whole life of a nation was submerged into a brand-new narrative. Once they were slaves, and then they were free. Once they were oppressed by King Pharaoh, and then they were redeemed by King YHWH.

The Exodus story of Israel influences practically every fiber of the biblical narrative all the way to Revelation. Key elements of the Exodus story occur time and time again[51] throughout scripture:

- Isaiah described the deliverance of Israel out of Babylonian captivity using Exodus themes

(Isaiah 43:19–21; 48:20–21; 52:11–12).

- Paul described our former life under sin as slavery (Romans 6:14; Galatians 4:8), and he cast our salvation in Exodus imagery (Colossians 1:13–14).

- Jesus used the Passover Feast as the occasion to mark his betrayal, trial, and execution (Matthew 26:2, 17–19; Luke 22:7; John 18:28).

Most importantly (at least for *The Kingdom Field Guide*), the New Testament makes the direct connection between the purpose of Moses' Exodus and the purpose of the greater Exodus led by Jesus, the Greater Moses. First, why did King YHWH lead Israel out of Egypt? It wasn't just to deliver them *from* enslavement in Pharaoh's kingdom, but also to deliver them *to* redemption in God's kingdom:

> *"Now therefore, if you will indeed obey my voice and keep my covenant, you shall be my treasured possession among all peoples, for all the earth is mine; **and you shall be to me a kingdom of priests** and a holy nation." These are the words that you shall speak to the people of Israel.*
> **—Exodus 19:5–6**

This passage is one of the great hinges of the entire story arc of the Bible. It captures what God is doing in all of history. He is making a kingdom of priests. He is gathering a people he dearly loves as a treasured possession. Shockingly, this scene is nearly always overlooked when telling the Exodus story. It gets overshadowed by the plagues that precede it or the Ten Commandments passage that follows.

Everybody knows what happened at the *top* of Mount

Sinai when God gave Moses the law. And everybody can quote some of those "Thou shalt not..." commandments. But only a tiny fraction of people, including Christians, remember what Moses spoke to the people at the *base* of Mount Sinai. Those words provide the whole context and framework for the commands given at the top of the mountain in the Law.

"You shall be to me a kingdom of priests" (Exodus 19:6) is the dye into which all of the fabric of Israel's nation was to be immersed. This is the story into which Israel was submerged when they left Egypt through the waters of the Red Sea. God wasn't just rescuing them *from* Pharaoh; he was rescuing them *for* himself as a treasured possession, as highly valued and deeply loved citizens of his kingdom. That very story continues with us today. God is still immersing us into that dye so that every fiber of our lives is colored by that same kingdom narrative.

The Apostle Peter made this explicitly clear, calling his formerly pagan audience "a chosen race, a royal priesthood, a holy nation, a people for [God's] own possession, ... sojourners and exiles" (1 Peter 2: 9, 11). Then, in the Revelation to the Apostle John, the whole narrative arc of the Bible concludes with an exclamation point. The ransomed throng of people from every tongue, tribe, and nation is identified as "a kingdom and priests to our God" (Revelation 5:10).

This is the Exodus story of God delivering his people *from* the kingdom of darkness and bringing them *to* the kingdom of light. This is the story into which Israel was baptized as they crossed the Red Sea. This is the story into which we have been baptized and the lens through which we ought to view every scene of our lives. All of the Bible, all of history, and our whole world, encompassing every person from every nation, is one grand kingdom story.

When the story in our heads aligns with reality, then and only then can we live a good life. Without this alignment, there is only frustration and wreckage. When the story in our heads is not aligned with reality, that's called being crazy. Christian faith without the very real kingdom narrative is craziness.

Imagine yourself as a Jew living in Egypt toward the end of a 430-year captivity. You can count back twenty generations of slaves. (If that's difficult to do, imagine if slavery hadn't been abolished in the United States and still persisted today as it did before the Civil War.) What would the narrative of your life be? What deeply ingrained story of oppression would dominate your world view and impact your daily existence? How would that shape your identity, forge your relationships, and color how you saw the world?

Now imagine that you're among the people who followed Moses through the Red Sea and were baptized into a new life after escaping Egypt. Imagine that at the base of Mount Sinai, you were told that God viewed you as part of his treasured possession and would include you as a citizen of his new kingdom of priests. Is it any wonder that the people of Israel had a hard time in the desert? Is it a surprise that some of them wanted to go back to Egypt to a familiar life of misery rather than face the uncertain future of a promised kingdom? It was incredibly difficult to change their narrative from slaves of King Pharaoh to sons of King YHWH.

The magnitude of the before and after of Israel's story is staggering. It must have felt like whiplash to the people. Put yourself in their place and notice the tectonic shifts:

- From ruthless slavery in the kingdom of Pharaoh to covenant freedom in the kingdom of YHWH (Exodus 1:13–14; 2:11)

- From the name of Pharaoh exalted in all of Egypt to the name of YHWH exalted in all the earth (Exodus 9:29; 14:17–18)

- From being distant from God, who had been hidden, to intimate knowledge of God's name of YHWH (Exodus 3:14–17) and God's presence manifested (Exodus 4:5, 29–30; 13:21–22; 14:13–14)

- From hatred and dread from King Pharaoh (Exodus 1:12) to being loved by King YHWH.

The overarching theme of this transformative story is from Exodus 19:6. God said, "You shall be to me a kingdom of priests and a holy nation." The Israelites needed to adopt that story in their minds and have it color every fiber of their lives.

Just as Israel needed to be baptized into their new narrative, our whole lives must be immersed in the kingdom story! It's worth a close look because God wants us to be baptized into this story as well. If we're baptized into Christ, how can we not be baptized into his story?

The Aimless Story

Peter called the church to live according to a new story and narrative (1 Peter 2:1–12).

You are a chosen race, a royal priesthood, a holy nation, a people for his own possession, that you may proclaim the excellencies of him who called you out of darkness into his marvelous light. Once you were not a people, but now you are God's people; once you had not received mercy, but now you have received mercy.

—1 Peter 2:9–10

This is a call to be immersed in a new narrative and to live according to a new script. It wasn't just about being *saved from* slavery. It was and is about being *saved for* a royal priesthood of God's kingdom. We have perfected the "saved from" storyline, but we've neglected the narrative of what we have been saved for. We try to live a story that has a beginning but no end. We know where we came from, but we have completely lost track of where we are going. We are no different from Israel. They wandered aimlessly for forty years, knowing full well where they had come from but forgetting where they were going.

This is the thrust of Paul's argument in his epistle to the Romans. He wasn't just teaching theology and doctrine; he was pleading for the readers to adopt a whole new life narrative. Romans 6 is littered with themes of the Israelites' baptism in their escape from slavery in Egypt. Paul urged the church to adopt the same life story so that they would no longer be aimless. Paul argued that we've been set free from the taskmaster of sin, so now we have a new lease on life through the goodness of Christ (Romans 6:3–7).

We haven't just been set free *from* sin; we've been set free *for* new life (Romans 6:8–14). We are under a new ruler, not the tyrant of sin and death. Our new dominion is the good, loving kingdom of the Christ. By baptism, we are immersed in Christ.

So then, when we get baptized into Christ, let's not leave off the core element of his story. When we are baptized into Christ, we take not just his moral fiber, but also his life story, his narrative, his purpose—his kingdom.

Side Trip: Kingdom Apps

Take a moment to go to the app store on your phone. Type in "kingdom" and look at the hundreds of games that have kingdom themes. Why is there such an obsession with kingdom content in our media and entertainment? We are desperate to ingest kingdom narratives. We are ravenous for them. Why? Because God wired that story into our DNA. He designed us to hunger and thirst for it. He created us to rule and reign with him in his kingdom. Take a quick inventory of your current media intake. What are the kingdom narratives you are feeding on?

CHAPTER SIX FIELD TRIP

The Home of Power

In this field trip, you will be searching for "palaces," the places where people of power live. Chances are that Buckingham is not a feasible location for you, so if you don't live near an actual palace, then look for other seats of power. This may be a state capitol building, a city hall, a courthouse, or the headquarters of a large company.

Once you find a place where a source of great authority and influence is housed, notice how that power is projected through the architecture, the symbols, and the buzz of important people serving that power. How do people dress there? How do they carry themselves? Does the building have an air of greatness? Pay attention to flags, logos, icons, or art pieces that proclaim the majesty of this "palace." Look at how the grounds or gardens are kept. Is there an immaculate attention to detail? Is beauty used to project importance?

Field Trip Details

Travel: If you don't live in a large city or urban hub, you may need to travel a bit to find an impressive center of power and authority.

Cost: Travel costs, if any. If possible, opt for a guided tour of your chosen "palace."

Time: A few hours, unless you want to make a road trip of it and travel to an international place of power, such as Washington, D.C. In that case, you'll want to spend multiple days exploring.

Physical Demands: Walking

Gear: Bring good shoes, a Bible, and a journal.

Key Scriptures to Guide Your Trip: Exodus 6:7; Leviticus 26:11–12; Isaiah 40:21–22; Isaiah 42:5; Jeremiah 31:33; John 1:1–5; 1 Corinthians 3:16; 1 Corinthians 6:18–20; 2 Corinthians 6:16; Ephesians 2:19–22; Revelation 21:1–4

Schedule this field trip now. Put it on your calendar!
Day: _____
Time: _____
People invited to join me: _____
_____
_____

Seeing the Kingdom Connection

The Bible says that we, believers, are the temple of God (1 Corinthians 3:16). We are the residence where he lives. How is it that the most powerful being in the cosmos would make his home in our hearts? How is it that the church is his palace, a center of his rule and worship? What does it mean that your own physical body is a temple of the Holy Spirit and an administrative center where the rule of God manifests his greatness and authority?

In the Old Testament, the temple was also the meeting place between God and man. It was the ground where heaven intersected earth. The words "I will be your God, and you shall be my people" (Jeremiah 7:23), found throughout scripture, are known in theology circles as the "covenant formula." This formula is used to capture the fullness of God's covenants (Ezekiel 14:11; Zechariah 8:8; 2 Corinthians 6:16; Hebrews 8:10; Jeremiah 32:38; Exodus 6:7; Leviticus 26:12; Revelation 21:7).

Wherever the covenant formula is found in the Bible, the reader should picture the intimate, loving, personal relationship between God and his people secured by covenant, just as a husband and wife secure their loving relationship with a marriage covenant. The covenant formula speaks of a loving union, not just a formal governing relationship, between the King and his citizens.

Questions for Reflection

1. What sticks out from this field trip or is a new idea for you?

2. What questions have come out of this field trip? What doesn't make sense to you?

3. How do you see Jesus and his kingdom in this experience?

4. How can you apply this to your life and take a next step?

5. What will you talk to God and other people about?

After this field trip, circle where you are right now in your journey to find God's kingdom as a hidden treasure.

Blind   Aware   Ponder   Value   Trap of Inaction   Prioritize   Own/Sell

Journal: Spend some time in your journal to record further thoughts.

SMALL GROUP GUIDE

Chapter Six Discussion Questions

Key Scripture:
A Kingdom of Priests
1 Peter 2:1–10

1. Think back to when you were first presented with the gospel. Were you told about Christ's kingdom? If so, was it presented as something real and present? Think about the ways you have been trained to share the gospel. How can you explain the reality of the kingdom to those who are not yet part of it?

2. Why is it important that Christ be recognized as more than a bridge girder? From scripture, list as many qualities, attributes, and titles of Christ as you can. Have you been following Christ in all of his fullness or just a few aspects of his person and work?

3. Consider the sphere of influence you have with friends, family members, co-workers, students, and neighbors. How have your relationships been shaped by the Bible's narrative of God's kingdom coming? What would change if the kingdom were to come more fully in and

through you?

4. *The restoration of our royalty is a major part of the restoration of humanity. Jesus came to restore our rightful place of ruling with him for eternity, beginning right here and now.* In light of this, how would you respond to a Christian who says, "I'm just a sinner saved by grace" or "I'm nobody special."

5. What are some of the most compelling stories (true or fictional) that have influenced your life? Think of your favorite books, movies, television series, etc. Analyze why these narratives resonate with you.

6. *When your story gets woven into the story of Jesus, then you can grow into the person God uniquely designed you to be.* What does it mean on a practical, daily level for your story to become part of the greater Jesus story? Do the narratives in your head about who you are and the meaning of your life reflect your place in Jesus' kingdom story? Why or why not?

7. What faulty personal narratives need to be replaced with true, kingdom-oriented narratives? What has God delivered you *from*? What has God delivered you *to*? How will you internalize these truths to make the story in your head align with the reality of the kingdom story?

8. Discuss your experience on the field trip. What did you learn? What surprised you? What challenged you?

Chapter Six Notes

CHAPTER SEVEN

Seeing the Kingdom Story of Scripture

The Bible's kingdom story is not a single, continuous narrative. Among the narratives, there are also histories, letters, poems, wisdom literature, prophecy, and genealogy. But as a whole, the various forms of literature trace the arc of one grand kingdom story. The story of the Bible is about God's kingdom. There are a thousand subplots and sub-stories within the sweeping narrative, but all of the stories fall beneath the larger movement of God's kingdom coming.

Granted, this story is intensely complex, sophisticated, detailed, and creative. About forty different human authors wrote in multiple languages to various audiences spanning at least fourteen centuries. The authors were not only inspired and moved along by God himself, but were also geniuses in their own rights, commanding a huge range of literary techniques, tools, and trades. Nevertheless, the Bible tells a single story.

Like all stories, the narrative arc of the Bible has an opening, a conflict, a climax, and a resolution. The last book of the Bible captures the essence of this kingdom story with one stroke:

> Then the seventh angel blew his trumpet, and there were loud voices in heaven, saying, "The kingdom of the world has become the kingdom of our Lord and of his Christ, and he shall reign forever and ever."
> —**Revelation 11:15**

That's it. There's the story. What was lost in Genesis is ultimately regained in Revelation. Everything in between is an outworking of this plan.

God is establishing his kingdom through the pages of the Bible. If you keep this in mind when you read, then scripture will become like a pop-up book, with kingdom themes previously unseen leaping from the page. If you haven't paid attention to the kingdom story of scripture, then the Bible will become brand new to you once you read it through this lens.

In one sense, it's a simple story: God's kingdom coming. On many levels, it is quite easy to understand, just like every other kingdom story. But pack your bags because we will need at least half of all eternity to explore the depth and greatness of this saga. This story is inscribed in our DNA. We were designed by God to live in his eternal kingdom. We are both the audience and the actors in this drama.

At three critical junctures in the story, the Bible clearly spells out what God is doing in history. Right after Israel was delivered from Egyptian slavery, God told Moses, "You shall be to me a kingdom of priests and a holy nation" (Exodus 19:6). Then the Apostle Peter told the fledgling church, "You are … a royal priesthood" (1 Peter 2:9). Finally, at the end of the Bible, the Revelation to John tells us that God has "made them a kingdom and priests" (Revelation 5:10). These three passages trace the arc of the biblical narrative.

God's purpose isn't just to make a priesthood; it's a *royal* priesthood. And God isn't just making a kingdom, but a kingdom of *priests*. As we unfold the narrative, you'll see that this is intensely relevant to your life because you, as a follower of Jesus, are called to be a royal priest in that kingdom.

The kingdom thread weaves through the whole story of scripture with two main strands: (1) kingdom authority and (2) temple. To identify the strand of *kingdom authority*, look for themes of reign, power, thrones, crowns, and kings. Kingdoms have kings who effectively reign and project power over citizens by the exercise of authority. Throughout the biblical narrative, King YHWH is seen commanding his people, directing military conquests, issuing decrees, establishing law, and delegating authority to his vice-regents. Why? That's what kings do, and the Bible is a kingdom story.

The second main strand is *temple*. Kings exercise authority from a physical place. In modern language, we speak of the palace of a king as the place where he resides. The palace has a throne room, the center from which the king's power is projected into the world. The throne is the seat in the throne room where the king encounters his citizens, dispatches orders to his ministers, and executes judgments. In biblical language, the tabernacle or temple is the palace of King YHWH, the place where his name and glory reside. The holiest of holies in the tabernacle or temple is the throne room, the inner sanctum and place of encounter between King YHWH and representatives of the people. The ark within the holiest of holies is the "mercy seat," the throne where King YHWH "sits." As we trace the story, there will be specific emphasis on the strands of kingdom authority exercised in and through the temple.

Clearly the story can't be fully retold here. I suspect that it can't be fully told through all eternity. Instead of making a comprehensive run-through of the kingdom story in *The Kingdom Field Guide*, I'll direct you to the superb book *The Drama of Scripture* by Craig Bartholomew and Michael Goheen.[52] They trace the narrative of God's kingdom with great detail through the scriptures. It's a thrilling condensation of the most epic saga ever told.

I do want to pull out four significant markers of the Bible's kingdom story. There are four main covenants between God and man in the Bible, and these four covenants have explicit kingdom purposes and greatly help us to see the story from Genesis to Revelation. In all of its brilliance, elegance, depth, wonder, and genius, God's story is a kingdom story, and we are invited to adopt this story as the story of our very lives. What we're about to look at is the story in stick-figure form. What can be shown here only in crude flannelgraph fashion will be worth a lifetime of study and enjoyment.

Cairns: Four Covenants Marking the Path

In 2006, I completed the most difficult physical challenge of my life: the Wonderland Trail. My friend Brian and I hiked around Mount Rainier, covering almost 100 miles with a cumulative vertical gain equal to climbing Mount Everest from sea level. The Wonderland Trail is wonderful—and brutal. Big ups. Big downs. Practically no flat sections at all. The ticket price for Rainier's stunningly beautiful trail is excruciating effort. I trained for a year to get in the best physical condition of my life, and the Wonderland Trail still drove me into the ground.

On the north side of Mount Rainier is a section of high alpine trail called Spray Park, except that there isn't any obvious trail you can follow in Spray Park. Sometimes

there is no beaten path, no worn rut or boot track. On this
section of the Wonderland, at times there's only bare rock.
It was on this section of trail that we found ourselves in a
dense fog and heavy rain. I couldn't see more than a few
yards in front of me. I was cold, wet, sore, and near a
breaking point. Brian had hiked ahead, so I was alone. It
was disturbing and dangerous to be hiking bare rock without a trail in these conditions, but every few hundred feet,
somebody had placed stacked rocks—called cairns—to
mark the route.

In my exhausted condition, all I could do was put one
foot in front of the other as I watched my steps carefully.
Every time I came upon a cairn, there was a huge relief, a
certainty that I wasn't lost. I knew where I was. Then I set
out again, guessing at the direction and hoping that I
wasn't wandering until the next cairn emerged from the

pea-soup fog. I was lost without those cairns. The stone markers let me know that I was on the right path.

The story of scripture can be like Spray Park. How many times have you read the Bible and just felt lost? Strange prophetic images, odd animal sacrifice rituals, and baffling dietary restrictions can create a dense fog that is disorienting. But there are rock stacks that mark the trail. The major covenants in scripture mark the path of the kingdom story in the Bible. The covenants are promises made between God and his people for the purpose of establishing the kingdom. When you see these covenants, just know that you're on the path tracing the kingdom narrative arc.

Authors Peter Gentry and Stephen Wellum provide a masterful treatment of this in their book *Kingdom Through Covenant*. In their graphic image, they say, "The biblical covenants serve as the framework and *backbone* to the entire narrative plot structure of Scripture."[54] The story doesn't stand without the covenants, and there is no story without the kingdom.

We're going to look at four of the covenant cairns that mark the trail of the kingdom story. In bronze-aged Mesopotamia, covenants were agreements that kings used to advance the agenda of their kingdoms. They were legally binding arrangements, typically between one powerful king and a lesser king or people group. In nearly every case, covenants were instruments of a king that secured and advanced the interests of his kingdom.

King YHWH established four major covenants,[55] all of which explicitly serve specific functions to advance his kingdom. These covenants stand as cairns to mark the kingdom story of scripture. Here's a summary of the four covenants that we'll look at in more detail:

Covenant	Kingdom Purpose	References
Abrahamic	-**Populate** the citizenry -**Locate** the territory -**Mandate** the mission	Genesis 12:1–3; 15:1–6; 17:1–8
Mosaic	-**Consecrate** the citizens -**Regulate** the relationships -**Cultivate** the bond of love	Exodus 19–24
Davidic	-**Coronate** the King -**Elevate** the King's glory -**Insulate** the King's realm	2 Samuel 7; 1 Chronicles 17:1–14
New Covenant	-**Commemorate** the King's triumph -**Anticipate** the King's return -**Delegate** power to the King's people	Matthew 26:26–29; Mark 14:22–25; Luke 22:14–20; 1 Corinthians 11:17–26

The covenants are not isolated promises floating independently. God isn't changing course by changing covenants as if he were a drunk driver swerving through history. Each covenant builds on the previous ones, and they are all interconnected, tightly woven together with directed purpose and intention, culminating in Jesus as the King of kings.

Scholars of Jewish literature note that ancient authors used a technique called "stringing pearls," whereby important ideas from various sources were strung together to make a beautiful whole.[56] The covenants as a whole are a stunning string of pearls with overlap and interconnectedness showing God's great purpose and plan through all of time to establish his kingdom. This chart shows a few of the themes woven through the covenants and the accounts of King YHWH establishing the promises:

Theme	Abrahamic Covenant	Mosaic Covenant	Davidic Covenant	"New" Covenant
Promised Land	X		X	X
People	X	X	X	X
Offspring	X		X	X
Royalty	X	X	X	X
Blessing	X	X	X	X
Curses	X	X		
Sacrifice	X	X		X
Global scope	X	X	X	X
A "Great Name"	X		X	
Eternal	X	X	X	
Belief	X	X		
Nations	X	X	X	
Possession	X	X	X	
Kingdom	X	X	X	X

Broadly, these covenants trace the movement of God in history to establish his kingdom. If you can see the purpose of God through these covenants, you'll see the kingdom narrative come alive in the Bible. And when you see the kingdom narrative come alive in the Bible, you'll see the kingdom come alive in the very world around you. You'll be swept up and carried along by that ultimate story of stories.

Let's revisit our comic strip. It has some elements of the good news: the cross, salvation, eternal life, and forgiveness.

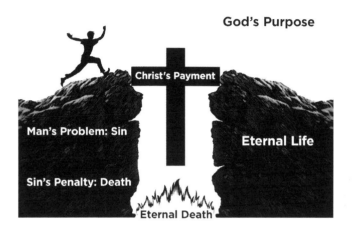

But this gospel picture is zoomed in too tightly. It places the emphasis on a lone individual and his struggle with sin. This is what theologian Dallas Willard calls the "Gospel of Sin Management," which leaves so much to be desired. If I respond to Christ on the basis of this gospel, what is to be done with the rest of my life? After I make my initial "leap of faith," what's left for the rest of my life on earth? Is "God's Purpose" for my life simply an act of crossing a fiery pit of death and then telling other people to do the same? The narrative arc of this story also ignores most of the story the Bible tells. Where are the covenants? Where are the ancient promises God faithfully keeps to every generation? Where is the grand culmination?

At the risk of bragging, may I say that my comic below is much better at presenting the gospel? Isn't it more useful for picturing the narrative of the Bible?

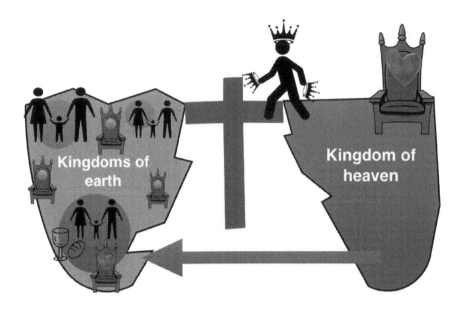

The real problem we face isn't a fiery pit prepared to toast sinners. The real problem is a rebellion of the kingdoms of earth against the kingdom of heaven. In cahoots with a demonic rebellion, humanity mutinied and set up competing thrones. The cross is the means by which the King of kings defeats evil, atones for sin, and brings his rule back to earth as it is in heaven. King Jesus is restoring all creation back to its good order under his sovereignty, and he carries crowns with him to restore humanity's role as vice-regents who rule and reign on his behalf. We become his agents and co-workers in the restoration of all things (2 Corinthians 5:18–19), uniting all things in heaven and on earth under his rule (Ephesians 1:7–10).

Does this comic capture the essence of the four major covenants to tell the kingdom story? Let's see.

The Abrahamic covenant? Check. YHWH promised to

Abraham a royal family and land that would be the source of blessing to all the families of the earth (Genesis 12:1–3). Jesus commissions us by his authority to bring the good news and good blessings of God's restored kingdom to all the earth (Matthew 28:16–20).

The Mosaic covenant? Check. YHWH promised to make a kingdom of priests governed by the law of love (Exodus 19:6). Jesus insisted that his followers keep the great commandments to love God and people (Matthew 22:36–40) and gave them a new command to love in the manner that Jesus loved (John 13:33–35). The primary means through which God's kingdom comes on earth as it is in heaven is by obedience to the royal law of love (James 2:8).

The Davidic covenant? Check. YHWH promised David that one of his descendants would sit on an eternal throne and rule an eternal kingdom (2 Samuel 7). Jesus is the Son of David (Matthew 1:1), who defeated death on the cross, was resurrected, and ascended to the Father's right hand to sit on a heavenly throne (Acts 2:29–36). Jesus is actively bringing his rule to bear on earth through his body, the church, in the power of the Holy Spirit.

The New Covenant? Check. On the evening before his crucifixion, Jesus gathered with his twelve disciples in an upper room. He gave them the cup and bread as a symbol to remind them of his victory secured on the cross and to anticipate his return and the future culmination of the kingdom. Four times in three accounts of the last supper, the writers of the Gospels made a direct connection between the communion sacrament and God's kingdom (Matthew 26:26–29; Mark 14:22–25; Luke 22:14–23).

After declaring faith and loyalty to King Jesus in this comic, what are we left to do? What's God's purpose for us? Plenty! In accordance with the Abrahamic covenant, we are to be busy being a blessing to the whole world. In accordance with the Mosaic covenant and the law of love, we are to love God, love our neighbors, and love each other as Jesus has loved us. In accordance with the Davidic covenant, we are to steward the authority that King Jesus, the Son of David, entrusts to us so his reign increases on earth. Finally, in accordance with the New Covenant, we are not to forget the victory of the cross, the future return of our King, and the ultimate consummation of his kingdom on earth as it is in heaven.

That is the good news of the kingdom. That is the story of the Bible. And that is to be the story of our lives. It's not the story of a lone soul hoping to avoid a fiery pit. It's the story of us, together, restoring all creation and bringing all things under the rule of King Jesus.

The quality of your Christian life depends greatly on how you adopt this kingdom narrative. The story in your head needs to align with the reality of God's really real kingdom in the world.

Seeking the Kingdom in the Bible

In order to see the kingdom come more and more fully in our lives, we need to tune our eyes to see the kingdom in the story of scripture. The four covenantal cairns mark the path of this story in the Bible, and the more you look for these markers, the more they will jump out at you. Familiar passages you've read perhaps a dozen times will become brand new as the kingdom story leaps and screams from the page.

Acts 13:13–41 records an incident in Antioch of Pisidia. What may seem like a typical account of one of Paul's missions is a treasure of the kingdom story hidden in the New Testament. By focusing your attention on the covenantal markers, you can pick out crucial details that connect to activity of King Jesus over millennia to establish his kingdom. Look at the covenantal connections Paul crammed into this short speech before a synagogue in Asia

Minor (with my commentary in bold):

Now Paul and his companions set sail from Paphos and came to Perga in Pamphylia. And John left them and returned to Jerusalem, but they went on from Perga and came to Antioch in Pisidia. [**Per the covenant with Abraham, God's blessing will extend to all of the nations, and here Paul was bringing God's goodness to a largely pagan area with a smattering of dispersed Jews.**] And on the Sabbath day they went into the synagogue and sat down. After the reading from the Law [**the Mosaic covenant**] and the Prophets, the rulers of the synagogue sent a message to them, saying, "Brothers, if you have any word of encouragement for the people, say it." So Paul stood up, and motioning with his hand said:

"Men of Israel and you who fear God, listen. The God of this people Israel chose our fathers and made the people great during their stay in the land of Egypt [**the Abrahamic covenant promises a multitude of people to populate the kingdom**], and with uplifted arm he led them out of it. And for about forty years he put up with them in the wilderness [**the people's stubbornness was in rebellion to the terms of the Mosaic covenant**]. And after destroying seven nations in the land of Canaan, he gave them their land as an inheritance [**the Abrahamic covenant promised this land for the kingdom territory**]. All this took about 450 years. And after that he gave them judges until Samuel the prophet. Then they asked for a king, and God gave them Saul the son of Kish, a man of the tribe of Benjamin, for forty years. And when he had removed him, he raised up David to be their king, of whom he testified and said, 'I have found in David the son of Jesse a man after my heart, who will do all my will.' Of this man's offspring God has brought to Israel a Savior, Jesus, as he promised [**the promise according to the Davidic covenant**]. Before his coming, John had proclaimed a baptism of repentance to all the people of Israel [**the royal family according to the Abrahamic covenant**]. And as John was finishing his course, he said, 'What do you suppose that I am? I am not he. No, but behold, after me one is coming, *the sandals of whose feet I am not worthy to untie.' [**The One to Come is the "Son of David" per the Davidic covenant.**]*

*"Brothers, sons of the family of Abraham [**by the Abrahamic covenant**], and those among you who fear God, to us has been sent the message of this salvation. For those who live in Jerusalem and their rulers, because they did not recognize him nor understand the utterances of the prophets, which are read every Sabbath, fulfilled them by condemning him. And though they found in him no guilt worthy of death, they asked Pilate to have him executed. And when they had carried out all that was written of him, they took him down from the tree and laid him in a tomb. But God raised him from the dead, and for many days he appeared to those who had come up with him from Galilee to Jerusalem, who are now his witnesses to the people [**both the people of Israel and the people of the nations according to the Abrahamic covenant**]. And we bring you the good news that what God promised to the fathers, this he has fulfilled to us their children by raising Jesus, as also it is written in the second Psalm,*

"'You are my Son, today I have begotten you.'

And as for the fact that he raised him from the dead, no more to return to corruption, he has spoken in this way,

*"'I will give you the holy and sure blessings of David' [**promised in the Davidic covenant**].*

Therefore he says also in another psalm,

"'You will not let your Holy One see corruption.'

For David, after he had served the purpose of God in his own generation, fell asleep and was laid with his fathers and saw corruption, but he whom God raised up did not see corruption. Let it be known to you therefore, brothers, that through this man forgiveness of sins is proclaimed to you, and by him everyone who believes is freed from everything from which you could not be freed by the law of

Moses *[Jew and Gentile alike, since God's purpose was al-*
ways worldwide blessing through his kingdom].
—*Acts 13:13–39*

Once you start looking for the covenant markers of the
kingdom story, you'll see them *everywhere* in scripture.
Passages you memorized decades ago may suddenly be
transformed and become brand new when you look at
them through the lens of the kingdom story. Even the
(sadly) all too familiar John 3:16–18 can be seen in a
brand-new light when viewed through the lens of the covenantal kingdom:

For God so loved the world *[by covenant with Abraham*
that the world would be blessed], that he gave his only Son
[the royal, eternally enthroned Son of God by covenant
with David], that whoever believes in him should not perish
but have eternal life. For God did not send his Son into the
world to condemn the world, but in order that the world
might be saved through him *[by covenant with Abraham]*.
Whoever believes in him is not condemned, but whoever
does not believe is condemned already, because he has not
believed in the name of the only Son of God *[the Anointed*
One with the unending reign on David's throne by cove-
nant].

The worn-out Christmas narrative in Luke springs to
new life when seen through the lens of the covenants. The
births of John and Jesus can become washed-out clichés
after being put through the meat grinder of countless Sunday school lectures and Charlie Brown TV specials. But
when you read the opening chapters of Luke with an eye
to the kingdom narrative told by the covenants, suddenly
there is a new vitality:

In the days of Herod, king of Judea, there was a priest named Zechariah, of the division of Abijah. [**According to the Mosaic covenant, God promised to make Israel a kingdom of priests.**] And he had a wife from the daughters of Aaron [**the first royal high priest**], and her name was Elizabeth. And they were both righteous before God, walking blamelessly in all the commandments and statutes of the Lord [**that govern YHWH's kingdom according to the Mosaic covenant**]. But they had no child, because Elizabeth was barren, and both were advanced in years.
—Luke 1:5–7

The author Luke set the table by drawing the reader into the old narrative that echoes back to the Mosaic covenant. After describing the pregnancy of Elizabeth with John the Baptist, Luke then launched into the birth narrative of Jesus. His account strongly connects to the Davidic covenant:

In the sixth month the angel Gabriel was sent from God to a city of Galilee named Nazareth, to a virgin betrothed to a man whose name was Joseph, of the house of David [**to whom God promised a son who would sit on his throne for eternity**]. And the virgin's name was Mary. And he came to her and said, "Greetings, O favored one, the Lord is with you!" But she was greatly troubled at the saying, and tried to discern what sort of greeting this might be. And the angel said to her, "Do not be afraid, Mary, for you have found favor with God. And behold, you will conceive in your womb and bear a son, and you shall call his name Jesus. He will be great and will be called the Son of the Most High. And the Lord God will give to him the throne of his father David, and he will reign over the house of Jacob forever, and of his kingdom there will be no end" [**according to the covenantal promise to David**].
—Luke 1:26–33

Then comes Mary's "Magnificat," a symphonic poem with the three major Old Testament covenants weaving in and out, layered carefully and beautifully together, with all of their promises culminating in Jesus:

> And Mary said, "My soul magnifies the Lord, and my spirit rejoices in God my Savior, for he has looked on the humble estate of his servant. For behold, from now on all generations will call me blessed; for he who is mighty has done great things for me, and holy is his name. And his mercy is for those who fear him from generation to generation. He has shown strength with his arm [**as in the account of Moses judging the Pharaoh of Egypt in Exodus 6:1, 6**]; he has scattered the proud in the thoughts of their hearts; he has brought down the mighty from their thrones and exalted those of humble estate [**as the lowly shepherd David was exalted to his throne**]; he has filled the hungry with good things, and the rich he has sent away empty. He has helped his servant Israel, in remembrance of his mercy, as he spoke to our fathers, to Abraham and to his offspring forever" [**through the covenantal promise to Abraham for a royal people in a promised land**].
>
> **—Luke 1:46–55**

The "Magnificat" of Mary is followed by the "Benedictus" poem of Zechariah celebrating the birth of his son, John. This poem continues to weave the covenants together in narrating the grand kingdom story:

> And his father Zechariah was filled with the Holy Spirit and prophesied, saying, "Blessed be the Lord God of Israel, for he has visited and redeemed his people [**out of Egyptian slavery as promised to Moses**] and has raised up a horn of salvation for us in the house of his servant David [**by his covenant**], as he spoke by the mouth of his holy prophets from

*of old, that we should be saved from our enemies and from the hand of all who hate us; to show the mercy promised to our fathers and to remember his holy covenant, the oath that he swore to our father Abraham [**to make a royal people who would bless the whole earth**], to grant us that we, being delivered from the hand of our enemies, might serve him without fear [**like the Israelites, who were set free from the terror of Egyptian slavery**], in holiness and righteousness before him all our days. And you, child, will be called the prophet of the Most High; for you will go before the Lord to prepare his ways, to give knowledge of salvation to his people in the forgiveness of their sins, because of the tender mercy of our God, whereby the sunrise shall visit us from on high to give light to those who sit in darkness and in the shadow of death [**both in Israel and in the whole world according to the Abrahamic covenant**], to guide our feet into the way of peace."*

—Luke 1:67–79

Luke continued to compose the covenantal symphony with a crescendo in the birth of Jesus, who is the culmination of all God's royal promises:

*In those days a decree went out from Caesar Augustus that all the world should be registered. This was the first registration when Quirinius was governor of Syria. And all went to be registered, each to his own town. And Joseph also went up from Galilee, from the town of Nazareth, to Judea, to the city of David, which is called Bethlehem, because he was of the house and lineage of David [**establishing Jesus' claim to be the Son of David and to inherit the covenantal eternal throne of David**], to be registered with Mary, his betrothed, who was with child. And while they were there, the time came for her to give birth. And she gave birth to her firstborn son and wrapped him in swaddling cloths and laid him in a manger, because there was no place for them in the inn.*

—Luke 2:1–7

As with the birth of any heir to a throne, the birth of Jesus was announced with great fanfare, in this case by a host of angels. And why not? All of the Old Testament kingdom narrative was wrapped up in swaddling cloths and lying in a Bethlehem manger. It was worth shouting from the heavens!

*And in the same region there were shepherds out in the field, keeping watch over their flock by night. And an angel of the Lord appeared to them, and the glory of the Lord shone around them, and they were filled with great fear. And the angel said to them, "Fear not, for behold, I bring you good news of great joy that will be for all the people [**because all of the families on earth will be blessed according to the Abrahamic covenant**]. For unto you is born this day in the city of David a Savior, who is Christ the Lord [**the covenantal heir of David who will sit on the eternal throne to rule an eternal kingdom based on the law of love**]. And this will be a sign for you: you will find a baby wrapped in swaddling cloths and lying in a manger." And suddenly there was with the angel a multitude of the heavenly host praising God and saying,*

*"Glory to God in the highest, and on earth peace among those with whom he is pleased!" [**True global peace is offered to all families and all nations by covenantal promise to Abraham.**]*

—Luke 2:8–14

Take a minute to reflect on the current Christmas narrative in your head about the birth of Jesus. Is that version of the story shaped more by Christmas traditions than by the Old Testament covenants? Is the origin story of Christ the King more informed by Sunday school pageants with cute kids and goats than by the great kingdom promises to the patriarchs Abraham, Moses, and David?

Something happens to the story of scripture when you look at it through the lens of the covenants. It moves from a rehearsed performance on a church stage to a three-dimensional narrative you can enter into and actually live in. What's bland becomes fantastic. What's boring becomes thrilling. What's confusing become clear. The more you engage with the kingdom narrative in scripture, the more you'll find God's kingdom becoming really real in your life.

Bible Trip: The Selfie

The lust to claim God's throne, resist God's authority, and rob God's glory is at the heart of every sin. The Bible is rife with that theme. Sin isn't just an "oops." Sin is rebellion against God's rule. For us to join the goodness of God's really real kingdom, we must face the reality of our rebellion.

For this Bible Trip, I'd like you to take a selfie with your smartphone (or find a picture of yourself in an album). Look at yourself in the picture. Really look. Who are you? Somewhere in your heart is a rebel. You want your kingdom for your glory and your name. You may not be completely a rebel. Perhaps only a small amount of your life is lived in rebellion. There may be much in your life that is good and admirable. But you don't need the entire meal to be moldy to call it spoiled. Just a little mold is enough to send it back to the chef.

Read the following Bible passages. Consider where you see your own past or present rebellion. Rebellion isn't just confined to the pages of the Bible. It leaps off the written words and seeps into the sinews of our bodies. It creeps into the idle thoughts of our minds and lurks within the depths of our hearts. Rebellion is the grabbing hand that seeks to tear our souls.

The warnings against rebellion pass from the Old Testament to the New Testament and from the New Testament to our world today. Please read these passages carefully: Psalm 2:1–3; Psalm 107:10–15; Proverbs 17:11; Isaiah 63:7–10; Hebrews 3:15; and 2 Thessalonians 2:3.

After reading those, look again at the picture of yourself. The gospel of the kingdom isn't just that you've rebelled; the gospel of the kingdom is that God invites all rebels to rule with him. He adopts rebels. He loves rebels. He makes rebels his heirs. He gives crowns to rebels.

God saves us from rebellion, and he saves us for his kingdom. Yes, there are still remnants of the rebellion living in our hearts, but under King Jesus, that rebellion is in the process of being replaced with his good rule and reign.

Small Group Guide

Talk about areas in your life where you have seen victory over the rebellion in your heart. What are your areas of current struggle? Spend time praying for one another for courage to continue the battles. Do not try to fix one another or judge. Be good listeners. This will likely be a very vulnerable small group discussion. Be sure that you reinforce confidentiality in your group. Do not ask people to share what they are not yet ready to share. If there are any significant needs or issues that surface in your life, be sure to contact a local pastor to find the next steps toward wholeness.

Credentials for a King

Jesus began his public ministry with the proclamation of his kingdom. After that, it was time to establish his credentials as the King. He claimed the titles of that kingship:

the Messiah, the Christ, the Son of God, the Son of Man, the Son of David, the Son of Abraham. If he was going to claim those names, he'd better have the goods to back it up. If somebody is going to sit on the eternal throne over God's eternal kingdom, it's probably a good idea to examine and scrutinize the candidate to make sure that there is a legitimate claim to the throne. This is actually a very normal process in any kingdom. When the question of the throne is up in the air, the royal succession must be legally established before a king can be crowned.

The New Testament spends an inordinate amount of effort establishing the credentials of Jesus for being the Christ, the rightful King. There are at least three types of evidence offered for Jesus' claim to the eternal throne over God's eternal kingdom on earth: (1) royal lineage, (2) the testimony of witnesses, and (3) works of power and authority.

Curiously, we often think that the purpose of the Bible is to prove that Jesus is God. There is some of that, no doubt, but the biblical authors made a far greater effort to prove that Jesus is King. It's worth looking at his credentials for the claim to the throne.

Royal Lineage

Real kingdoms are obsessed with genealogies. They have to be since the throne is passed along family dynasties. Royal lineage is important to establish who may legally reign in a kingdom.

Have you ever wondered why the Bible wastes so much ink on obscure names and boring lists of unpronounceable family trees? In large part, this is because the Bible is a kingdom story, and the lineage must be carefully examined and preserved to establish who can rightfully rule over YHWH's kingdom of priests.

Because God's kingdom is really real, it follows that it

would be obsessed with lineage. Somehow the story all traces back to the covenant with Abraham and the promise that he would have a family as numerous as the stars in the sky. This family would be a dynasty of kings, and from this line of kings, there would be worldwide blessing.

That promise of a royal dynasty then passed from Abraham to Isaac and from Isaac to Jacob. Jacob was renamed "Israel" and had twelve sons. From his sons came the twelve tribes of Israel. Going all the way back to the book of Genesis, God decreed the royal lineage to pass to Judah, one of the twelve sons of Jacob:

> Judah, your brothers shall praise you; your hand shall be on the neck of your enemies; your father's sons shall bow down before you. Judah is a lion's cub; from the prey, my son, you have gone up. He stooped down; he crouched as a lion and as a lioness; who dares rouse him? The scepter shall not depart from Judah, nor the ruler's staff from between his feet, until tribute comes to him; and to him shall be the obedience of the peoples.
>
> **—Genesis 49:8–10**

From the beginning, it was determined that the King over YHWH's kingdom must follow this lineage in order to carry the royal scepter: (1) a son of Abraham, Isaac, and Jacob and (2) a descendant of Judah from Israel's tribes. Stick with me because Christ's family tree is only as boring as you make it.

When God made his covenant with David, he said that the eternal King sitting on an eternal throne would be a descendant of David, the "son of David." So now we can sum up the royal lineage of the Christ, the rightful heir to the throne, as: (1) son of Abraham, (2) tribe of Judah, and (3) son of David. This explains why the New Testament opens with this "boring family tree" that Matthew records so specifically:

> *The book of the genealogy of Jesus Christ, the son of David, the son of Abraham.*
>
> *Abraham was the father of Isaac, and Isaac the father of Jacob, and Jacob the father of Judah and his brothers, and Judah the father of Perez and Zerah by Tamar, and Perez the father of Hezron, and Hezron the father of Ram, and Ram the father of Amminadab, and Amminadab the father of Nahshon, and Nahshon the father of Salmon, and Salmon the father of Boaz by Rahab, and Boaz the father of Obed by Ruth, and Obed the father of Jesse, and Jesse the father of David the king.*
>
> **—Matthew 1:1–6a**

If Matthew was claiming that Jesus was the King of kings, he had to establish the legal title with an impeccable royal lineage. If Jesus were not a son of Abraham, not of the tribe of Judah, or not a descendant of David, then he would easily have been proven an imposter to the throne. Then he would have been rightly killed for insurrection in trying to take a throne that wasn't legally his.

But the lineage of Jesus establishes the credentials for Jesus to be the Christ, the Son of David, who can rightfully claim David's eternal throne and eternal kingdom according to the promise. This is the good news. This is the story the New Testament is telling. This is the gospel of the kingdom.

Picture a royal herald shouting in the streets, accompanied by trumpets: "Hear ye, hear ye! [Trumpets blast.] The King has been born! [More trumpets] The Christ has arrived! And it is Jesus of Nazareth! [Trumpets again] His lineage proves that this news is true! [Trumpets go on for days…]"

Okay, buddy, let's just put that trumpet down now.

Testimony of Witnesses

When establishing the legal claim to a throne, lineage is important, but when there is a dispute over the claims to a throne, then a legal proceeding must be held with witnesses called to testify to the credentials of a potential king.

The New Testament emphasis of "witnessing" to Christ dates back to an Old Testament scene in which God established a legal global court hearing to assert his right to rule. He set up a trial, a *fair* trial, in which both sides were allowed to call their witnesses to testify regarding who was the rightful king. Was the rightful king of the cosmos one of the world's pagan gods, or was it YHWH? Pay attention to the legal scene in this global courtroom drama of Isaiah 43:

Bring out the people who are blind, yet have eyes, who are deaf, yet have ears! All the nations gather together, and the peoples assemble. Who among them can declare this, and show us the former things? Let them bring their witnesses to prove them right, and let them hear and say, It is true. "You are my witnesses," declares the LORD, "and my servant whom I have chosen, that you may know and believe me and understand that I am he. Before me no god was formed, nor shall there be any after me. I, I am the LORD, and besides me there is no savior. I declared and saved and proclaimed, when there was no strange god among you; and you are my witnesses," declares the LORD, "and I am God. Also henceforth I am he; there is none who can deliver from my hand; I work, and who can turn it back?"

Thus says the LORD, your Redeemer, the Holy One of Israel: "For your sake I send to Babylon and bring them all down as

fugitives, even the Chaldeans, in the ships in which they re-
joice. I am the LORD, your Holy One, the Creator of Israel,
your King."
                                                    —Isaiah 43:8–15

This courtroom adjudicated a battle with YHWH against every other person or god who claimed to be king, savior, or lord. The whole world assembled; all the nations packed together in the courtroom. Both sides were called to bring forth witnesses and testify. The issue at hand boiled down to "Who's in charge of the cosmos? Who's the top dog? Who is king?"

This Isaiah courtroom drama is critically important for understanding the context of the New Testament, especially the early church. Jesus made reference to this court trial in the book of Acts, just before his ascension. He said to his disciples:

But you will receive power when the Holy Spirit has come
*upon you, and **you will be my witnesses** in Jerusalem and in*
all Judea and Samaria, and to the end of the earth.
                                                    —Acts 1:8

Why did Jesus need witnesses? Just as it was in Isaiah, the stage was being set for a global jury to be established in the legal dispute. The witnesses (the disciples) would testify that Jesus is the Christ. He is the one who has the legal right to rule. In many ways, the New Testament is the outworking of the legal drama initiated in Isaiah 43. YHWH desired to assert his legal right as king over the universe he created, and Jesus had the same agenda here.

Look at some of the passages from Acts that are scenes in this courtroom dispute. Peter's interpretation of the Pentecost scene centered not on the Spirit, but on Jesus' claim to be the Christ. His speech to the people in that upper room was framed as the legal testimony of a witness for Jesus' legal claim to be King (Acts 2:32–36). Take a moment to read that passage. Notice that when Peter was sharing the gospel, he wasn't just telling people that their sins could be forgiven. Rather, he was testifying as a legal witness in a global court of appeals that Jesus is the Christ and has the legal right to sit on David's throne at the right hand of God.

Later, when Peter was called before a legal hearing of the Jewish Sanhedrin and was literally being examined as a witness in a criminal trial, he continued the testimony that Jesus is the Savior:

> Then Peter, filled with the Holy Spirit, said to them, "Rulers of the people and elders, if we are being examined today concerning a good deed done to a crippled man, by what means this man has been healed, let it be known to all of you and to all the people of Israel that by the name of Jesus Christ of Nazareth, whom you crucified, whom God raised from the dead—by him this man is standing before you well."
>
> —Acts 4:8–10

Shortly thereafter, Peter and other disciples were brought before the Jewish leadership for another legal hearing. Peter served as a faithful witness as he testified again that Jesus is the Christ (Acts 5:25–32).

Eventually, the disciples were released from their captivity, and they continued to be witnesses. The specific message they were compelled to share without end was that "the Christ is Jesus" (Acts 5:42). That was their witness. That was the legal claim they were asserting in their testimony. They were saying something like, "This man from Nazareth, this carpenter born to Mary in Bethlehem, he is the one who has the right to rule and sit on David's throne. This Galilean is YHWH from Isaiah 43, who claims that he is the only King ruling the cosmos."

Can you see why it was so contentious for the disciples to claim that Jesus is the Christ? This is why they were imprisoned, beaten, and eventually killed. By testifying as witnesses that Jesus is the Christ, they made a legal claim that all other rulers, all other kings, all authorities on earth fall below the feet of Jesus.

Even when the disciple Stephen was being stoned to death, he provided eyewitness testimony that Jesus is not only the Christ, but the very Son of Man at God's right hand. Remember the passage from Daniel:

> I saw in the night visions, and behold, with the clouds of heaven there came one like a son of man, and he came to the Ancient of Days and was presented before him. And to him was given dominion and glory and a kingdom, that all peoples, nations, and languages should serve him; his do-minion is an everlasting dominion, which shall not pass away, and his kingdom one that shall not be destroyed.
> —*Daniel 7:13–14*

Now compare that to Stephen's eyewitness testimony at his stoning:

> Now when they heard these things they were enraged, and they ground their teeth at [Stephen]. But he, full of the Holy Spirit, gazed into heaven and saw the glory of God, and Je-sus standing at the right hand of God. And he said, "Behold, I see the heavens opened, and the Son of Man standing at the right hand of God."
> —*Acts 7:54–56*

Stephen was yet one more witness in God's grand Isaiah 43 legal dispute over who is King. Then, in a dramatic twist, the Apostle Paul was added as a witness, continuing the testimony.

The courtroom battle of all human history is about a claim to be the rightful king. Who has a legal claim to the ultimate throne over all the universe? This witnessing was and is so much more than "believe in Jesus and be forgiven for your sins." There's much, much more at stake.

Modern-day apologetics (defense of the faith) is often centered on proving the deity of Jesus, but the early church had a different focus. They were concerned with "proving that Jesus was the Christ" (Acts 9:19b–22). They were urgently and constantly bolstering Jesus' credentials for being King.

As the book of Acts proceeds, it follows the course set by Jesus for the Apostles to be his "witnesses in Jerusalem and in all Judea and Samaria, and to the end of the earth" (Acts 1:8). The testimony that Jesus is Christ the King wasn't just for Jews, but for Gentiles as well. They were witnesses that Jesus wasn't just King of the Jews, but King of the whole world. The latter half of Acts shows the witnesses spreading out to the rest of the world. In city after city, the legal court hearing continued. The dispute was not about Jesus' divinity but about who was king.

Now when [Paul and Silas] had passed through Amphipolis and Apollonia, they came to Thessalonica, where there was a synagogue of the Jews. And Paul went in, as was his custom, and on three Sabbath days he reasoned with them from the Scriptures, explaining and proving that it was necessary for the Christ to suffer and to rise from the dead, and saying, "This Jesus, whom I proclaim to you, is the Christ." And some of them were persuaded and joined Paul and Silas, as did a great many of the devout Greeks and not a few of the leading women. But the Jews were jealous, and taking some wicked men of the rabble, they formed a mob, set the city in an uproar, and attacked the house of Jason, seeking to bring them out to the crowd. And when they could not

find them, they dragged Jason and some of the brothers be-
fore the city authorities, shouting, "These men who have
turned the world upside down have come here also, and Ja-
son has received them, and they are all acting

against the decrees of Caesar, saying that **there is another**
king, Jesus."

—Acts 17:1–7

The irony of this scene is that the Jewish mob that attacked poor Jason got the message loud and clear. Paul's
message was that Jesus is the Christ. The rabble of the city
understood perfectly the testimony of the witnesses:
"There is another king, Jesus."

This is the heart of the gospel; this is good news of the
kingdom. The mob didn't like it, but at least they understood what was being proclaimed. Both Jews and Gentiles
heard and believed that Jesus is the Christ, the King.

The rest of the book of Acts is a continuation of the
courtroom dispute. The apostles continued to testify that
Jesus is the Christ. They were faithful witnesses to the
ends of the earth.

If we take a quick survey of the rest of the New Testament, we can see that a huge number of witnesses testified
that Jesus is the Christ. Here is a small sampling of the
roster:

- Angels (Luke 2:10–14)

- Peter, the best friend of Jesus (Matthew 16:13–
  17)

- The demonic realm (Luke 4:40–41)

- A Samaritan woman (John 4:25–30)

- Crowds of people (John 7:25–31)

- Martha (John 11:25–27)
- Apollos (Acts 18:24–28)
- The Apostle John (John 20:30–31)
- Jesus himself (Mark 14:61–62).

God packed the courtroom. He had an impeccable roster of eyewitnesses. Their testimonies were airtight. The credentials were indisputable to assert that Jesus is the Christ, the King. And yet, the court is still in order. The global hearing continues to this day. God is still calling witnesses to testify that Jesus is the Christ. Your very own life is called to be a witness and provide testimony that Jesus is the King.

Works of Power and Authority

Jesus has the right lineage to be King, and there is more than enough testimony by credible witnesses to support his claim to the ultimate throne. But the New Testament offers another line of evidence: the miraculous powers of Jesus.

Real kings have real power and authority. The greater the king, the greater his power. If Jesus is claiming to be the ultimate ruler, the King of kings, then that claim ought to be backed up by a demonstration of ultimate power and authority. The New Testament does just that.

The miracles of Jesus are not just spectacular parlor tricks. They have a purpose. In performing signs and wonders, Jesus made a direct claim to be YHWH himself—the embodied God, Creator, and King of Israel come to rule on earth in the flesh.

John explicitly stated the purpose of writing his Gospel and recording the great works of Jesus:

> *Now Jesus did many other signs in the presence of the disciples, which are not written in this book; but these are written **so that you may believe that Jesus is the Christ**, the Son of God, and that by believing you may have life in his name.*
> **—John 20:30–31**

John didn't want his readers to have a vague, general faith in Jesus. He didn't want them merely to believe that Jesus exists or that Jesus has a divine origin. No, John was clear. He presented the record of miraculous signs so we would give loyalty and "may believe that Jesus is the Christ."

Let's look at a cross-section of the types of authority and power manifested by Jesus.

Power Over Nature

- Calmed a raging storm, wind, and sea (Matthew 8:23–27; Mark 4:35–41)

- Turned water into wine (John 2:1–11)

- Multiplied loaves and fish (Matthew 14:15–21)

- Walked on water (Matthew 14:25)

- Commanded fish (Matthew 17:27; Luke 5:1–11)

Power of Miraculous Healing

- Healed disease by speaking from a distance (John 4:46–54)

- Cured insanity (Mark 5:1–20)

- Cured leprosy (Matthew 8:1–4; Luke 17:11–

19)

- Cured paralysis (Mark 2:1–12)
- Restored a withered hand (Mark 3:1–6)

- Restored speech, sight, and hearing (Matthew 9:32–33; Mark 7:31–37; Mark 8:22–26; John 9:1–39)

Power Over the Demonic Realm

- Cast out demons and commanded them to obedience (Mark 5:1–20; 9:14–29)
- Bound the power of Satan (Mark 3:22–27)
- Cast Satan down from heaven (Revelation 12:7–9)
- Cast Satan into the lake of fire (Revelation 20:10)

Other Demonstrations of Authority

- Exercised authority to forgive sins (Mark 2:1–12)
- Renamed people (Mark 3:16–19; John 1:42)
- Commissioned and sent people (Matthew 10; Matthew 28:16–20; John 17:18)
- Delegated power and authority to his disciples (Mark 6:7; Luke 9:1–2)
- Sent the Holy Spirit (John 16:7)
- Sent angels (Matthew 13:41–43; Acts 12:11;

Revelation 22:16)

- Taught of his own authority (Mark 1:22; Luke 4:31–32)

- Claimed to be Lord of the Sabbath (Matthew 12:1–8)

Power of Life and Death

- Raised people from the dead (Matthew 9:18–26; Luke 7:11–17; John 11:1–46)

- Predicted and fulfilled his own resurrection (Luke 24:5–7)

The greatness of a king is reflected by the greatness of his power and authority. Jesus demonstrated his power and authority during his public ministry for a purpose: to establish his credentials as the King over heaven and earth. By this indisputable power, Jesus takes the title "Christ" and claims the eternal throne of David to be his very own.

Jesus, the King, is inviting *you* to rule on his behalf so that his kingdom comes in and through you. That is good news. That is the good news of the kingdom. And all of this is only part—merely one golden bauble—of the treasure hidden in the field.

CHAPTER SEVEN FIELD TRIP

Finding Your Lost Family Stories

For this field trip, you will hunt for lost family stories. Most of us know a fair number of stories about our parents, but we often know less about our grandparents and practically nothing about our great-grandparents. For this field trip, your journey will be through time, exploring the unknown territory of your personal history.

As you search through the past, keep a journal or record about the genealogical gems you find.

Field Trip Details

Travel: Minimal to extensive

Cost: Minimal

Time: Minimal to extensive

Physical Demands: Minimal

Gear: Minimal

Key Scriptures to Guide Your Trip: Matthew 1:1–17; Matthew 6:9–14; John 1:12; John 13:33–34; Romans 4:16–18; Galatians 3:7–9, 26–29; Ephesians 2:19–22; Ephesians 5:1; 1 John 3:1–2

*Schedule this field trip now. Put it on your calendar!
Day: _____
Time: _____
People invited to join me: _____
_____
_____

Interview your parents, grandparents, aunts, uncles, and cousins about stories they remember. Ask *who*, *what*, *when*, *where*, and *why* questions. Dig for details, the more specific the better. For example:

- Who was your favorite teacher and why?

- What are some favorite stories from your vacations?

- What was your hometown like?

- What were some of the challenges when you were growing up?

- How did you meet your spouse?

- Describe your military service.

- How was faith lived out in your family?

- What did you do for fun?

Often only a few open-ended questions are enough to open the floodgates for stories.

Genealogical software, such as Ancestry.com, may prove helpful for filling in the family tree beyond three to four generations. Services such as this usually have a subscription fee but can often provide history going back centuries. Numerous online guides are available to collect family stories and history as you fill in biographical details.

Always have pen and paper handy to capture details of the stories that are told. Consider making videos or audio recordings of the interviews, but always ask permission first. Face-to-face interviews are always best. Personal connection adds richness.

Perhaps you'll want to take your grandmother to one of her favorite vacation spots from childhood or revisit a town where your grandfather used to live. Car trips can prompt stories as people drive through old neighborhoods. Consider interviewing your parents at the church where they got married or an uncle in the bleachers of the high school stadium where he played football. Be creative!

When you're on location, engage all of your senses to experience the surroundings. What are the sights, sounds, and smells? Take off your shoes to feel the sand on the beach where your parents first met. Run your hand over the rough wood walls of the barn at your great-grand-mother's homestead. Listen carefully to the forest sounds where your grandfather used to hunt. The cumulative effect of these small details makes stories come alive and feel more real.

Genealogy can be a lifelong journey or a just a quick query on an ancestry website. Even a short phone call to a grandparent may uncover interesting family stories that haven't yet been told.

Seeing the Kingdom Connection

Use this adventure as a reminder that you are part of a larger story connected to God's kingdom. If you have given your loyalty to Jesus as King, then you've already been adopted into his royal family. You are now an heir, and your royal family story traces all the way back to Abraham, the father of faith:

Know then that it is those of faith who are the sons of Abraham. And the Scripture, foreseeing that God would justify the Gentiles by faith, preached the gospel beforehand to Abraham, saying, "In you shall all the nations be blessed." So then, those who are of faith are blessed along with Abraham, the man of faith.

—Galatians 3:7–9

...for in Christ Jesus you are all sons of God, through faith. For as many of you as were baptized into Christ have put on Christ. There is neither Jew nor Greek, there is neither slave nor free, there is no male and female, for you are all one in Christ Jesus. And if you are Christ's, then you are Abraham's offspring, heirs according to promise.

—Galatians 3:26–29

That is why it depends on faith, in order that the promise may rest on grace and be guaranteed to all his offspring— not only to the adherent of the law but also to the one who shares the faith of Abraham, who is the father of us all, as it is written, "I have made you the father of many nations"— in the presence of the God in whom he believed, who gives life to the dead and calls into existence the things that do not exist. In hope he believed against hope, that he should become the father of many nations, as he had been told, "So shall your offspring be."

—Romans 4:16–18

The kingdom story of the Bible is *your* family story. As you talk to your parents and grandparents about their stories, allow your own personal narrative to be shaped by the kingdom story. Just as you are a part of your great-grandparents' legacy, continuing their name and story, so are you also part of the royal legacy started by Abraham to bring the blessings of God's kingdom to the whole

world.
The Difficult Road

Some people have family stories with significant trauma or dysfunction, and your journey into the past may not be comfortable or fun. In many cases, the search for family history may need to be accompanied by professional counseling to help process old wounds that have yet to heal. Often a genogram, a chart of family emotional connections, can shed important light on psychological issues traced to your family of origin.

If you have yet to explore difficult parts of your family history, I highly recommend first gathering a support team around you that includes trusted friends, pastoral care in your church, and a professional counselor with experience in family dynamics. I also recommend the book *Emotionally Healthy Spirituality* by Peter Scazzero as a companion resource for this part of your journey.[57]

But do not neglect this field trip just because it is difficult. The Trap of Inaction is lurking and waiting to squash this journey. God may intend this hard work to bring you to a new place of thriving in his good kingdom. After all, the story of God's family in scripture is by no means whitewashed. In the Bible's saga of God's kingdom coming, we find murder, polygamy, serial lying, incest, idolatry, cowardice, prostitution, slavery, adultery, and every flavor of evil. All of this is in the family lineage of Jesus, the King.

If God uses any of us to advance any of his kingdom one inch, then it will be to *his* glory and a testament to *his* mercy, kindness, favor, and power. Our fallenness is not a disqualification from being ambassadors and stewards of God's kingdom.

Your difficult journey through the mess of your own family history may just be a part of that great project of restoration, in which God makes all things new and brings all of the world under the rule of Christ. Your courage to lean into the good, bad, and ugly of your family may end up being a significant answer to your own prayers of "Your kingdom come, your will be done, on earth as it is in heaven" (Matthew 6:10). Invite Jesus along. Be present with him. Ask the Holy Spirit to give you wisdom, courage, forgiveness, mercy, and patience as you work with God to restore what has been lost in your family.

Questions for Reflection

1. What sticks out from this field trip or is a new idea for you?

2. What questions have come out of this field trip? What doesn't make sense to you?

3. How do you see Jesus and his kingdom in this experience?

4. How can you apply this to your life and take a next step?

5. What will you talk to God and other people about?

After this field trip, circle where you are right now in your journey to find God's kingdom as a hidden treasure.

| Blind | Aware | Ponder | Value | Trap of Inaction | Prioritize | Own/Sell |

Journal: Spend some time in your journal to record further thoughts.

SMALL GROUP GUIDE

Chapter Seven Discussion Questions

> **Key Scripture:**
> Throne, Throne, Throne
> Revelation 4:1–5:14

1. Read Revelation chapters 4–5 and pay careful attention to the kingdom themes in this passage. What language does the Apostle John use to show that this narrative is about the kingdom? When a Bible writer repeats a word two or three times, it typically means that it has special importance. How many times does the word *throne* appear in these two chapters? Why is that important? How can you become more aware of the kingdom theme of scripture as you read through the Bible?

2. What does it mean to you personally to be part of a kingdom of priests (1 Peter 2:9)? How should this impact your daily life as well as your devotional life?

3. Why is a gospel that focuses only on the individual and leaves out the message of God's covenants and kingdom incomplete?

4. What are Christ's credentials to be the King of kings? How can you support his claim to be King through your testimony as a witness?

5. What is the current "story of your life" that runs through your mind? Is the kingdom narrative woven into your everyday life and embodied in your actions? How can you make the story in your head better align with the reality of God's kingdom in the world?

6. Discuss your experience on the field trip. What did you learn? What surprised you? What challenged you?

Chapter Seven Notes

_____

_____

_____

_____

_____

_____

_____

_____

_____

_____

_____

_____

_____

_____

_____

_____

_____

_____

_____

_____

_____

_____

_____

_____

CHAPTER EIGHT

The Kingdom Comes Through Prayer and Faith

In the early 1900s, the British Empire reached its peak glory as history's greatest kingdom. At this high-water mark, almost 500 million people were under Great Britain's rule. A quarter of the earth's landmass came under that throne's dominion. And all of this began in fourth century BC, crawling from the muck and mire of an Iron Age Celtic tribe. How did that happen? In short, the British kingdom grew and flourished above and beyond all competitors. The Britons captured territory, secured resources, provided for people, defeated enemies, and expanded their reach. Laws were established and enforced. They were able to perpetuate a throne with real authority, exercising real power in the world. That's how kingdoms come.

Because God's kingdom is a really real kingdom, that's also how his kingdom comes—with some twists. You could say that the humble origins of the kingdom of Christ started in the backwater towns of Bethlehem and Nazareth, the places where the promised king of the promised kingdom was born and raised. When he left earth to take his throne, this King had only about 120 devoted followers in his kingdom (Acts 1:15). That's not a great result and far from a superpower or empire. Yet today there are over one billion people alive who claim allegiance to King Jesus. The kingdom of Christ dwarfs any and every competitor. The British Empire is but a toy compared to the kingdom of Christ. How did this happen? It all started in and through those few disciples. From those 120 kingdom citizens sprang a world-capturing kingdom that will be eternal and have no end.

God's kingdom comes in and through those people who direct their loyalty, trust, and confidence toward that Jewish carpenter who became King. You're reading *The Kingdom Field Guide* because you don't just want to see God's kingdom; you want to see God's kingdom come. One of your deepest desires and most painful longings is for the good life of God's rule to spread all around you. You may not be able to name it, but that desperate hunger for all things beautiful, true, right, pure, good, and just is a desperate hunger for God's kingdom to come more and more.

Up to this point, this book has focused on seeing God's kingdom. Now it's time to zero in on how to see God's kingdom come—in you and through you. It starts with a deceptively simple prayer.

In and Through Prayer

One day, the disciples came to Jesus and asked him to teach them to pray. He gave a short prayer—a meager ten lines—that is surprisingly simple but incredibly powerful:

Our Father in heaven, hallowed be your name. Your kingdom come, your will be done, on earth as it is in heaven. Give us this day our daily bread, and forgive us our debts, as we also have forgiven our debtors. And lead us not into temptation, but deliver us from evil.

—Matthew 6:9–13

Like me, you might have prayed this prayer hundreds or thousands of times yet never guessed the endless depth, complexity, and grandeur of these few words. If you want to see God's kingdom come in and through you, you'll be an explorer of this prayer for the rest of your life. It won't be just a bedtime ritual, but a lifetime pursuit. You won't just pray this prayer; you'll live in and through it. It will shape not only what you do for God's kingdom, but also who you really are in God's kingdom.

The Lord's Prayer captures our identity and purpose from the beginning of creation. Peter J. Gentry and Stephen J. Wellum, authors of *Kingdom Through Covenant*, explain how God forged our identity as recorded in the Genesis narrative. In relation to God, we are *sons*,[58] deeply loved by him and called to a personal relationship with him. In relation to creation, we are *kings* ruling on behalf of God and stewarding what's been entrusted to us on earth.[59] Together, this is how we are to live as a kingdom of *priests* who worship and serve God (Exodus 19:6; 1 Peter 2:9–10).

Incredibly, this rich trifold identity of sons, priests, and kings is encompassed within the first three lines of the Lord's Prayer.

- "Our Father in heaven" ==> shapes our identity as beloved *sons* of God in a loving relationship.

- "Hallowed be your name" ==> shapes our identity as *priests* who worship God and exalt his name.

- "Your kingdom come" ==> shapes our identity as *kings* with delegated authority from God over creation to bring his royal rule "on earth as it is in heaven."

In less than a few dozen words, Jesus gave us a prayer that encompasses not only the entire narrative arc of the Old Testament, but the entire arc of all of history, from creation to the eternal age to come.

If you want to see God's kingdom come in and through you, the Lord's Prayer is the starting place. It shapes your identity as a true, whole person. Look at how even just these three lines help us to become healthy and integrated in the full identity God has for us. The diagram below is oversimplified, but it makes the point:

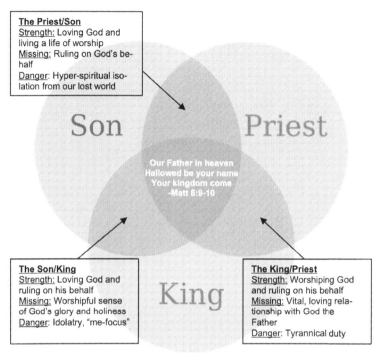

The Priest/Son
Strength: Loving God and living a life of worship
Missing: Ruling on God's behalf
Danger: Hyper-spiritual isolation from our lost world

Son

Priest

Our Father in heaven
Hallowed be your name
Your kingdom come
-Matt 6:9-10

The Son/King
Strength: Loving God and ruling on his behalf
Missing: Worshipful sense of God's glory and holiness
Danger: Idolatry, "me-focus"

King

The King/Priest
Strength: Worshiping God and ruling on his behalf
Missing: Vital, loving relationship with God the Father
Danger: Tyrannical duty

The fall of humanity in the Garden of Eden wasn't just a moral "oops." It was a rebellion against our Maker and his design. Our identity was disintegrated. We became malformed creatures with parts of our core humanity missing or muted. Dangers lurk when either son, priest, or king drops from who we are and how we live. The train wreck of human history stems from our imbalanced identity. Think of the tyrannical kings who have no regard for loving relationships and have craved God's glory for themselves. Consider the ruin caused by religious authorities who deny people a personal intimacy with God and have forgotten that their authority is only valid as they live under God's rule. Witness the futility of navel-gazing, hyper-spiritualists who love being loved but neglect their responsibility of stewardship over creation and right worship of the Creator.

As we pray *and live* the Lord's Prayer, we are restored to balance in our identity as sons, priests, and kings. The Lord's Prayer will direct our wayward course back to genuine love, right worship, and good stewardship under God's rule.

Of course, the Lord's Prayer is not the only prayer that leads us to see God's kingdom come. Jesus also modeled the trifold identity of son-king-priest in his famous "High Priestly Prayer" recorded in John 17:

> When Jesus had spoken these words, he lifted up his eyes to heaven, and said, "Father, the hour has come; glorify your Son that the Son may glorify you, since you have given him authority over all flesh, to give eternal life to all whom you have given him. And this is eternal life, that they know you, the only true God, and Jesus Christ whom you have sent. I glorified you on earth, having accomplished the work that you gave me to do. And now, Father, glorify me in your own presence with the glory that I had with you before the world existed.
>
> **—John 17:1–5**

You can't see what you're not looking for, but when you start seeing human identity as son-king-priest, the themes leap out of Jesus' prayer. His *sonship* is manifested with the intimate relation to God as Father. His *kingship* is evident in the authority he received from the Father and exercised to accomplish work in the world. His *priesthood* is clearly displayed as he intercedes for a fallen world and brings glory to God. Jesus is the true man—humanity in the fullness originally intended. Is it strange that his kingdom would come through prayer that reveals our true design?

In 2012, I was dating my now wife, Katie. Part of my vetting process as a potential spouse was to meet her whole family, especially her great-uncle, Dr. Jerry Kirk. Jerry is not only a patriarch in the family, but also an international leader in the Christian world. When the family gathered around the table, Jerry introduced us to a prayer that has completely changed my life.

For over forty years, Jerry has developed what he calls "The Prayer Covenant."[60] This discipleship tool guides people to pray for one another for at least forty days. I've prayed this prayer with dozens of people since 2012, almost daily. It's probably not coincidental that within the same time period, I have grown more as a whole person than at any other time of my life. Read this prayer slowly and consider praying it daily for yourself and others:

- *Grace*: Dear Father, thank you for your grace that has made me one of your dearly loved children.

- *Love*: By your grace, make being with you, loving you, and obeying you my highest priority.

- *Compassion*: Empower me to love others the way you love me.

- *Repentance*: Wash me clean from every sin.

- *Worship*: Enable me to praise you, O Lord, with all my heart.

- *Commitment*: Jesus, be Lord of my life today in new ways and change me any way you want!

- *Dependence*: Fill me with your Holy Spirit.

- *Influence*: Make me an instrument of your grace, truth, forgiveness, righteousness, and justice.

- *Discipleship*: Use me today for your glory, as a witness to your kingdom, and to invite others to follow Jesus Christ as Lord.

- *Authority*: Gracious Father, I pray in the name of Jesus Christ, our Savior, and in the power of the Holy Spirit. Amen.

Can you see the three elements of *sonship*, *priesthood*, and *kingship* within these few lines? This prayer has shaped me. It's simple but profound and supremely challenging to pray in faith. Year by year, the Lord has used this prayer to restore my identity. Through prayer, I've been recovering what's been lost. I'm being made whole as a son, priest, and king beneath King Jesus. I've seen God's kingdom come in and through me. Of course, more than prayer is needed to see God's kingdom come in and through you, but it's the place to start. Next, let's see how you can see God's kingdom come through faith.

In and Through Faith

As a child, I believed in Santa Claus. And why not? Around early December, I started behaving especially good. I wrote out a Christmas list, and on Christmas day, some of those things on the list magically appeared beneath the tree with a card that read, "From Santa." Clearly it was reasonable to believe.

My son, Kai, also believed in Santa. And why not? On Christmas morning, the plate of cookies was half-eaten by the fireplace, and a trail of sparkles led to presents under the Christmas tree. Sometimes that sparkle trail went from the fireplace to the bathroom. Who else could have done that but Santa? There was good evidence to believe that he existed, so Kai believed, too.

For much of my adult Christian life, my faith in Jesus was too much like my faith in Santa. I believed that Jesus existed. I believed that if I was good enough and prayed just right, he would give me stuff. My faith also included agreement with a checklist of statements about Jesus:

- ✓ Jesus is God.
- ✓ Jesus died for me.
- ✓ Jesus rose from the dead.
- ✓ Jesus forgave my sins.
- ✓ I can go to heaven because I agree with the four statements above.

I even had some Bible verses mostly memorized that summed up this good news, such as Romans 10:9:

> *...if you confess with your mouth that Jesus is Lord and believe in your heart that God raised him from the dead, you will be saved.*

I confessed Jesus as Lord and believed that God raised him from the dead, so I knew that I would be saved. But I had no idea about God's kingdom and was unable to see his kingdom come in and through me. Why? My faith in Jesus was too much like faith in Santa Claus. If I'm good enough, he'll give me stuff.

It's not that the Romans 10:9 aspects of Christian faith are wrong; they are absolutely true. But the faith of our twenty-first-century Western culture has become centered primarily on a few elements:

1. Agreement that Jesus exists

2. Agreement with a list of theological statements about Jesus

3. "Being good" by attending church, reading the Bible, praying, and giving money

4. Telling other people the good news about items 1–3

5. Going to heaven to be with God when you die

6. Jumping on a cloud and strumming that harp.

This kind of belief is only a small pixel in the full picture of faith the Bible paints, and it almost always leaves people scratching their heads about the kingdom. Biblical faith has a much closer analogy to General George Patton than it does Santa Claus. Let me explain.

In World War II, General Patton led his Third Army in what's arguably the most daring, brilliant, and staggering military campaign of the modern era. With the 101st Airborne Division pinned down in Bastogne, Patton marshaled his troops through 100 miles of enemy territory in miserable winter conditions. Arriving in the strategic Belgium crossroads, he relieved the 101st Division, who would likely otherwise have perished from German attack or starvation.

Now picture yourself in Patton's Third Army, heading from danger to danger. You believe in your General, but your belief is so much deeper than merely agreeing that he exists. Your belief in him far surpasses mental agreement with some statements about him. Belief in Patton means that you are supremely loyal to him. Your belief in him means that you obey his every command. Your belief means that you have a fierce dedication to him that will not be deterred by danger, extreme winter, misery, fear, or exhaustion. Your belief means that you trust Patton's command even though you can't see the big picture. Your faith in Patton means that under his command, you will be faithful to your enlistment oath sworn upon entering the military.

This kind of loyal, trusting, obedient commitment is a much better picture of Christian faith. It's through this kind of faith in Jesus that you'll begin to see God's kingdom come in and through you. The Christian church is not called to defeat enemies on a military battlefield,[61] but Jesus is a commander, the Supreme Commander. One of his titles revealed in the Old Testament is "Lord of hosts," which includes being the commander of the armies of God. Over 261 times, YHWH is named with this highest military rank (for example, 1 Samuel 1:3; Psalm 80:19; Isaiah 31:4–5).

One of David's poems captures God's identity as the King who is also the most-high military commander:

Lift up your heads, O gates! And be lifted up, O ancient doors, that the King of glory may come in. Who is this King of glory? The LORD, strong and mighty, the LORD, mighty in battle! Lift up your heads, O gates! And lift them up, O ancient doors, that the King of glory may come in. Who is this King of glory? The LORD of hosts, he is the King of glory!
—Psalm 24:7–10

When King Hezekiah was surrounded by the armies of the wicked Assyrian King Sennacherib, he prayed to God and called on him as the Lord of hosts, commander of the armies of heaven, to defeat his enemy on earth (Isaiah 37:15–20).

When Israel had faith in YHWH, the Lord of hosts, they trusted him, were loyal to him, and obeyed him, much like an army follows a general. The Exodus narrative of Israel coming out of Egypt and being led through the desert wilderness is written, in part, as a story of military preparation (Numbers 1:1–3; 45–46). Entering the promised land after crossing the River Jordan is cast as a military conquest commanded by YHWH (Joshua 4:11–14). Shortly after entering the promised land, Joshua had a famous encounter with "the commander of the army of the LORD," whom we now know to be a theophany of Jesus (Joshua 5:13–15).

I'm not giving you this background as an argument to say that the Christian church must take up arms and stockpile ammunition. Rather, we need to understand this background to provide some depth to the biblical idea of faith. Faith means so much more than believing that Jesus exists and agreeing with a list of stated facts about him. Jesus is our King of kings and Lord of hosts. Faith in Jesus means that we are utterly loyal to him, obedient to him, true in our allegiance to him, faithful in carrying out his commands, and trusting in the plan for his kingdom to come.

Our faith means that fear, doubt, hardship, and pain will not dissuade us from following Jesus. In fact, strong faith isn't an absence of fear or doubt. Strong faith means loyalty to Jesus in the face of fear and doubt. The soldiers in Patton's Third Army weren't machines. They had considerable feelings of uncertainty and dread of what was around the corner, but they were faithful to General Patton because they followed him despite uncertainty. That's the biblical picture of faith in Christ: trusting loyalty and loving obedience regardless of our real doubts and the frailty of unknowing.

Returning to the Romans 10:9 passage, when we "confess … that Jesus is Lord," it goes far beyond a mental acknowledgement of Christ's existence. It's an oath of enlistment binding us to be loyal to his every command given as King and the Lord of hosts.

This is the picture of the resurrected Christ before his ascension in Acts 1. Luke records that Jesus "had given commands" and that "he ordered [his disciples] not to depart from Jerusalem" (Acts 1:1–5).

Do you think the disciples experienced fears or doubts? Plenty. The most dramatic display of doubt came at the Great Commission. The resurrected Jesus was standing on a mountain with his disciples, and he commanded them, "Go therefore and make disciples of all nations..." (Matthew 28:18–20). There's a part of this picture which is often overlooked: doubt. Before Jesus issued the charge for worldwide ministry, the author, Matthew, included this important context:

> Now the eleven disciples went to Galilee, to the mountain to which Jesus had directed them. And when they saw him they worshiped him, **but some doubted**.
> **—Matthew 28:16–17**

The enemies of Jesus in the religious establishment had murder in their hearts. The disciples' trusting loyalty to King Jesus would cost many of them their lives because following Jesus was considered a betrayal to Caesar. Many of their families hated them. Many of the disciples left their businesses or sources of predictable income. Of course there was doubt among the disciples. How could there not be? But they didn't allow their uncertainty to keep them from following the orders and commands of the resurrected King Jesus. They followed his dictates *in faith*.

To this day, people are being persecuted for their faith in Jesus—their allegiance and loyalty to Jesus. In the Western world, we typically don't face hostility on this scale. Nonetheless, we are faced with countless small forks in the road where we must decide if we will be faithful to Christ.

Every dollar spent is a moment for faith. Will we steward our resources faithfully to honor what King Jesus has entrusted to us?

Every word spoken is a moment for faith. Will we speak in a way that brings honor to the name of King Jesus, or will we be disloyal to his great name through deceit?

Every hour of the day is a moment for faith. Will we spend our time wisely in obedience to King Jesus' command to love one another as he loved us, or will we squander our lives in isolated Netflix binges or endless Instagram scrolling?

If you think I'm getting high and mighty, the finger also points at me. I had to wean myself from a backgammon addiction after playing over 5,000 games on my phone. I'm not proud of that. Surely I could have spent some of that time more *faith-fully* instead of using a phone to numb myself.

Consider the sobering kingdom parable told by King Jesus about the man who went on a journey and entrusted property to his servants (Matthew 25:14–30). Some of the servants used the money to generate more income for their master. They were commended with "Well done, good and faithful servant. You have been faithful over a little; I will set you over much." But the lazy servant who hid the money out of fear was cast out into darkness.

When we are loyal to Jesus, we are faith-filled. When we are obedient to Jesus, we are faith-filled. When we trust Jesus, we are faith-filled. When we are good stewards of the resources of Jesus, we are faith-filled. When we are allied to Jesus, we are faith-filled. When we are faith-filled, we are faithful. And when we are faithful, we will see God's kingdom come in and through us.

CHAPTER EIGHT FIELD TRIP

Looking for Loyalty

Loyalty is a key element of faith in Jesus. As we are devoted to his rule, his kingdom will come in our lives. As we are aligned with his commands, his character is formed in us. As we show devotion to his name, we become his light in the world.

This field trip will take place over the length of a week. You're going to be searching for examples of loyalty all around you. Carry a journal wherever you go and pay attention to displays of loyalty at work, at home, on your commute, in your entertainment, and on the news. Be alert. Record what you see and when you see it.

There is *brand loyalty*, for example. Look for company logos on clothes, hats, and bumper stickers. Also look for *group loyalty*. When somebody wears a sports jersey, say a Jordan 23, the person is showing devotion to that athlete and team. Try to identify displays of *political loyalty* in bumper stickers and t-shirt slogans. Look for country flags flown in yards or in front of government offices.

Pay attention to *personal loyalty*. This is when somebody shows devotion to another person. Is there an employee who goes above and beyond for the boss? Listen closely to wedding vows as the bride and groom swear lifetime faithfulness to each other.

Finally, after you've looked for signs of loyalty in other people, notice your own devotions. Is there a store you are dedicated to buying food from? A gas station where you *must* fuel up? What TV show is a "can't miss" in your schedule? When your phone rings, what name on your caller ID will have you picking up and answering every time? Look for patterns of "likes" when you're scrolling through social media. What grabs your attention? Whom are you following? Whose Instagram feed is feeding you?

If you have a tough time seeing your own loyalties, pay attention to your calendar, wallet, and personal energy. The way you spend your time, money, and effort is a huge clue to the allegiances in your life. Then consider: How much of your loyalty is given to the King of kings?

Field Trip Details

Travel: Turn your normal life routine into a week-long field trip. Go where you normally go in the rhythm of work, home, and social life.

Cost: Zero

Time: Spend as much time as you can paying attention to loyalty.

Physical Demands: Zero

Gear: Journal to record your observations of loyalty

Key Scriptures to Guide Your Trip: Matthew 21:22; Romans 10:17; Galatians 2:16–20; Ephesians 2:8–9; Ephesians 3:16–17; 2 Timothy 4:7; 1 Peter 1:8–9; 1 John 5:4

Schedule this field trip now. Put it on your calendar!
Day: _____
Time: _____
People invited to join me: _____

_____

_____

Seeing the Kingdom Connection

As the King of kings, Jesus commands complete loyalty from us. Our faith in Christ is so much more than a mental agreement that he exists. Jesus calls us to lay down our lives for him. Why? Because in his ultimate display of loyalty to *us*, he laid down *his* life.

There must not be any loyalty greater than our devotion to the kingdom of God. If you are more devoted to your sports team than to Jesus, then you have some work to do. If you can proudly wear a company logo but dare not utter the name of Jesus in public, then it's time to re-evaluate your loyalties. If you have time to binge-watch *Game of Thrones* but don't have time to serve in a church ministry, then it's time to check your faithfulness to the throne of Christ. Does a political loyalty for a candidate commandeer more mindshare than Christ?

Jesus was clear that his followers must give their highest devotion to him alone. This call to ultimate loyalty is what Jesus meant when he said:

> *If anyone comes to me and does not hate his own father and mother and wife and children and brothers and sisters, yes, and even his own life, he cannot be my disciple. Whoever does not bear his own cross and come after me cannot be my disciple. ... So therefore, any one of you who does not renounce all that he has cannot be my disciple.*
> **—Luke 14:26–27, 33**

Questions for Reflection

1. What sticks out from this field trip or is a new idea for you?

2. What questions have come out of this field trip? What doesn't make sense to you?

3. How do you see Jesus and his kingdom in this experience?

4. How can you apply this to your life and take a next step?

5. What will you talk to God and other people about?

After this field trip, circle where you are right now in your journey to find God's kingdom as a hidden treasure.

Journal: Spend some time in your journal to record further thoughts.

SMALL GROUP GUIDE

Chapter Eight Discussion Questions

> **Key Scripture:**
> Filled with the Fullness of God
> Ephesians 3:14–21

1. How did the Apostle Paul connect faith (verse 17) to the fullness of God (verse 19) in the Ephesians passage? Why do we need strength from the Holy Spirit for Christ to dwell in our hearts? Why did Paul say that love is essential for a life of fullness?

2. Consider your trifold identify as a son, priest, and king. Which of these resonates most with you? Which do you struggle most to accept and embrace? What specific danger do you face by not understanding and appropriating your full identity in Christ's kingdom?

3. Is your faith in Jesus more like a child's faith in Santa Claus or a soldier's faith in his leader? How might your faith respond to tests, such as persecution, difficulties, or doubts? Does King Jesus have your unconditional loyalty and obedience? Why or why not? What is needed in your life for faith in Christ to grow?

4. Discuss your experience on the field trip. What did you learn? What surprised you? What challenged you?

Chapter Eight Notes

CHAPTER NINE

See the Kingdom Come
Through Worship

If you want to see God's kingdom come in and through you, you will worship God. This means so much more than singing a few songs on Sunday morning. Worship will become your one job as you live in God's kingdom.

Real kingdoms have real occupations for the citizens. Ultimately, however, no matter the duty, job, or assignment, every citizen is tasked with the one job of making the name of the king great. Every action of each person either adds to or detracts from the reputation of the kingdom throughout the land. There's a word for actions that bring glory to a king. It's *worship*.

It's no coincidence that two major biblical words for worship carry the sense of work and service. The Hebrew word *avodah* means worship, work, and service.[62] The Greek word *latreia* means worship and service.[63]

In the Old Testament, God called priests from the lineage of Levi to perform the work of the tabernacle and the temple. Their work was often physically challenging and very demanding. As the Israelites wandered in the desert, the Levitical priests were tasked with setting up, tearing down, and transporting the tabernacle. This was hard, back-breaking work. Picture them pounding stakes into hardened desert soil and rocks. See them sweating as they carried materials that weighed thousands of pounds. For forty years, they toiled, moving that tent. The Levites were God's carneys. Set up the tent. Take it down. Move it. Do it again. And again. And again—for forty years! But this work was considered worship. The work of the tabernacle was to bring glory and honor to the name of King YHWH among them. Work was worship. It was an honor to carry the tabernacle.

King YHWH commanded excellence in everything because he is the King of All. His "home," the tabernacle, was the place of his rule among his people. The tabernacle was the palace of the King of the Universe. All of the priests' work needed to be conducted in a way that spread the fame, glory, and honor of the King among the nations. The priests had different roles and functions. Some carried, some built, some sacrificed, and some entered the holiest of holies. But they all had one job: worship.

In biblical languages, the root words for *worship* also carry the sense of bowing or bending the knee before somebody. This makes sense in kingdom settings. When people appear before a king or a queen in the throne room, the men bow, and the women curtsey. Their knees are bent in reverence. They lower themselves physically as a sign of exalting the ruler and the throne. As a sign of obedience and loyalty, they may even reply to a king, "Yes, your Worship."

Throughout the kingdom narrative in the Bible, we are called royal priests (Exodus 19:5–6; 1 Peter 2:9–10; Revelation 5:9–10). As priests, we have one job: worship. Our work is worship. In everything we do, we are to "bow the knee" to acknowledge the greatness and goodness of our King.

The occupation of citizens in any kingdom is to glorify

the king. This is the case in God's really real kingdom as well. In every part of our public and private lives, we are to glorify God. Our inner thoughts and outer actions are to enhance and exalt the name of God. Our one job is to worship.

You Had One Job

When you visit London, there is a massive workforce that tends to the royal household. At the time of this writing, these were some of the vacancies[64] of real job positions:

- Marketing Manager at St. James Palace
- Finance Manager at Buckingham Palace
- Housekeeping Assistant at the Palace of Holyroodhouse
- Chauffeur at Kensington Palace
- Web Developer at Buckingham Palace

The full list of occupations supporting the royal family would itself fill a book, and every position—from security to food prep—has one job: to make the name of the Queen great. Every action and execution of duty *must* reflect well on the reputation and honor of the monarch.

The full regal name of the Queen is actually "Her Majesty Elizabeth the Second, by the Grace of God of the United Kingdom of Great Britain and Northern Ireland and of Her other Realms and Territories Queen, Head of the Commonwealth, Defender of the Faith."[65] Imagine if your boss had that title! Regardless of whether you were trimming a tree, driving a car, or cooking an omelet, all would be done for the honor of that name. Why? Because shoddy work would project a shoddy reputation to the world. And if you personally knew Her Majesty, your love for her would compel you even more to strive for excellence to guard and enhance her greatness.

Because the kingdom of God is really real, it also has real work for its citizens, and the job of every citizen is to make the name of the King of kings shine. Our one task is to enhance the reputation of Jesus, to project his greatness to the world and reflect back to him the praises of all creation. This is worship, and worship is our one job in the kingdom of God. Regardless of your earthly occupation—teacher, street sweeper, parent, pastor, or athlete—your one job is to worship, enhancing the greatness of the name of King Jesus to the world around you.

Let's look at some scriptures that establish your one job of worship:

I will bless the LORD at all times; his praise shall continually be in my mouth.

—Psalm 34:1

So, whether you eat or drink, or whatever you do, do all to the glory of God.

—1 Corinthians 10:31

And whatever you do, in word or deed, do everything in the name of the Lord Jesus, giving thanks to God the Father through him.

—Colossians 3:17

As each has received a gift, use it to serve one another, as good stewards of God's varied grace: whoever speaks, as one who speaks oracles of God; whoever serves, as one who

*serves by the strength that God supplies—in order that in
everything God may be glorified through Jesus Christ. To
him belong glory and dominion forever and ever. Amen.*
—1 Peter 4:10–11

One of my favorite internet memes is "You Had One
Job." The meme captures hilarious pictures of people
clearly failing in the one task assigned to them. This is my
own "one job" scene I saw at a store.

*C'mon, Banana Guy! You had one job! Don't stock the
oranges where the bananas go!*

If you haven't seen these memes, just do a quick internet search for "one job meme" to see some colossal goofs
when people had a single job to do but missed the mark.
I'm usually laughing with tears when I flip through those
memes. Think of lines on a road that are terribly crooked.
C'mon, road line guy! You had one job to do! Or the Pepsi
can that ends up on the Coke display. *C'mon, Coke guy!
You had one job!*

Now think of people serving the true King Jesus who
fail to give him glory when the world is watching closest.

C'mon, Christian, your one job is to worship the Christ! Sheesh.

If Jesus were doing his public ministry in the twenty-first century instead of the first, I'm convinced that he'd use this meme. Often. Listen to Jesus' admonition to his disciples and picture the "You Had One Job" meme in the background:

> *You are the salt of the earth, but if salt has lost its taste, how shall its saltiness be restored? It is no longer good for anything except to be thrown out and trampled under people's feet.*
>
> *You are the light of the world. A city set on a hill cannot be hidden. Nor do people light a lamp and put it under a basket, but on a stand, and it gives light to all in the house. In the same way, let your light shine before others, so that they may see your good works and give glory to your Father who is in heaven.*
>
> **—Matthew 5:13–16**

What's the job of salt? To be salty. What's the job of light? To give light. What do we say to diluted salt and dim light? *You had one job!* The job of a kingdom citizen is to magnify the glory of the King and his kingdom. If we're not enhancing the reputation of Jesus as we pay our taxes, love our neighbors, and drive our cars, we're not doing our one job.

Side Trip: A Prayer for Showing Up

I'd like you to pray a prayer every day for forty days. It's a prayer for showing up. God created you uniquely to bring him glory. You have a unique personality, design, and gifting. You have unique experiences, passions, and talents. You can live your life in a way that others "may see your good works and give glory to your Father who is in heaven" (Matthew 5:16). But you must show up. You must bring your personality to each encounter. You must not shy away from offering your gifts to a world that desperately needs them. You must not try to be somebody else because you are guaranteed to stink at being somebody else.

When you just try to be you, there will be new energy and vitality available in your life because a huge weight will be lifted. For this Side Trip, take a few minutes every day to pray this prayer for showing up. Set a daily alarm as a reminder. This has the promise of being a game changer.

I wrote this prayer based on 1 Peter 4:7–10. May it be a regular blessing to you as it has been to me.

Dear Father, in showing up today, thank you
that I'll waste the **least** amount of energy
when I bring you the **most** glory.
Father, your kingdom come as I become like Jesus
in choosing the **lowest** place of service
with the **highest** use of my gifting.
Father, form me to be the **best** version
of myself you created me to be
as we, together, destroy the **worst** idolatry
lurking in worry, fear, envy, and pride.
By your Spirit, enable me to enjoy the **broadest** life
within the boundaries of your **narrowest** purpose for me
in the body of Christ,
by the strength of Christ,
with the love of Christ,
for the name of Christ,
Amen.

Toasting Bagels with the Space Shuttle

We've established that in God's kingdom, we have only one primary occupation. We were designed and created for this one job: worship. When we operate according to design, when we do the job we were created to do, it brings glory, praise, and honor to the creator.

Let me give you an example. The space shuttle has been called one of the most complex machines ever built by mankind. Let's look at some of the specs:

- Peak velocity in orbit: 17,500 miles per hour

- Maximum temperature on reentry: 1,650 degrees F

- Combined odometer of the five space shuttles over the lifespan of the shuttles: 513 million miles

- Temperature of rocket system on take-off: 5,600 degrees.

When the shuttle worked as planned, there was a huge celebration at NASA. People gave high fives, fist bumps, and backslaps. When the shuttle did its job, the people who designed the shuttle received glory, honor, and praise. Why? When something becomes what it is meant to be, it brings glory to the creator of that thing.

We all must eventually face this profound question: "What did God design me to be?" Jesus doesn't want us just to follow a set of rules or go to church or even "be good." Jesus wants to align our very nature with his design of who were meant to be.

Your greatest joy in life is found when you become what you're meant to be, and your biggest sorrows arise when your life isn't aligned with your design. There is tragedy when the space shuttle doesn't work as designed, and there's tragedy when you don't work as designed.

So who are we designed to be? Jesus said it clearly:

> **You are the light of the world.** ... *In the same way, let your light shine before others, so that they may see your good works and give glory to your Father who is in heaven.*
> —**Matthew 5:14–16**

Our whole purpose in God's kingdom is to shine like a light so that people will see us and then give glory to God in heaven. Why did Jesus go through all of the trouble to make the universe, populate it with billions of people, and then redeem those billions of people by his death on the cross? He did it so the Father may receive glory!

As a citizen of the kingdom, you are meant to become a person who brings glory to God. This is worship. This is our one job.

Now let's go back to the space shuttle. It was created for one job: to take people and stuff to space and return safely. When that happens, it brings glory to the creators of the shuttle. But what if people were to use a space shuttle for something for which it wasn't designed? Let's say that Congress passed a law that the space shuttle could be used only to toast bagels.

In 2013, I combined my geekiness and love for bagels in a strange twist of events. I wondered what it would be like to turn a space shuttle into a bagel toaster. This led to what I thought was a really simple question: How far away from the space shuttle rockets would you need to place a bagel in order to toast it to perfection?

This seems like an easy question. The rockets burn at about 5,600 degrees Fahrenheit while a toaster works at 450 degrees. Shouldn't it be an easy calculation to figure out how far away the bagel needs to be?

To answer the question, I did exhaustive research. (I spent five minutes and clicked a few Google links.) Not coming up with an easy internet answer, I decided to do some empirical research. I performed a scaled-down experiment with a blow torch and a bagel. This is me with the scorched bagel on the left.

I had immense satisfaction in turning a bagel into a black, charred lump of coal, but unfortunately, I didn't find out how far away the bagel needed to be from the space shuttle to turn it a nice golden brown.

I decided to post the question to social media. I thought this was a simple question with an easy answer, but I ended up setting off a *firestorm*. The "Space Shuttle Bagel Toaster" question spread through social media to hundreds of people, and I started getting responses from an actual NASA engineer, an old friend from high school, and scientists in the physics department at Western Washington University. I actually spoke with a rocket scientist who worked on a space shuttle!

This simple question turned into a raging debate because the Space Shuttle Bagel Toaster question, as it turns out, is very complicated. People went at it, spending chunks of time trying to figure out this complicated question. The most satisfying and seemingly reliable answer came from a personal interaction I had with Devlin Baker, a brilliant man who came out of the WWU physics department. I quote his solution in full because it's worth the ink:

This is slightly tricky, as the air around the rocket is not a closed system like an oven, and does not reach a fixed temperature (i.e., 450 degrees) due to convection, air currents, etc. Rather, the rocket would cook the bagel in the manner that an open-topped toaster does, by infrared (blackbody) radiation.

Toaster elements are only around 900K, and have an emission surface area of a few square centimeters, so we can work out the average surface flux on the bagel pretty easily.

L = sigma* T^4 * A_elements

F = L/A_bagel

Where sigma is the Stefan Boltzmann constant, T is the temperature in K, and "A_elements" is the surface area of the elements, and "A_bagel" is the surface area of the bagel. An average bagel has a surface area of around 30cm^2, so the total flux on a bagel in your average toaster is around 1,000 watts per square centimeter. So at what distance does the blackbody radiation due to the rocket provide that surface flux?

We can assume that the exhaust stream is about the same as the rocket nozzle, or 2.4 meters, and drops below 5600F after about 10 times that distance, giving a total emission area of ~25m^2. We can see that at distances approximately equal to the sectional area of the exhaust stream, the flux will be many times higher than the toaster. We have to move much farther away, where the inverse square law takes effect.

F = L / 4 * pi * r^2

Where r is the distance, L is the luminosity of the rocket exhaust, and F is the desired flux of 1,000 watts per square meter. All we have to do is solve for r!

r = sqrt(L/4*pi*F) = **426 meters away**

That assumes you want to cook it nicely, and about the same time as a toaster does.

I can't decide if the biggest thrill is that a real physicist actually performed calculations on toasting a bagel with a space shuttle or that his answer begins, "This is slightly tricky," or that he took the time to measure the surface area of a bagel!

Joking aside, if somebody actually were to use a space shuttle to toast a bagel, it would be a shame and a huge loss because of the tremendous cost to produce a space shuttle. There have been millions of labor hours poured into the program. Each space shuttle mission costs about 2 billion dollars when you take into account the specialized materials, the design, the engineering, the testing, and the training.

What would the creators of the space shuttle think if their brilliant and amazing work were only used to toast a bagel? Would there be high fives, celebrations, and back-slapping if their grand finale were 60 grams of toasted carbs?

Not even close. It would be tragically sad. There would be a huge sense of loss and waste because—here it is— the space shuttle *wasn't designed to be* a toaster.

There is an even greater loss when we don't live according to our design. Let's go back to the words of Jesus:

You are the light of the world. … In the same way, let your light shine before others, so that they may see your good works and give glory to your Father who is in heaven.
—*Matthew 5:14–16*

We are designed to be a light that brings glory to God. If we fail to live as designed, the loss is tragic. Why? Because there was a great cost to making us light. NASA spent billions to design and make the space shuttle. Consider the cost to the Father, Son, and Holy Spirit in making us the light of the world.

First, look at the cost to Jesus, God the Son. Jesus left his Father's side in heaven and took on a body for eternity. He lived among sinful men. He was placed at the mercy of Satan. Jesus bore the punishment of all sins for all people for all time and incurred the wrath of the Almighty God on the cross. Jesus was despised and rejected by his own people. God the Son received a new body when he was raised from the dead, but part of the cost of our redemption is that he will have scars in his hands, feet, and side for all eternity! The only scars in eternity will be the scars of Jesus. This is part of the cost for us to become the light of the world.

Next, let's look at the cost to God the Father. The Father loves the Son. He has loved his Son for all eternity past, but the cost to redeem us was the Father giving up the life of his Son in sacrifice. I'm a dad, and I know the pain of seeing my son suffer. It's unbearable. But God the Father poured out his wrath on his own Son, who stood in our place for our sin. This is a terrible price to pay and an exceedingly high cost. God the Father willingly paid this cost so that we could become the light of the world.

Finally, let's look at the cost paid by God the Spirit. He is the Holy One who must dwell in imperfect, sinful people. Think about that. The Spirit is grieved, squelched, and blasphemed among human beings. Let's acknowledge that a holy and pure God dwelling in sinful man is a tremendous cost.

The cost God paid to redeem us makes the space shuttle costs look like chump change!

If we aren't being light and living so that God receives glory, then we are not living according to design. Are you toasting bagels with a space shuttle? Don't you know what you are meant to become? Let's read it again:

> You are the light of the world. ... In the same way, let your light shine before others, so that they may see your good works and give glory to your Father who is in heaven.
> —*Matthew 5:14–16*

When we fail in this design, there is such a wasted cost. But when we live in a way that brings glory to God, it's worth the price of investment!

We weren't created and redeemed so that our existence could be spent avoiding being toasted in the fires of hell. We were created ultimately to give glory to God, to worship him, and to declare the greatness of his name. That's our purpose. We were designed to worship. We've got one job.

Do you want to see God's kingdom come in and through you? Then worship with your whole life. Steward all of your time, resources, relationships, passions, talents, and energy in a way that exalts the reputation of Jesus. Proclaim the goodness of God through your public and private conduct. Allow your external actions and internal motivations to be brought under the rule of Jesus Christ so that when people see your life, they can't help but glorify God.

Are you toasting bagels with a space shuttle rocket?

You were designed for so much more. You are the light of the world.

CHAPTER NINE FIELD TRIP

Hunting for Idols

Go on a hunt for the idols in the world around you. An idol is anything, real or imagined, that wrongly receives worship rightly belonging to God alone.

N. T. Wright argues that idolatry is at the root of every sin.[68] Our failings aren't just a moral "oops." Rather, sin is a rebellion against our original design to be worshippers of the one true God. In his book *The Day the Revolution Began*, Wright explains the devastation of idolatry:

> Humans are called not just to keep certain moral standards in the present and to enjoy God's presence here and hereafter, but to celebrate, worship, procreate, and take responsibility within the rich, vivid developing life of creation. According to Genesis, that is what humans were made for.

> The diagnosis of the human plight is then not simply that humans have broken God's moral law, offending and insulting the Creator, whose image they bear—though that is true as well. This lawbreaking is a symptom of a much more serious disease. Morality is important, but it isn't the whole story. Called to responsibility and authority within and over the creation, humans have turned their vocation upside

down, giving worship and allegiance to forces and powers within creation itself. The name for this is idolatry. The result is slavery and finally death.

When our worship is misaligned, everything else in our lives falls into disorder and ruin.

In this field trip, you are going on a hunt for the idols in the world around you. How do you recognize an idol? Look for what people bow down to. There may not be literal bowing, but when somebody places top priority on something and makes sacrifices of time, energy, and money to that thing, then it is an idol.

Your hometown sports team can be an idol. When everything is less important than game time, there's probably some misplaced worship. If sacrifices are made so the team is followed *no matter what*, there's idolatry lurking beneath the surface.

Your bank account can be an idol if it receives more attention and devotion than God. Do you bow down to serve your 401(k) statement?

Your family can be an idol. If you worship the idea of a happy home more than you worship God, then you are missing your vocation in God's kingdom of priests.

James K. A. Smith rightly identifies shopping malls as centers of worship, complete with a secular liturgy[69] and a priesthood that receives your tithes and offerings at the cash register.

Look for these altars that we have set up for our idols.

Look for situations where people mimic Mike Meyer and Dana Carvey in the movie *Wayne's World* when they bow down to Alice Cooper and chant, "We're not worthy."[70] That movie scene is hilariously exaggerated, but it has a disturbing kernel of truth. In reality, we do bow down in worship to people, institutions, and creation. We'll give glory to *anything* instead of God, the Maker of everything.

Field Trip Details

Travel: Travel around your hometown to hunt for idols. Go to places of power, entertainment, or commerce.

Cost: Zero

Time: Take at least half a day for this trip. Really look and pay attention. There are idols everywhere, perhaps even in your own home.

Physical Demands: Zero

Gear: Take your journal to record observations of idolatry.

Key Scriptures to Guide Your Trip: Exodus 20:1–7; Isaiah 45:20; Matthew 4:8–10; Romans 1:18–25; 1 Corinthians 10:7–14; Galatians 4:8; Colossians 3:5; 1 John 5:21; Revelation 9:20

Schedule this field trip now. Put it on your calendar!
Day: _____
Time: _____
People invited to join me: _____
_____
_____

Seeing the Kingdom Connection

All glory, honor, and power belong to Jesus, the King of kings (Revelation 4:11). He alone deserves our worship and devotion. Jesus has the name that is exalted above every name (Philippians 2:9–10). He occupies the eternal throne as the Son of David and rules over an eternal kingdom without end (Daniel 7:13–14). Before true worship can be fully offered to the true God, you need to become aware of the idols in your life and in the world around you. When you discover that you're offering worship to something other than God, you need to smash that idol.

Eventually, one day, *every* knee will bow to Jesus (Romans 14:11). But we don't need to wait for that day. As you bow your knee to Jesus now, his kingdom will come more and more in your life.

Questions for Reflection

1. What sticks out from this field trip or is a new idea for you?

2. What questions have come out of this field trip? What doesn't make sense to you?

3. How do you see Jesus and his kingdom in this experience?

4. How can you apply this to your life and take a next step?

5. What will you talk to God and other people about?

After this field trip, circle where you are right now in your journey to find God's kingdom as a hidden treasure.

Blind   Aware   Ponder   Value   Trap of Inaction   Prioritize   Own/Sell

Journal: Spend some time in your journal to record further thoughts.

SMALL GROUP GUIDE

Chapter Nine Discussion Questions

Key Scripture:
Worship in a Cave
Psalm 34:1–22

1. King David wrote Psalm 34 when he was fleeing for his life, under persecution, and living in a cave. He was able to worship God during one of the lowest points of his life (verses 1–3). Put yourself in that terrible cave experience with David. How would you be feeling? What fears might arise? What doubts? What would worship look like under those circumstances? Describe the experiences of worship growing up in your family and now in your life.

2. *In everything we do, we are to "bow the knee" to acknowledge the greatness and goodness of our King.* How can this attitude of worship permeate your daily life? Make a list of your routine daily activities, including chores, occupation, family time, and volunteer and leisure activities. How can you build more worship into your daily life?

3. Are you living up to the purpose for which God has created you? Are you living as the light and the salt that he designed you to be? In what ways is your life glorifying the God who made and redeemed you? Are there areas of your life that are not being used according to God's design? What are those areas, and how can you bring them into alignment with their true God-given purpose?

4. What are the idols in your life that rob God of worship? What demands too much of your time, attention, energy, and resources? The main idols of our culture are usually in the areas of money, sex, and power. Which of these is a strong temptation for you?

5. In the area of worship, where are you stuck in the Trap of Inaction? Have you fallen into a rut? Has worship become dull or a duty? How can you breathe new vitality into your worship?

6. Discuss your experience on the field trip. What did you learn? What surprised you? What challenged you?

Chapter Nine Notes

CHAPTER TEN

See the Kingdom Come Through Stewardship

Real kingdoms have real economies, systems of exchange of goods and services. When Joe has a chicken, and Sally has a sack of grain, a healthy economy allows for equitable and reliable trade of grain for the chicken.

All of the kingdoms of this world have economies based on scarcity. There's not enough grain to go around, so a kingdom establishes a trusted and stable system of allocating those scarce goods. Kingdoms or countries that are successful in allocating scarce goods have healthy economies with a thriving exchange of goods and services. Countries that have unstable economies end up with food lines.

Even during the coronavirus crisis in 2020, the stable economy of the United States yielded mass rushes on toilet paper and hand sanitizer. That tiny virus revealed a huge scarcity mindset as people made mad dashes to Costco.

Because God's kingdom is really real, it also has a real economy. However, in God's kingdom, the economy isn't based on scarcity. God's economy is based on abundance.

God literally owns everything. Every penny, every ounce of gold, every sack of grain, and every chicken is his. He is the rightful and legal owner of it all. This is the clear testimony of scripture:

The earth is the LORD's and the fullness thereof, the world and those who dwell therein, for he has founded it upon the seas and established it upon the rivers.
—Psalm 24:1–2

Who has first given to me, that I should repay him? Whatever is under the whole heaven is mine.
—Job 41:11

For every beast of the forest is mine, the cattle on a thousand hills. I know all the birds of the hills, and all that moves in the field is mine.

If I were hungry, I would not tell you, for the world and its fullness are mine.
—Psalm 50:10–12

The God who made the world and everything in it, being Lord of heaven and earth, does not live in temples made by man, nor is he served by human hands, as though he needed anything, since he himself gives to all mankind life and breath and everything.
—Acts 17:24–25

Let's be clear. You own nothing, not one penny. Your house isn't yours. The shirt on your back isn't yours. Your bank account isn't yours. The breath in your lungs isn't yours. The burger on your plate isn't yours, nor the plate.

Everything you have comes from God and belongs to God. Your body, talents, and time aren't yours. Even your soul belongs to God, as we'll see later.

What you have God has entrusted to you as a steward. All of your resources, time, and abilities have been given to you on loan, and you are expected to use everything wisely, generously, and in love. As you give to God and others a portion of your paycheck, you are trading in God's kingdom economy. As you give others time and service, you are accruing "treasure in heaven" (Matthew 6:19–20). As you use your talents for the good of God and the good of your neighbor, you are being a good steward.

The more you participate in God's kingdom economy through good stewardship, the more you will see that it is an economy of abundance. You may never be rich according to the standards of the world, but you will find *true* riches, both in this life and the next.

If you want to see God's kingdom come in your life, you'll learn to be an excellent steward of the abundant resources entrusted to you. You'll become adept at trading in God's kingdom economy. Let's look more at what that means.

Playing Monopoly

God's kingdom economy is more real than all of the economies of this earth. After making that statement, all respectable bankers, investors, and stock market traders probably think I'm crazy. If so, they are in peril of being shown to be great fools. [Warning: I'm about to turn your world upside down. Stop reading right now if you don't want the rug to be pulled out from under you.]

Let's begin with the game of Monopoly. It's often mistaken for just a box with dice, title deeds, money, and pewter figurines that provide fun and recreation. But this board game is actually a full-blown, real economy.

First, it's real because it has real money. For a while, Monopoly players agree that the rainbow assortment of cash bills have value. The money is used to buy and sell property, pay fines, build houses, and secure a host of goods. There is faith that the money has value inside of the game. Players trust that the $200 payday received at "GO" will have future value to buy property or pay debts. As in a real economy, there's a player who is the banker and controls the flow of cash. There's also a system of taxes. If you play like I do, then there's a type of lottery you can win by landing on Free Parking and scoring the huge pile of cash in the center of the board. All of this works because the players agree that the currency has value. They place faith and trust in that value for future transactions. They have confidence that if they save enough money, it can be used to secure future assets or pay future rents should they land on another player's property. The money is just paper, but it's backed by common trust among all of the players participating in the Monopoly economy.

Second, Monopoly is real because it has real assets. The properties, houses, and hotels are real. A physical deed proves ownership of a property and entitles you to collect rent based on the amount of investment into that property. As in real life, Monopoly real estate is all based on location, location, location. If you've ever placed hotels on Boardwalk and Park Place, then you know the thrill and exhilaration. It doesn't matter that the property is only a few square inches instead of acres. It's not important that the houses are thimble-sized instead of house-sized. They are real assets people acquire using the real currency.

Finally, Monopoly has a real goal: to win. Gain as much as you can. Amass a fortune that exceeds everyone else's. This goal drives you to make deals, steward resources well, be wise with your spending, and always be calculating risk versus reward.

But then something drastic and dramatic inevitably happens—the game ends. The thriving and flourishing economy collapses and fails in an instant. When the game is over, all of the cash becomes worthless, all investments fail and lose the ability to secure income, and every trade is nullified. The property which you formerly owned has a voided title deed. In the blink of an eye, the whole economy is swept back into the box. Then, as if transported by magic, you enter into the "more real" economy of your world. You join an economy in which all the cash bills are green and there's a different set of title deeds, another system of trusted currency, new properties, assets, and bills to pay.

Only a fool would take Monopoly money and try to secure a mortgage through Bank of America. You'd be scoffed at. All of the properties in Monopoly are named for real places in this world, but if you were to take your Monopoly deed to Boardwalk or Park Place and try to collect rent, you'd be locked up as a lunatic. If you were to take a plastic Monopoly hotel and try to use it as collateral for a loan, you'd be tossed out onto the streets. Just try to take a yellow $100 Monopoly bill and hand it to the cashier at the grocery store. You'll be arrested if you try to leave the store with a filled cart.

When the Monopoly game ends, the economy instantly collapses. Faith in the currency fails, and nothing of value in the game's real economy can be brought into the "more real" economy of our daily lives. This is all very obvious, and you know it innately, even if you haven't voiced it.

Here's where you're in peril of becoming a fool. Just like in Monopoly, the economy of this world requires faith and common trust in the currencies of trade. We have a common agreement and mutual confidence that when we swipe a credit card, exchange small tokens of silver and copper, or hand over crumpled bills, all of this money has value and can be transferred from one entity to another while maintaining worth for future transactions. It's not much different from all of the same tokens in Monopoly, but we believe that it's "more real" because, after all, Monopoly is just a game that always ends.

In real life, just like in Monopoly, we are constantly making improvements to property we've acquired. We add rooms to the house, upgrade appliances, and knock down old buildings to build what's bigger and better. We look down on properties that are overgrown and shake our heads at unimproved lots that are claimed by weeds. We admire people who build luxury condos and are able to command top dollar for rent. And the drumbeat of "location, location, location" marches us from mortgage to mortgage in hopes of living behind gates, guard houses, and security systems on Park Place.

When the Monopoly game ends, you go back to a world where you steward your resources, work hard, save money, and invest in land or entrepreneurial ventures so that your investment can grow. In the "more real" economy of this life, there's a pursuit to amass more and more; there's a drive to "win" by filling the coffers.

But then, in the blink of an eye, the economy of this life will inevitably vanish like withered grass. At the end of your life, everything you held to be of value will suddenly lose all value. All of the confidence, faith, and trust you'd placed in the binary digits, coins, and bills will be instantly proven worthless. All of your rights to property will be voided because after your final breath, you'll step into the "more real" economy of the kingdom of God. There, none of your earthly title deeds will be honored. They'll be nullified, and you'll find that none of your possessions were ever yours.

Side Trip: Monopoly Money

Find a Monopoly bill and put it in your wallet or purse. For the next month, every time you spend money, look at the Monopoly money as a reminder that the economy of this world is a game that will instantly vanish at the end of your life. But also remind yourself that you have the ability to create treasure in heaven by the way you steward your money. Are you using your resources wisely, generously, in love, and as a blessing to others in Jesus' name? You can convert the money of this life into currency with eternal value in the age to come.

Small Group Guide

Do this activity together as a small group. Compare your experiences as you pay attention to how you spend money. Talk about what it means to live according to the economy of God's really real kingdom. Jesus *always* entrusts to us the finances we need to be generous and loving toward others. How does your view of money change when you live as if every dollar in your bank account actually belongs to King Jesus?

You may think that I'm getting a bit carried away with the Monopoly analogy, but Jesus made this precise point in his parable of the rich fool. It's worth taking some time right now to read Luke 12:13–21. Don't rush through this teaching of Jesus'. There is far too much at stake to think that God's really real kingdom doesn't have a really real economy.

There are more than a few salient points in the parable of the rich fool, but let's touch on some of the big ones. First, we need to hear this parable through the ears of the first-century Jewish audience. To them, the rich fool's land was far more than a random chunk of real estate. Jesus spoke this parable in the *promised land* given to

Abraham and his royal family by covenant way back in Genesis (12:1–4). And by covenant, when this royal family was obedient to the royal law of love, there would be abundance and blessing from their King YHWH to the people. This included a land that was fruitful and over-flowing:

> And if you faithfully obey the voice of the LORD your God, being careful to do all his commandments that I command you today, the LORD your God will set you high above all the nations of the earth. And all these blessings shall come upon you and overtake you, if you obey the voice of the LORD your God. Blessed shall you be in the city, and blessed shall you be in the field. Blessed shall be the fruit of your womb and the fruit of your ground and the fruit of your cattle, the increase of your herds and the young of your flock. Blessed shall be your basket and your kneading bowl. Blessed shall you be when you come in, and blessed shall you be when you go out.
>
> The LORD will cause your enemies who rise against you to be defeated before you. They shall come out against you one way and flee before you seven ways. The LORD will command the blessing on you in your barns and in all that you undertake. And he will bless you in the land that the LORD your God is giving you.
>
> **—Deuteronomy 28:1–8**

When Jesus said, "The land of a rich man produced plentifully" (Luke 12:16), it was another way of saying that God was being generous and abundant in his provision. The rich fool of the parable was receiving a covenant blessing of abundance because King YHWH was pouring out his favor through the promised land. What was the fatal error this affluent chump made? He thought that the abundance was his. Count how many times he said "I" or "my" in his conversation with himself:

*"What shall I do, for I have nowhere to store **my** crops?" And
he said, "I will do this: I will tear down **my** barns and build
larger ones, and there I will store all **my** grain and **my** goods.
And I will say to **my** soul, 'Soul, you have ample goods laid
up for many years; relax, eat, drink, be merry.'"*
—*Luke 12:17–19*

We need to read this parable through the lens of the
kingdom story as told by the covenants. Go back to the
Abrahamic covenant and remember that the mandate of
this royal family was to be a blessing to all of the nations
of the earth (Genesis 12:1–4). If they were faithful to
YHWH and kept the covenant as a kingdom of priests
(Exodus 19:6), then YHWH would bless them abundantly
(Deuteronomy 28:1–8). In receiving such a blessing, they
weren't meant to hoard it for themselves, but to turn it toward others and be a blessing to the whole world. This is
the kingdom economy of abundance. God always gives
his people what they need to be generous! But when his
people think that it belongs only to them, they become
fools.

In the parable, the Monopoly game ended, and everything the fool thought he had instantly lost value.
Everything vanished, and he was left completely bank-
rupt. His fully stocked barns and abundance vanished with
his last breath. He learned that none of his possessions
ever truly belonged to him; they were a blessing entrusted
to his stewardship, that he would use them to bless others.

Being "rich toward God" (Luke 12:21) means that we
are to manage our abundance with generosity, kindness,
love, and goodness to others. Nothing we have is ours. It's
all entrusted to us in stewardship.

The parable ends on a chilling and sobering note. When
the rich man appeared before God, the King of the

Universe said, "Fool! This night your soul is required of you" (Luke 12:20). In the original language, the words used are similar to a loan being called back by the bank. Even our souls don't belong to us! Our very souls are on loan to us, entrusted to us by God, and one day the loan will be called in. We will give an account of how we stewarded our very souls loaned to us by our King. *Gulp.*

God doesn't just own our bank accounts, houses, and cars. As our Creator and King, he holds the title deed to our very souls, and how we spend our lives on earth matters very much in the kingdom economy. *Double gulp.*

I'm tempted to apologize for calling you a fool if you live this life as a barn-stuffer, but I won't. And shouldn't. You'd be right to call me a fool if I were wasting my soul to hoard temporarily a stack of gold or grain.

> Then Jesus told his disciples, "If anyone would come after me, let him deny himself and take up his cross and follow me. For whoever would save his life will lose it, but whoever loses his life for my sake will find it. For what will it profit a man if he gains the whole world and forfeits his soul? Or what shall a man give in return for his soul? For the Son of Man is going to come with his angels in the glory of his Father, and then he will repay each person according to what he has done. Truly, I say to you, there are some standing here who will not taste death until they see the Son of Man coming in his kingdom."
> **—Matthew 16:24–28**

Look again at how Jesus uses the language of the kingdom economy in this stern and loving warning: profit, save, lose, gain, forfeit, give, return, repay. These are financial terms of a rightful King exerting sovereignty over his own resources distributed throughout his realm. The Son of Man is coming again in his kingdom, but his rule and reign are not on pause, waiting for that day. His kingdom can also come right now in and through us when we are good stewards of his resources entrusted to us.

The Father's Day Gift

When my son, Kai, was young, he wanted to give me a Father's Day present. Being the resourceful kid that he was, he asked me for $10 and then bought me a belt. At first glance, this doesn't seem like much of a gift. After all, I gave him the money to buy me a gift. So, was it really a gift? Yes, it was a gift I'll never forget. Kai returned to me what I'd given him *with love*. He took time to go to the mall, spending his own energy and effort in an act of kindness and honor. Every penny he had for that gift he received from me, but he gave back to me more than I'd given him. I gave him money. He gave me love. Kai was rich toward his father.

This is precisely how God's kingdom economy works. God's kingdom comes through our practical, daily actions exercised through love in God's kingdom economy. Everything we have belongs to the Lord. Everything. Our wallets, houses, cars, clothes, food, toys, and tools—everything is stamped, "From God." But, strangely, when we give back to God in worship, love, and generosity what we've received as a gift, it becomes a blessing to God. As we steward what we've been given in love and generosity, we shall see God's kingdom come in and through us—big time.

This precise dynamic is clearly shown on the occasion when King David led Israel to provide for the construction of the Temple. He said:

> Yours, O LORD, is the greatness and the power and the glory and the victory and the majesty, for all that is in the heavens and in the earth is yours. ... For all things come from you, and of your own have we given you. ... O LORD our God, all this abundance that we have provided for building you

*a house for your holy name comes from your hand and is all
your own.*
—*1 Chronicles 29:11, 14, 16*

Both King David and the people of Israel gave generously to God for the provision of the Temple construction,
but they were simply giving to God what they had already
received from him. They gave it back with worship, generosity, and love, and those things gave value to the gift.

The provision for Solomon's temple in Jerusalem was
a carbon copy of the provision for Moses' tabernacle in
the desert after the Israelites left Egypt. The Israelites gave
an overflowing of gold, silver, bronze, linens, oils, animal
skins, rare jewels, and incense for the tabernacle.

Where did a ragtag bunch of former Egyptian slaves
get such abundance and wealth for the construction of the
tabernacle? God *gave it to them.* In the plunder won
through the battle against Pharaoh, Israel was given fabu-
lous wealth from the very Egyptians who once enslaved
them (Exodus 12:33–36).

This is how the economy of God's kingdom works. It's
not based on scarcity but on abundance. Because everything we have comes from God, we have nothing to lose
in giving generously, for what we have is not truly ours. A
proverb captures the essence of the kingdom economy
perfectly:

*One gives freely, yet grows all the richer; another withholds
what he should give, and only suffers want.*
—*Proverbs 11:24*

If we give from a heart of worship, love, and generosity, we'll find that our lives will be made rich.

The lavish resources God has given us go far beyond money, shelter, clothing, and food. Look at the embarrassment of riches Paul highlighted for the church in Ephesians. We are "blessed … in Christ with every spiritual blessing in the heavenly places … according to the riches of his grace, which he lavished upon us" (Ephesians 1:3, 7–8).

Take a moment to read Ephesians 1. Paul shows us the overflowing spiritual resources that build us up into a spiritual temple for God. This abundant provision is arguably greater than the provision for Moses' tabernacle in the desert and Solomon's temple in Jerusalem. God has given us lavish abundance in Christ so that we can return it to him with love and worship.

In his posthumous book *Life Without Lack*, Dallas Willard wrote about the very presence of Jesus in heaven and the abundance of God's kingdom economy on earth:[71]

> The glorious, eternal, all-sufficient omnipotent Creator of the universe whose greatness surpasses anything we could ever imagine. Unlimited in resources, just as he is unlimited in love, he is the Good Shepherd who generously provides for our every need.

Everything we have comes from Jesus, and because of the great gifts from the kind hand of this Good Shepherd, we can say, "I shall not want" and "my cup overflows" (Psalm 23:1, 5).

When Jesus told the parable of the rich fool (Luke 12:13–21), the indictment was that the man had basked in the Lord's abundance but laid up treasure for himself and failed to be "rich toward God." This would be the equivalent of me giving Kai $10, but instead of buying me a gift, he'd kept the money for himself. Instead of returning from the mall with a bow-wrapped belt, he'd come home with pockets stuffed with empty candy wrappers. He'd probably have a certain level of temporary satisfaction. After all, he had catered to his whims and desires, but he would have saddened and hurt his father.

The cost is too great when we don't give to God what's already his. We suffer a tremendous loss in our souls when we fail to be "rich toward God" by returning to him even a little of what's been given to us. God expects his kingdom citizens to participate in his economy of abundance— not only in receiving, but also in giving with a heart of worship, love, and generosity. The proverb is worth reading again:

One gives freely, yet grows all the richer; another withholds what he should give, and only suffers want.
—Proverbs 11:24

A life aligned with God's kingdom economy of abundance requires confidence that the King of kings will always give us what we need to be generous. Always. No matter how much or little we have, Jesus continuously provides enough for us to be rich toward God and others. Always.

The key is not to live in greed or anxiously scramble for resources of the kingdom. Instead, seek the kingdom first, having a calm trust that the resources will be provided (Luke 12:22–31). God feeds the ravens, and aren't we more valuable than birds? God clothes the flowers, so how much more will he clothe us?

Jesus' teaching about the kingdom economy does not end with personal provision, though that is remarkable and a reason for his disciples to cast off fear, anxiety, and insecurity. In his next breath, Jesus moved from personal provision to generosity:

> *Fear not, little flock, for it is your Father's good pleasure to give you the kingdom. Sell your possessions, and give to the needy. Provide yourselves with moneybags that do not grow old, with a treasure in the heavens that does not fail, where no thief approaches and no moth destroys. For where your treasure is, there will your heart be also.*
>
> **—Luke 12:32–34**

Can we be generous if we are given the kingdom? Absolutely. And as we give freely, we shall only grow all the richer. This is the kingdom economy of abundance. *God always gives us what we need to be generous.* Everything we have comes from him. Everything we hold belongs to him. It is God's *pleasure* to give us the kingdom, and we grow all the richer as we humbly and generously give back what the Father has given to us.

Today is Father's Day. God has given you a ten-dollar bill. Now get to the mall and buy him that belt! When you steward God's resources with loving generosity, you will see God's kingdom coming in and through you.

The Giving God

There's a passage in the book of Nehemiah that is very easy to miss, like one strand in a pile of yarn. But pull that thread and you'll find that it connects to a massive tapestry woven through the rest of scripture.

The prophet Nehemiah told the story of Israel in chapter 9 of the book of Nehemiah. He started with creation, establishing YHWH as the Creator and the King over the heavens and the earth (verse 6). Then Nehemiah recounted the establishment of God's royal family through Abraham (verses 7–8). Next, he moved to their exodus from slavery in Egypt (verses 9–11) and the forty years of wandering in the desert (verses 12–21). As he described

the royal family entering the promised land, the prophet dropped this little gem:

> And you gave them kingdoms and peoples and allotted to them every corner. So they took possession of the land of Sihon king of Heshbon and the land of Og king of Bashan. You multiplied their children as the stars of heaven, and you brought them into the land that you had told their fathers to enter and possess. So the descendants went in and possessed the land, and you subdued before them the inhabitants of the land, the Canaanites, and gave them into their hand, with their kings and the peoples of the land, that they might do with them as they would. And they captured fortified cities and a rich land, and took possession of houses full of all good things, cisterns already hewn, vineyards, olive orchards and fruit trees in abundance. So they ate and were filled and became fat and delighted themselves in your great goodness.
>
> **—Nehemiah 9:22–25**

Did you catch it? Nehemiah said, "You gave them kingdoms." Pull on that little thread and you'll find that it's woven into the majestic tapestry of all history.

What God did on a small scale in the promised land of Canaan, he is doing on a massive scale throughout the whole human story. And just what is that? He is making a kingdom so he can give it away.

God makes a kingdom to give a kingdom. He is not on a power trip, although he has all power. He intends to give away the kingdom that he has labored throughout all of history to build.

Just as Israel conquered the kingdoms in Canaan, all of the kingdoms of the earth will be conquered by King Jesus:

> *Then the seventh angel blew his trumpet, and there were loud voices in heaven, saying, "The kingdom of the world has become the kingdom of our Lord and of his Christ, and he shall reign forever and ever."*
> **—Revelation 11:15**

What will King Jesus do with these kingdoms? He will give them away. Look at how this theme is woven through scripture:

> *And the kingdom and the dominion and the greatness of the kingdoms under the whole heaven **shall be given** to the people of the saints of the Most High; his kingdom shall be an everlasting kingdom, and all dominions shall serve and obey him.*
> **—Daniel 7:27**

> *Blessed are the poor in spirit, for theirs is the kingdom of heaven. ... Blessed are those who are persecuted for righteousness' sake, for theirs is the kingdom of heaven.*
> **—Matthew 5:3, 10**

> *And they sang a new song, saying, "Worthy are you to take the scroll and to open its seals, for you were slain, and by your blood you ransomed people for God from every tribe and language and people and nation, and you have made them a kingdom and priests to our God, and they shall reign on the earth."*
> **—Revelation 5:9–10**

At the end of the age, God will give his glorious

kingdom to his people. He is the giving King. He gives us a kingdom built and established through the law of love.

But we have a problem. We don't just want something; we want everything. We have an insatiable desire for more. All our lives, we desire everything. No matter how much we have, it's never enough. Why do we have this desire? *Because God designed us to receive everything.* If you are designed to receive everything, then *something* will never be enough.

In the beginning, humanity was created for everything. Our union with God was full, and in his love, he gave us a whole world of delight in the Garden of Eden. But in taking and eating the fruit of the tree, we traded everything for *something*.

Now, in our fallen condition, we are constantly empty. No matter how much we take, we still have only something, and something will never fill us because we were created for everything.

But Jesus, who had everything with God, gave himself on the tree of the cross. Jesus became *nothing*. Now we are restored to everything, not by receiving something, but by receiving *Someone*. In Jesus, we return to the fullness of God's love, purpose, and delight. *Someone* became *nothing* to save us from the emptiness of *something* and restore us to *everything*.

We desperately want power because he designed us to reign. We want glory because he designed us to share in his glory. We want fame because he designed us to carry the name of Jesus, the most exalted name, at which every knee shall bow. But it's not just stuff, power, or fame that's the inheritance of God's people. It's the love of God himself!

God is making a kingdom, governed by love, and then giving that kingdom to his people for them to reign over for eternity. This is how the infinite, good, omnipotent God says, "I love you." He bends the history of all people in all time and place to establish a kingdom of love, and then he gives it to them. God's gift of the kingdom made possible through the sacrificial gift of his Son is a grand statement of "I love you" that brings us into the adventure of his kingdom.

This is why the parable of the hidden treasure makes sense:

> *The kingdom of heaven is like treasure hidden in a field, which a man found and covered up. Then in his joy he goes and sells all that he has and buys that field.*
> **—Matthew 13:44**

This is the gospel of the kingdom. This gospel captures us and compels us to join King Jesus in the grandest, boldest, and most challenging saga of all time. He invites us to join this narrative arc as one jumping into a thundering, rushing river at flood stage. This is the gospel of the kingdom. We get to receive everything the giving God has to offer us. In return, we give him everything we are and have: our love, our devotion, our hearts, minds, bodies, and souls. He gives us a place to rule at his side. We give him our obedience and adoration. He gives us his kingdom, and we give him our loyalty, trust, and confidence.

Where's George?

"Where's George?" is a game that makes spending paper money a new kind of adventure. Using serial numbers as trackers, you can log a dollar bill into the game's website (www.wheresgeorge.com) and then follow the progress as the bill moves throughout the country. Join thousands of other people who are also finding and logging bills on the website.

Field Trip Details

Travel: None

Cost: Minimal

Time: Minimal

Physical Demands: None

Gear: Minimal

Key Scriptures to Guide Your Trip: Ecclesiastes 5:10; Malachi 3:10; Matthew 6:1–4, 19–24; Matthew 13:22; Mark 12:41–44; Luke 12:13–21; Philippians 4:11–13; 1 Timothy 6:3–10, 17–19; Hebrews 13:5; 1 John 2:15–17

Schedule this field trip now. Put it on your calendar!
Day: _____
Time: _____
People invited to join me: _____
_____
_____

The game is simple but fun. There are three steps. First, enter the serial number of a dollar bill on the website. Second, subtly mark the bill by writing, "Where's George?"[72] Third, spend the bill to return it to natural circulation. When other people find your bill, they will log it in the website, and you'll be notified. When you find a bill someone else has marked, you simply log in the serial number, and that person will be notified. You'll be able to follow the natural flow of money as it's circulated. If you really want to dive in, then enter the race for top-ranked players based on how many bills have been found and tracked. Currently, "Iguana Girl" holds the top spot with over 300,000(!) bills with "hits."[73]

The "Where's George" game will take you to the unexplored world of your own money. You didn't know it, but there's a treasure hunt lurking in your wallet. The game will pop up anywhere you give and receive currency. Your grocery store, coffee shop, bank, and favorite restaurant get folded into the game as you start paying attention to the money you circulate. Normal places become part of an adventure in a national game of hide-and-seek.

Seeing the Kingdom Connection

The "Where's George" game will help you to be mindful about something that's been operative all around you but you probably never noticed. Almost 300 million bills are being tracked by "Where's George." Thousands of bills are registered every day. There's an excellent chance that you've been a carrier of this harmlessly marked currency, but since you can't see what you're not seeking, the game has been hiding out in the open—in your own wallet, most likely!

By joining the "Where's George" game, you will train your spending habits to look for marked bills. You'll begin to see what's been invisible. There will be a layer of extraordinary imposed on what's ordinary.

I mentioned "Iguana Girl" as the top-ranked player in the world. She has released over 1.2 million bills, and more than 25% of them have been found and logged by others. It may be that she's taken the game a tad too far, but clearly this game is a very high priority to her. Now I don't know the first thing about "Iguana Girl" (she may not be a girl or an iguana), but we can safely say that she's focused at least some of her attention on this game. For her, I'm sure that looking for marked bills has become second nature. Every bill she gets is reflexively scanned and marked. I'd not be surprised if much of her world view is dominated by "Where's George." Can't you picture her with a big "WG" tattoo on her right forearm and Washington's furtive eyes from the one-dollar bill on her left?

Jesus wants us to become an "Iguana Girl" when it comes to seeking the really real kingdom all around us. When he said to "seek first the kingdom" (Matthew 6:33), he meant for our attention, focus, and energy to be dedicated toward seeking and seeing the advance of God's rule in the world all around us. Jesus wants us to bend our minds reflexively toward the extraordinary goodness of God's reign in the ordinary substance of our lives.

Use the "Where's George" game as a daily reminder to seek first the best possible life under God's good blessings. For a while, turn every bill that passes through your wallet into a prompt about the really real kingdom right under your nose.

Every dollar that you have literally belongs to God. It

is his. All of it. Our money is entrusted to us as a resource of God's kingdom economy. He wants us to be generous and to store up treasures in heaven (Matthew 6:19–20) by using our resources wisely, generously, and in love.

Questions for Reflection

1. What sticks out from this field trip or is a new idea for you?

2. What questions have come out of this field trip? What doesn't make sense to you?

3. How do you see Jesus and his kingdom in this experience?

4. How can you apply this to your life and take a next step?

5. What will you talk to God and other people about?

After this field trip, circle where you are right now in your journey to find God's kingdom as a hidden treasure.

| Blind | Aware | Ponder | Value | Trap of Inaction | Prioritize | Own/Sell |

Journal: Spend some time in your journal to record further thoughts.

SMALL GROUP GUIDE

Chapter Ten Discussion Questions

Key Scripture:
Parable of the Rich Fool
Luke 12:13–21

1. When and where have you seen generosity in others? Who has most influenced you to be generous and why? What is a story in your life when you experienced the generosity of another person?

2. Take an inventory of your material possessions: money and investments, home and household goods, vehicle(s), clothing, food, etc. Stop and acknowledge that each of these belongs to God. Thank him for allowing you to be the steward of it. Then ask him to show you if you are using that commodity to its fullest potential in his economy. Are you being a blessing to others with the blessings that God has bestowed on you?

3. Consider your deepest desires. Do you long for love, honor, fame, power, or riches? How is this desire part of a God-given longing for his kingdom? How does his kingdom meet the otherwise insatiable needs of your

heart? Are you ready to give everything to him to receive everything from him? Are you ready to sell all for the treasure in the field?

4. How do you react when you consider that God the Father gave his own Son for you? What emotions does this provoke? How does this challenge your thinking? How real is this gift to you?

5. Discuss your experience on the field trip. What did you learn? What surprised you? What challenged you?

Chapter Ten Notes

CHAPTER ELEVEN

See the Kingdom Come Through Love and Goodness

I'm going to make an utterly profound theological statement in three words that you will instantly downplay. Ready? Here it is:

God is good.

That's it. Most likely a giant "*Duh!*" is filling the thought bubble above your head. So I'll say it again.

God is good.

You may be nodding your head, agreeing with me, but you still don't get it.

God is good.

Now you're thinking, "Yes. Of course. I know God is good." But you're missing it.

God *is* good!

Now you're getting frustrated, maybe a bit angry. "How does the author know I don't get it? Obviously I get it. Why doesn't he move on?!" You may even be ready to put the book away, but please don't, because you're still a long way off from understanding. A long way.

God is *good*!

How do I know that you don't understand these three

little, simple words? Because *I* don't understand them. Not by a long shot.

All of us will spend all of eternity straining to capture the greatness of God's goodness. Why? Because—

God is good.

The eternal One. The all-powerful One. The all-loving One. The all-knowing One. The One who is completely just, righteous, and merciful. The One who is always present everywhere at all times. The essence of goodness is made up of the essence of Godness.

Out of God comes good—only good—and all good comes from God. There is not anything that is good that does not have some root connection to God. Why? Because God made everything, and when everything was made, God called it very good (Genesis 1:31). Take a moment right now to read the creation account in the first chapter of Genesis. Pay careful attention to how God declared the goodness of what he had made.

The Genesis account is written in the form of a King giving order to chaos to bring goodness to his realm. What happened when God's rule was carried out at creation? Good happened. That is the result of God's work.

We need to return to G. K. Chesterton's earth-shattering quote:[74]

> The more I considered Christianity, the more I found that while it had established a rule and order, the chief aim of that order was to **give room for good things to run wild**.

Good running wild is the result of God's rule and work. God is good. You don't know how profound this is, and neither do I. Ruth Haley Barton said, "God's goodness is his greatest glory and it's what we need the most."[75]

When Paul addressed a pagan crowd who mistook him for a god, he tried to redirect their worship to the one true

God, who is truly good:

> ...we bring you **good news**, that you should turn from these vain things to a living God, who made the heaven and the earth and the sea and all that is in them. In past generations he allowed all the nations to walk in their own ways. Yet he did not leave himself without witness, **for he did good by giving you rains from heaven and fruitful seasons, satisfying your hearts with food and gladness**.
> —*Acts 14:15–17*

What has God been doing as he rules over all creation? He is doing good with every drop of rain, every harvest, every meal, every smile on your face. That's from God, and that's good.

When Peter explained the life work of Jesus to a Roman soldier, he said:

> Truly I understand that God shows no partiality, but in every nation anyone who fears him and does what is right is acceptable to him. As for the word that he sent to Israel, preaching **good news** of peace through Jesus Christ (he is Lord of all), you yourselves know what happened throughout all Judea, beginning from Galilee after the baptism that John proclaimed: how God anointed Jesus of Nazareth with the Holy Spirit and with power. **He went about doing good** and healing all who were oppressed by the devil, for God was with him.
> —*Acts 10:34–38*

When we read that passage, most often we focus on the spectacular battle against the demonic realm. When we think of the story of Jesus, we are usually preoccupied with his displays of power over nature, healing, walking on water, and raising the dead. No doubt these acts of

Jesus are compelling and worth considering, but don't miss the fact that "he went about doing good."

We may be tempted to say, "*Duh!*" when we hear that Jesus went about doing good. Of course he did good! But we are missing something too big, too wonderful if we don't dwell on that.

When the God of the universe took on flesh and came to earth, what did he do? He did good, and not just once or twice. Doing good was a primary focus of his daily life. In every conversation, every situation, every conflict, every moment of every day, Jesus "went about doing good."

Quite likely, Peter might have had an Old Testament prophecy in mind when he summed up the life of Jesus as "doing good." Ponder this passage about the new covenant from Jeremiah:

> And they shall be my people, and I will be their God. I will give them one heart and one way, that they may fear me forever, **for their own good and the good of their children after them**. I will make with them an everlasting covenant, that I will not turn away from doing good to them. And I will put the fear of me in their hearts, that they may not turn from me. **I will rejoice in doing them good**, and I will plant them in this land in faithfulness, with all my heart and all my soul.
>
> **—Jeremiah 32:38–41**

Twenty-trillion years from now, there will still be massive *aha!* moments of discovery as we uncover more of God's delight in doing good.

Please permit me a slight detour to Mars to help explain. Imagine that humanity has landed on the red planet and begun colonization. Now picture a scene in which one of the astronauts crests over a red hill and finds a single blade of grass. There would be a thrill, wonder, and explosion of awe that would grip the world. The news would captivate the old and the young, and there would be rapture that would grip us for decades. That single blade of Martian grass would literally change everything.

So why doesn't the grass in your own backyard provoke equal awe and wonder? Just because it is ordinary? Because of God's goodness in what's created, there is just as much thrill packed into a blade of grass in Manitoba as on Mars. Anything that is good is worthy of wonder, admiration, delight, and fascination. Just because there are trillions of grass blades on earth, should their glory be diminished? Why shouldn't the goodness of grass be magnified? Let's not let the abundance of goodness all around us fade simply because it is all around us. God is good, and if we are surrounded by goodness, we ought to be filled with wonder because that goodness constantly points us to God.

Doing Good

Your role in God's kingdom coming is not complicated, nor is it easy. But it is simple. How?

Do good. That's it.

Do you want to see the rule of Jesus spread to people in your workplace? Do good to your co-workers. Do you want the reign of Christ to break into your neighborhood? Do good to your neighbors. Do you want the kingdom of God to flourish in your family? Do good to your spouse, children, siblings, and parents. Goodness is what comes from keeping the royal law of love (James 2:8), and the kingdom comes from good.

Unfortunately, "good" has been saddled with some bad baggage. People who are the "holier-than-thou," hyper-religious types are often called "do-gooders." The prim and annoying moralist is called a "goody two shoes" and will spoil any fun in a five-mile radius. Every kid knows food that is "good for you" tastes disgusting and looks like green slop. The "good old boys" are a group of backward hicks conspiring to keep strangers out. "No good deed goes unpunished" is a common saying when kindness backfires. Author Jim Collins wrote the classic leadership book *Good to Great* based on the principle that good is the enemy of great and a sign of mediocrity.

Given all this, who wants to do good? And how can good be any good in bringing God's kingdom? Jesus must have known something that we don't because he taught that good is great. He commanded his disciples, "Love your enemies, do good to those who hate you" (Luke 6:27, 35).

In the business world, perhaps good can be considered the enemy of great, but in God's kingdom, God *is* good. When you love people, you are simply taking actions to bring good to their lives. By bringing in that good, you're expanding God's kingdom. *God's kingdom comes when it's your deepest joy to address a desperate need and create the most good.*

Jesus placed a high value on the good we bring to those around us. He taught that love is the action that brings good. He taught that God is love and God is good; therefore, loving people and doing good is showing them God.

How important is this to the kingdom of Jesus? Take a few minutes to read the parable of the sheep and goats in Matthew 25:31–46. In this story, one group of people represents the inheritors of the kingdom. By doing good to others—feeding them, clothing them, visiting them, and offering them drink—the group *did good to Jesus*. The King commended them, saying, "As you did it to one of the least of these my brothers, you did it to me" (Matthew 25:40).

The other group of people neglected to do good to people on earth. As a result, they neglected to do good to the King. Ultimately, they were shunned by the King (verses

41–46).

This ought to make us uncomfortable! Love is the law of Jesus' kingdom. When we love, we bring good to others and good to King Jesus.

Love Brings Good

We've established that God is good, but to these three little words, we need to add three more simple but powerful words:

God is love.

God *is* love.

God is *love*.

God is love.

Rather than spending another three pages trying to convince you that none of us truly understands the magnitude of that statement, will you just trust me? Or, if you don't trust me, will you trust the testimony of billions of Jesus followers who have found it to be true? If that's not enough, will you trust the testimony of scripture (Deuteronomy 7:9; Psalm 36:7; Psalm 86:15; Psalm 136:26; Ephesians 2:4–5; John 3:16–18; John 15:9–10; Romans 5:6–8; 1 John 3:1; 1 John 4:8, 16)?

Good. Thank you.

Now let's combine these six words into a core foundation for the kingdom of God. These two basic truths establish a primary channel for how we see God's kingdom come in and through us: God is good. God is love.

Let's see how scripture elevates these two ideas in combination. They are practically inseparable.

Oh give thanks to the LORD, for he is good; for his steadfast love endures forever!

—1 Chronicles 16:34

The trumpeters and musicians joined in unison to give praise and thanks to the LORD. Accompanied by trumpets, cymbals and other instruments, the singers raised their voices in praise to the LORD and sang:

"He is good; his love endures forever."

Then the temple of the LORD was filled with the cloud, and the priests could not perform their service because of the cloud, for the glory of the LORD filled the temple of God.
—2 Chronicles 5:13–14 *(NIV)*

That's just a small sample. Your meditation on other passages connecting God's love and goodness will be well rewarded. Take some time to consider these scriptures and pay attention to the intertwined themes of good and love: 2 Chronicles 7:3; Ezra 3:11; Psalm 100:4–5; Psalm 136:1–3.

The tragic story of Israel's rebellion and idolatry recorded in the book of Judges makes the same connection between steadfast love and goodness, only in a negative example:

As soon as Gideon died, the people of Israel turned again and whored after the Baals and made Baal-berith their god. And the people of Israel did not remember the LORD their God, who had delivered them from the hand of all their enemies on every side, **and they did not show steadfast love to the family of Jerubbaal (that is, Gideon) in return for all the good that he had done to Israel.**
—Judges 8:33–35

The goodness of God is entirely enmeshed in and entangled with the love of God. This theme continues clearly in the New Testament:

And we know that for those who love God all things work together for good, for those who are called according to his purpose.

—Romans 8:28

For you were called to freedom, brothers. Only do not use your freedom as an opportunity for the flesh, but **through love serve one another. For the whole law is fulfilled in one word: "You shall love your neighbor as yourself."** *But if you bite and devour one another, watch out that you are not consumed by one another....*

And let us not grow weary of doing good, *for in due season we will reap, if we do not give up. So then, as we have opportunity,* **let us do good to everyone,** *and especially to those who are of the household of faith.*

—Galatians 5:13–15; 6:9–10

Love is the action that brings good to another, and this is precisely how God's kingdom comes. God's love is the action that brings goodness into the world. That's how God rules. He rules through loving acts that result in goodness spreading to creation and creature alike. Good is the imprint and product of God's love.

Perhaps one of the most important Old Testament showcases connecting love with goodness is in Deuteronomy 6. Here the *Shema* (bolded below) is the peak of covenant faithfulness between YHWH and his people. It's so important that to this day, thousands of years later, many Jewish people still affix the Shema to their doorposts:

Hear, O Israel: The LORD our God, the LORD is one. **You shall love the LORD your God with all your heart and with all your soul and with all your might.** *And these words that I command you today shall be on your heart. You shall teach them* *diligently to your children, and shall talk of them when you sit in your house, and when you walk by the way, and when you lie down, and when you rise. You shall bind them as a sign on your hand, and they shall be as frontlets between your eyes. You shall write them on the doorposts of your house and on your gates.*

—Deuteronomy 6:4–9

This injunction for wholehearted love in the Shema is what Jesus would later call "the great and first commandment" (Matthew 22:36–40). But what's often overlooked are the many statements of goodness that connect to a life of faithful, covenantal love (Deuteronomy 6:10–12; 18–19; 24–25). The goodness of this world comes from God's active love being both given and received. It's no wonder that perhaps the most important statement about love in the Old Testament is followed by descriptions of rich goodness as a result of that love.

Please don't miss the connection between God's love and God's goodness, because this is how God's kingdom comes. Using Chesterton's language again, when God's loving rule and reign create order out of chaos, then room is made for good things to run wild. As we love God and others, his kingdom comes more and more, resulting in good things running wild on earth and in our lives.

Do you want to see God's kingdom come in your life? Then at every opportunity, in every part of your life, take actions of love that bring good to others. In love, make active decisions that result in good coming to a neighbor. In love, intentionally take steps that lead to good increasing in your workplace and home. Where love increases, goodness results. And where goodness results, God's kingdom has come.

How important, how fundamental is this? The Apostle Peter, who was personally taught the Lord's Prayer by the Lord himself, was crystal clear on the matter. How many times did Peter pray, "Your kingdom come, your will be done, on earth as it is in heaven"? Thousands of times, I imagine. It was likely on his lips constantly. And when Peter wrote his first epistle, how did he describe the will of God to those he had just called the kingdom of priests? He wrote, "For this is the will of God, that *by doing good* you should put to silence the ignorance of foolish people" (1 Peter 2:15).

The Apostle Paul also connected God's will to God's goodness, saying, "Do not be conformed to this world, but be transformed by the renewal of your mind, that by testing you may discern what is the will of God, *what is good* and acceptable and perfect" (Romans 12:2). In our renewed minds, we will pray, "Your kingdom come, your will be done." According to Paul, we discern God's will, in large part, by what is good.

God's kingdom comes through his goodness. That is his will on earth as it is in heaven. He rules and reigns through loving actions that result in an abundance of goodness covering the world. As the psalmist wrote:

On the glorious splendor of your majesty, and on your wondrous works, I will meditate. They shall speak of the might of your awesome deeds, and I will declare your greatness. They shall pour forth the fame of your abundant goodness and shall sing aloud of your righteousness.

*The LORD is gracious and merciful, slow to anger and **abounding in steadfast love**. The LORD is **good** to all, and his mercy is over all that he has made.*
—*Psalm 145:5–9*

God is good. God is love. These truths are foundational for seeing God's kingdom come in and through you. Look for God's goodness all around you. That's his kingdom. Look for how God's love is made manifest in the world.

That's his kingdom. And look for ways to extend his goodness and love in your life and the lives of others. That's God's kingdom coming in and through you.

The Apostle Paul presented the church in Rome with an Oreo cookie of "good" sandwiched between "love":

> Let **love** be genuine.
> Abhor what is evil; hold fast to what is **good**.
> **Love** one another with brotherly affection.
> **—Romans 12:9–10**

I'll close this section with another injunction from the Apostle Peter that I believe is prophetically crucial for our world today—not because I think that the world will end soon (though it might), but because we need to establish what our highest priorities, *above all*, ought to be:

> The end of all things is at hand; therefore be self-controlled and sober-minded for the sake of your prayers. **Above all, keep loving one another earnestly**, since love covers a multitude of sins. **Show hospitality to one another without grumbling. As each has received a gift, use it to serve one another, as good stewards of God's varied grace**: whoever speaks, as one who speaks oracles of God; whoever serves, as one who serves by the strength that God supplies—in order that in everything God may be glorified through Jesus Christ. To him belong glory and dominion forever and ever. Amen.
> **—1 Peter 4:7–11**

CHAPTER ELEVEN FIELD TRIP

A Full Day to Enjoy God's Goodness

This final field trip will last a full 24-hour period. This is a full day to enjoy God's goodness. You'll want to carve out a day in your calendar that begins one evening and lasts all the way through the next evening. Give yourself permission to set your worries, cares, and concerns aside during this period. If necessary, imagine that you are placing every weight you are carrying in the hands of Jesus. Commit all of the unfinished projects, all of the broken relationships, and all of the shortcomings into the caring hands of the King. Trust him with your to-do list. Rest assured that you are not so vital to the world that it can't last just one day without you.

On this day, your goal is to see God's goodness, really see it. Soak it in. Savor it. Delight in what is delightful. Take in the beauty by looking at the fine details. Listen to the sounds that fill the silence.

Pray and invite Jesus to join you during this day. This is a day for delight, enjoyment, play, good food, and worship—all together in the presence of God.

This can be a day at the beach or a stroll through the

woods or a city park. You may want to delight in the garden in your yard, soaking in all of the incredible details and beauty of God's creation. For this full 24-hour period, don't set your alarm clock in the morning; sleep as long as you want. Move slowly through the day. Savor each bite of food; taste the flavors. Be present in conversation. Be present in your life.

Unplug from your devices. Leave the phone at home if at all possible. Don't check emails, texts, or social media. This is a day to connect directly with God in his creation.

Use Psalm 145 as your field guide for this day.

> *On the glorious splendor of your majesty, and on your wondrous works, I will meditate. They shall speak of the might of your awesome deeds, and I will declare your greatness. They shall pour forth the fame of your abundant goodness and shall sing aloud of your righteousness.*
> **—Psalm 145:5–7**

Field Trip Details

Travel: Go to places that are beautiful. Find settings where God's creation can be enjoyed. Find locations that are set apart from the busy bustle of the frantic life.

Cost: Travel costs, food costs

Time: 24 hours

Physical Demands: Vary

Gear: Bring what you need to rest and delight in the setting of your choice. Good food is a bonus.

Key Scriptures to Guide Your Trip: Genesis 1–2; Exodus 20:8–11; Psalm 145; Isaiah 58:13–14; Hebrews 4:1–11

Schedule this field trip now. Put it on your calendar!
Day: _____
Time: _____
People invited to join me: _____

_____

_____

Seeing the Kingdom Connection

The goodness of the Ruler is shown in how he rules. The glory of the Creator is displayed in what is created. The majesty of the Maker is revealed in what is made. When we search for the goodness revealed in God's world, we find that God is so good. There are wondrous works right below your nose. Meditate on them. There are awesome deeds done by Jesus at your feet. Declare the greatness of him. God's works are gushing with God's goodness. Worship him for what he has made.

> *All your works shall give thanks to you, O LORD, and all your saints shall bless you! They shall speak of the glory of your kingdom and tell of your power, to make known to the children of man your mighty deeds, and the glorious splendor of your kingdom. Your kingdom is an everlasting kingdom, and your dominion endures throughout all generations.*
> **—Psalm 145:10–13**

This field trip is an ancient practice called Sabbath. I strongly encourage you to work this rhythm of rest and delight into your weekly schedule. If you can't take a full 24-hour Sabbath every week, then start with what is doable in your schedule, even if it's a few hours in a day. Start there, then slowly build up to a full 24-hour day set apart from the crazy busy life.

God has given Sabbath to us as a gift. This day of savoring God's goodness is one of the most profound spiritual disciplines. The more you enjoy God's goodness through a rhythm of rest, the more you will see God's kingdom coming in and through you. To learn more about the restoring power of a regular Sabbath, I highly recommend the book *The Rest of God* by Mark Buchanan.

Questions for Reflection

1. What sticks out from this field trip or is a new idea for you?

2. What questions have come out of this field trip? What doesn't make sense to you?

3. How do you see Jesus and his kingdom in this experience?

4. How can you apply this to your life and take a next step?

5. What will you talk to God and other people about?

After this field trip, circle where you are right now in your journey to find God's kingdom as a hidden treasure.

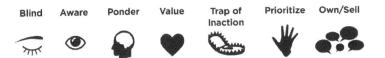

| Blind | Aware | Ponder | Value | Trap of Inaction | Prioritize | Own/Sell |

Journal: Spend some time in your journal to record further thoughts.

SMALL GROUP GUIDE

Chapter Eleven Discussion Questions

> **Key Scripture:**
> The Song of Loving Goodness
> Psalm 136:1–26

1. Spend several moments reflecting on God's goodness. What are some ways you see his goodness reflected in the world around you? How has God shown his goodness to you personally?

2. Describe a person you know (or know of) who has spent his or her life doing good. How does this person's life bring glory to God? What happens when a person does good out of a motive other than God's love? Is it possible to love truly without doing good?

3. What has been your experience with Sabbath? Discuss ways you have seen a Sabbath rest practiced. What would need to happen in your life to set aside a day for rest, play, delight, and worship? If a full Sabbath day per week isn't practical, how much time can you begin with to establish a rhythm of rest? Can you create a plan to increase that time so that you build up to a full

day of Sabbath every week? What are the obstacles in your way?

4. Discuss your experience on the field trip. What did you learn? What surprised you? What challenged you?

Chapter Eleven Notes

CONCLUSION

The Hidden Treasure

We end *The Kingdom Field Guide* by going back to where we started: hidden treasure.

> *The kingdom of heaven is like treasure hidden in a field, which a man found and covered up. Then in his joy he goes and sells all that he has and buys that field.*
> **—Matthew 13:44**

Recall that this parable maps the journey of a person who started *blind*. He stubbed his toe on the treasure and became *aware*. Then he *pondered* and *valued* what he found. After overcoming the *Trap of Inaction*, he *prioritized* his life. Finally, he enjoyed *owning/selling* the treasure.

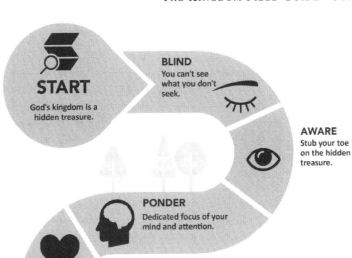

START
God's kingdom is a hidden treasure.

BLIND
You can't see what you don't seek.

AWARE
Stub your toe on the hidden treasure.

PONDER
Dedicated focus of your mind and attention.

VALUE
Discover the treasure's exceeding worth.

The Path to Finding God's Kingdom

The path to finding hidden treasure isn't easy, but it's always good. Where are you on this journey? What's your next step?

TRAP OF INACTION
Stuck with nothing changing in your life.

PRIORITIZE
Arrange your life so God's kingdom comes first.

OWN (SELL)
Delight in God's kingdom coming and sharing it with others.

With incredible detail, the author Luke traced this path through the crucifixion and resurrection narratives of Jesus in Luke chapters 23 and 24 and the book of Acts. He also recaptured the grand story of kingdom creation in Genesis.

Luke's narrative shows that *Jesus himself* is the treasure hidden in the field. Grab your Bible and read Luke chapters 23 and 24. Read this passage slowly and pay careful attention to the initial themes of being blind, becoming aware, pondering, and valuing.

Chapter 23 begins with the death of Jesus. The crucifixion scene is pictured as a reversal of Genesis, when God first created his kingdom. A criminal said to Jesus, "Remember me when you come into your kingdom" (Luke 23:42). Jesus' reply set up the new Eden within his new creation and promised a paradise that was available to the criminal that very day (Luke 23:43). From there, we embark on the path to finding hidden treasure.

Blind: Just before Christ's death, a darkness covered the land (Luke 23:44). Jesus' body was then buried—hidden like a treasure—in a dark tomb (Luke 23:50–56). Who buried Jesus? Joseph of Arimathea, a man who "was looking for the kingdom of God" (Luke 23:51). The disciples searched for Jesus but could not find him. He was hidden (Luke 24:1–12).

Aware: Finally, a group of women saw Jesus and reported back to the disciples. But still there was doubt. Still there was blindness. The big reveal came as some disciples were walking to Emmaus and Jesus joined them. As they went along, Jesus explained how all of scripture was fulfilled in him (Luke 24:13–27). Finally, the disciples' eyes were opened (Luke 24:28–31). Then, when all of the disciples were gathered, Jesus appeared before them (Luke 24:36–43). The disciples were fully aware.

Ponder: Jesus didn't just open the eyes of the disciples; he also opened their minds. He wanted to engage their thinking so they could ponder his resurrection in view of the full kingdom narrative of scripture.

At this point, the disciples had stubbed their toes on the hidden treasure, but that wasn't enough. They needed to rewrite the story in their heads to align with the grand story of Jesus throughout biblical history. Luke said that Jesus "opened their minds to understand the Scriptures" (Luke 24:26–27, 44–47).

Sadly, Luke didn't record the specifics of how Jesus unpacked all of the Law and the Prophets, but we can be reasonably confident that Jesus would have explained how he was the fulfillment and culmination of all of the covenants. As the Son of Abraham, Jesus was the one to bring God's blessing to all of the families of the world according to the Abrahamic covenant. Jesus must have told them how his New Commandment to love one another was the fullness of the Mosaic covenant commandments to love God and others. Jesus must have had the disciples ponder how his law of love enabled them to be his kingdom of priests, his holy nation, his chosen people. In tracing the story of scripture, Jesus certainly would have shown that he fulfilled the Davidic covenant as the Son of David claiming his eternal throne and ruling an eternal kingdom. And as the King of kings, Jesus must have revealed how his New Covenant brought the story of every tongue, tribe, and nation into his story of his kingdom coming on earth as it is in heaven.

Or perhaps the disciples were already keenly aware of this. After all, they had lived their entire lives pondering and living under the covenants. Perhaps Jesus' fulfillment of those covenants was as obvious as the statement "God is good."

Value: After engaging the minds of the disciples, Jesus captured their hearts. After Jesus unfolded the story along the road to Emmaus, Luke included a critically important detail. Some of the disciples said, "Did not our hearts burn within us while he talked to us on the road, while he opened to us the Scriptures?" (Luke 24:32). They went from depression after their Messiah's crucifixion to thrill after his resurrection. They found the treasure, and where the treasure is, there the heart will also be (Matthew 6:21).

We know that the disciples valued that treasure based on their response to Jesus: worship (Luke 24:50–53). They weren't just thinking about Jesus; they showed loyalty, commitment, and wholehearted devotion to him through worship, praise, and adoration. Worship shows value. In finding the resurrected Christ as a hidden treasure, their worship revealed the deepest value of their hearts.

Trap of Inaction: Then Jesus departed from them. He told the disciples to wait in Jerusalem, and he ascended to heaven (Luke 24:49–51).

Jesus left the disciples in the Trap of Inaction at the close of the book of Luke. He gave them a grand commission to bring his message to all nations (Luke 24:47), but at the same time, he told them to wait for the Holy Spirit and the power that was to come.

Jesus didn't want them charging off on their own. He knew that they didn't have the power, wisdom, and authority on their own to bring God's kingdom. He didn't want them to repeat the same sad Old Testament stories of rebellion. Without the Spirit, the disciples would fail, just as every kingdom emissary ultimately failed in the Old Testament narrative.

Jesus held them in the Trap of Inaction so they could be filled by the Holy Spirit. God's plan was for the Spirit of Christ to dwell *in them*. And from that indwelling, the disciples would become the body of Christ. That path— an indwelling of the Holy Spirit that leads to becoming the body of Christ—is our great hope of escaping the Trap of Inaction.

Prioritize: Luke continued the story in the book of

Acts and filled in some details. He showed that Jesus' priority after his resurrection was to speak about the kingdom for forty days (Acts 1:3). There was no message more important, no sermon more vital, no teaching more essential. In his waning weeks on earth, Jesus focused entirely on one priority: his kingdom.

With this context established, the disciples, being filled by the Spirit, had crossed the Trap of Inaction, and their new top priority was to be ambassadors of the kingdom. Luke's account unfolds with the disciples waiting (Acts 1), receiving power from the Holy Spirit (Acts 2), and then literally selling all (Acts 3–4). Their whole lives were reordered, and the coming of God's kingdom had utmost importance. Nothing was more important than doing the King's business. Look at how they prioritized their lives. In their joy, they sold all:

And they devoted themselves to the apostles' teaching and the fellowship, to the breaking of bread and the prayers. And awe came upon every soul, and many wonders and signs were being done through the apostles. And all who believed were together and had all things in common. And they were selling their possessions and belongings and distributing the proceeds to all, as any had need. And day by day, attending the temple together and breaking bread in their homes, they received their food with glad and generous hearts, praising God and having favor with all the people. And the Lord added to their number day by day those who were being saved.

—Acts 2:42–47

Own/Sell: The disciples found the kingdom in finding their resurrected King Jesus. They "owned" his rule and reign by offering their lives in service to their King. The treasure was theirs. All of the goodness of the kingdom was before them. Their whole lives were immersed in the

King and his kingdom. His story was their story. In selling everything they had, the disciples received everything Jesus had. Jesus himself took up royal residence in their hearts by the Holy Spirit. The church became the temple of the living God. The kingdom was within them because the King was in them. Jesus became a treasure hidden in the disciples' hearts!

The rest of the book of Acts is a record of how the disciples "sold" the kingdom to the rest of the world. The gospel of the kingdom moved from Jerusalem, Judea, and Samaria to the ends of the earth (Acts 1:8). The disciples gave testimony in ever-increasing circles as legal witnesses in a global courtroom. They testified that Jesus is the Christ (Acts 2:32–36; 4:8–10; 5:29–32, 41–42; 9:19–22; 17:1–7). They put up the "For Sale" sign so others could stub their toes on the treasure hidden in the field.

Luke concluded the book of Acts with the story of Paul, arguably the most influential ambassador of Jesus. Paul reached Rome, the capital of the most powerful kingdom on earth, and the book of Acts ends with this statement:

> [Paul] lived there two whole years at his own expense, and welcomed all who came to him, **proclaiming the kingdom of God** and teaching about the Lord Jesus Christ with all boldness and without hindrance.
>
> **—Acts 28:30–31**

The kingdom of Rome was the enemy of Christ's kingdom, but through Paul, that enemy kingdom became a field where people found hidden treasure. And from Rome, the good news of the kingdom spread to all the world.

Bible Trip: Your New Best Friend—Matthew

For this last Bible Trip, read and explore the whole Gospel of Matthew in one sitting. Set apart a couple of hours in your schedule to do this. Find a quiet space and turn off your phone. Remove all distractions.

Matthew has something to tell you. He knows something. Matthew found the hidden treasure, and he wants to show it to you. He is eager to be your new best friend because Matthew's Gospel is a giant neon sign pointing to Christ the King and his good kingdom.

As you read, look for the kingdom story. That story is not only the story of the Bible, but also the story of the real world right now. We've talked at length about how the story in your head needs to be aligned with the reality of God's kingdom in the world.

Before you read, pray this prayer:

Dear Father,
Your Son, Jesus, is the treasure hidden in the field.
Please give me eyes to see him
And ears to hear him.
Bring understanding to my mind
And worship of Christ to my heart.
Deliver me from the Trap of Inaction.
Help me to prioritize my life
So that seeking your kingdom is first.
And empower me, in my joy, to sell all for the treasure.
Use me as an ambassador of your loving reign
So I will be a blessing to the world around me.
I pray in the name of Jesus Christ, the King.
Amen.

Now be prepared for your eyes to be opened, for your priorities to change completely, and for your life never to be the same.

> **Small Group Guide**
> What does it mean that Jesus himself is the treasure hidden in the field? Is he your greatest value? What is the main obstacle right now to your "selling all" for the sake of Jesus? What does it mean practically to share the good news of the kingdom with other people? How can you embed the above kingdom prayer into your daily routine?

Jesus Is the Treasure

Jesus is the one who was hidden, overlooked, and seemingly worthless. He is also the one who can be found. He is the one who is waiting to be found.

God's kingdom is really real. Jesus is the really real King. His love alone exceeds all of the world's riches and power.

Our King commands us to seek first his kingdom. Jesus is worth more than every goal, possession, or loyalty you have or could have.

Remember that God's kingdom comes when your deepest joy meets a most desperate need and brings the greatest good in the world around you.

May the Lord's Prayer become the prayer of your life as you stub your toe on an overlooked box in the field, then sell all for the treasure hidden inside.

Our Father in heaven, hallowed be your name. Your kingdom come, your will be done, on earth as it is in heaven. Give us this day our daily bread, and forgive us our debts, as we also have forgiven our debtors. And lead us not into temptation, but deliver us from evil.

—Matthew 6:9–13

I hope you find delight as you live in God's kingdom. The treasure is waiting before your very eyes, but you can't see what you don't seek.

Conclusion Discussion Questions

1. Where are you now in regards to God's kingdom: blind, aware, pondering, valuing, in the Trap of Inaction, prioritizing, or owning/selling?

2. Jesus himself is the treasure. Is your life characterized by a pursuit of Jesus at any cost? What are the distractions in your life that keep you from seeking God's kingdom first?

3. If you missed any of the Field Trips, Bible Trips, or Side Trips in this book, when will you revisit them? Agree together as a small group on the date of your next field trip. In your personal life, write down on your calendar the next time you will engage in one of the Bible Trips or Side Trips.

4. There is a danger of setting this book down and nothing changing in your life. What is your plan, together as a small group, to avoid the Trap of Inaction? How can you continue to follow Jesus together in order to get beyond the Trap of Inaction to establish new priorities in your lives?

5. How can you pass on to others what you have learned

from *The Kingdom Field Guide*? Write down the names of three people you think may be ready to stub their toes on the hidden treasure. Pray for them daily. Also, write down your plan for contacting them. Extend an invitation to take the journey with you. Share your plan with others in your small group.

I commit to praying for these three people and inviting them to seek God's kingdom with me:

1. _____

2. _____

3. _____

This is my plan to learn about God's kingdom together with them:

_____

_____

_____

_____

_____

_____

_____

Conclusion Notes

_____

_____

_____

_____

_____

_____

_____

_____

_____

_____

_____

_____

_____

_____

_____

_____

_____

_____

_____

_____

_____

_____

_____

APPENDIX A

Checklists

Checklist of Field Trips

☐ A Walk Around Town (p. 29)

☐ Bird Watching (p. 66)

☐ Geocaching (p. 97)

☐ People-Watching (p. 118)

☐ Creating Order (p. 141)

☐ The Home of Power (p. 174)

☐ Finding Your Lost Family Stories (p. 215)

☐ Looking for Loyalty (p. 239)

☐ Hunting for Idols (p. 261)

☐ Where's George? (p. 288)

☐ A Full Day to Enjoy God's Goodness (p. 307)

Checklist of Side Trips

- ☐ Breathe (p. 20)
- ☐ "Ordinary" Objects (p. 43)
- ☐ Think About These Things (p. 45)
- ☐ Crashing Thoughts (p. 49)
- ☐ Under the Whole Heaven (p. 53)
- ☐ Wind (p. 85)
- ☐ Seeds (p. 94)
- ☐ Resources (p. 131)
- ☐ Deep Joy (p. 138)
- ☐ Six-Word Story (p. 163)
- ☐ Kingdom Apps (p. 173)
- ☐ A Prayer for Showing Up (p. 252)
- ☐ Monopoly Money (p. 275)

Checklist of Bible Trips

- ☐ The Big Bag of Seeds (p. 47)
- ☐ No Longer a Slave (p. 128)
- ☐ Here and Now (p. 133)
- ☐ Theirs Is the Kingdom (p. 158)
- ☐ The Story in Your Head (p. 161)
- ☐ Gaps and Ambiguities (p. 165)
- ☐ The Selfie (p. 200)
- ☐ Your New Best Friend—Matthew (p. 322)

Special Thanks

Special thanks belong to friends, family, and professionals who helped this book reach a deeply satisfying form.

Caleb Breakey, Debbie Oliver, Maria Floros, and the team at Renown Publishing have been good partners in the great adventure of publishing. They made the book shine and the process enjoyable.

Incredible friends provided solid feedback as beta-readers. A truckload of thanks belongs to Doug Scoggins, Thom LeCompte, Dick Matilla, Candy Marballi, and Dr. Jason Hubbard. Eric Young turned a small office with two red chairs into a place of great relationship, challenge, and inspiration.

When the book was still rough and wild, Kayli Thompson provided heroic developmental edits, and Belinda Ivy helped with graphics.

The staff at Christ the King Community Church give me the priceless gift of authentic Christian community. The Small Group Team shows me how to live Jesus' new commandment of love: Kevin Brearley, Ryan Ervin, Julie Burleson, Jayne Doll, Ron Walton, and Keith Bouma. Grant Fishbook teaches me about the heart of a shepherd who serves best when circumstances are the worst. Melonie Kemp gives me a crystal-clear picture of showing up as a whole person. Garret Shelsta, Derek

Archer, Chad Hoffman, and Todd King significantly nourished my thinking about the kingdom. Shawna Walton models a life of faithful service in a way that boggles the mind. Wendy Powell helps me hear from God.

Other people have shaped not just the book, but my life. Jerry Kirk continues to show me the sheer joy of following Jesus together with others. Daniel Frlan opened my eyes to flourishing in a kingdom of peace. Jack Faulkner, Jeff Condon, and Father Bryan Dolejsi are three legs of a stool—they supported me through some of the most difficult times of my life.

Josh Yates has deeply influenced my life as a disciple of Jesus. I've seen him stub his toe on the hidden treasure and sell all. There is nobody I know better suited than Josh to write the foreword to this book, especially because anything a Yates creates is beautiful and excellent.

Without the care of Carolyn Thomas-Chandler, I literally would not be here today.

I'm so grateful for my family: Julie, Rob, Ryder, Cole, Courtney, Mark, Rachel, and Jackson. The new family of Kai, Melody, and Sienna already brings me a deep joy.

Without the sacrificial love of Mom and Dad, I would not be who I am.

Finally, to Katie, my Beloved—you have been more than patient, more than loving, more than giving, more than supportive. You make me a better Brian. I love you more today. And I like you. Psalm 34:3.

REFERENCES

Notes

1. *Blue Letter Bible*, "Kingdom" (search results). https://www.biblegateway.com/quicksearch/?qs_version=ESV&quicksearch=Kingdom&begin=47&end=73.

2. Brown, Francis, Edward Robinson, Samuel Rolles Driver, and Charles Augustus Briggs. *A Hebrew and English Lexicon of the Old Testament*. Houghton Mifflin, 1906, p. 1022.

3. Brown, Robinson, Driver, and Briggs, *A Hebrew and English Lexicon*, p. 688.

4. Imes, Carmen. *Bearing God's Name*. InterVarsity Press, 2019, p. 31.

5. Chesterton, Gilbert Keith. *Orthodoxy*. John Lane Company, 1908, p. 18.

6. Ortberg, John. *Soul Keeping: Caring for the Most Important Part of You*. Zondervan, 2014, p. 20.

7. YHWH is God's revealed, personal name that he gave in his role

as King over his people in the Old Testament.

8. Scazzero, Peter. *The Emotionally Healthy Leader*. Zondervan, 2015.

9. G., Deyan. "How Much Time Does the Average American Spend on Their Phone?" TechJury.net. July 28, 2020. https://techjury.net/blog/how-much-time-does-the-average-american-spend-on-their-phone/#gref.

10. Swart, Tara, Kitty Chisolm, and Paul Brown. *Neuroscience for Leadership: Harnessing the Brain Gain Advantage*. Palgrave Macmillan, 2015.

11. Jones, Bruce. "Exceeding Guest Expectations: It's All in the Details." Disney. January 24, 2019. https://www.disneyinstitute.com/blog/exceeding-guest-expectations-its-all-in-the-details/.

12. Cosper, Mike. *Recapturing the Wonder: Transcendent Faith in a Disenchanted World*. Intervarsity Press, 2017, p. 24.

13. Authors Eric Bloom and Peter Scazzero call it the "Gap of Inaction," but "Trap of Inaction" sounds more sinister and is better suited for our purposes.

14. Strong, James. "G5485: charis." *A Concise Dictionary of the Words in the Greek Testament and the Hebrew Bible*. Faithlife, 2019.

15. Rocke, Chris, and Joel Van Dyke. *Geography of Grace: Doing Theology from Below*." Center for Transforming Mission, 2012, p. 246.

16. Photo credit: Brian Steele, 2018.

17. Photo credit: Brian Steele, 2018.

18. Schmalz, Timothy P. "Homeless Jesus." Sculpture by Timothy P. Schmalz. 2018. https://www.sculpturebytps.com/large-bronze-statues-and-sculptures/homeless-jesus/.

19. DeGrey, Laura, and Paul K. Link. "Lake Missoula Floods." Digital Geology of Idaho. http://geology.isu.edu/Digital_Geology_Idaho/Module13/mod13.htm.

20. Soennichsen, John. *Bretz's Flood: The Remarkable Story of a Rebel Geologist and the World's Greatest Flood.* Sasquatch Books, 2009.

21. Ragnar Events. 2020. https://runragnar.com.

22. "The Numbers: Where Data and the Movie Business Meet." Nash Information Services, LLC. http://www.the-numbers.com/movies/franchises/.

23. Otterson, Joe. "'Game of Thrones' Season Premiere Shatters HBO Ratings Records." Variety. July 17, 2017. http://variety.com/2017/tv/news/game-of-thrones-season-7-premiere-ratings-1202497751/.

24. Klein, Christopher. "Fooling Hitler: The Elaborate Ruse Behind D-Day." History. June 3, 2014. Updated August 30, 2018. http://www.history.com/news/fooling-hitler-the-elaborate-ruse-behind-d-day.

25. Kelly, Henry Ansgar. *Satan: A Biography.* Cambridge University Press, 2006.

26. Wolf, Jessica. "Give the Devil His Due." UCLA Newsroom. February 16, 2018. https://newsroom.ucla.edu/stories/give-the-devil-his-due.

27. Murdoch, Lindsay. "The Lost City." The Age. June 14, 2013. https://www.theage.com.au/world/the-lost-city-20130614-2o9k7.html#ixzz2WECSfBaD.

28. BBC Studios. "Cordyceps: Attack of the Killer Fungi—Planet Earth Attenborough BBC Wildlife." YouTube video. November 3, 2008. https://www.youtube.com/watch?v=XuKjBIBBAL8.

29. Handheld GPS units have become very affordable. The Geocaching website lists latitude/longitude coordinates that you plug into the GPS unit to direct you to the cache you'd like to find. If you don't have a GPS unit, bring along a friend who does have one. Caution: Geocaching is highly addictive. Trust me. If you get into it, you'll likely want to buy your own gear before long.

30. Brand, Paul, and Phillip Yancey. *Fearfully and Wonderfully Made*. Zondervan, 1997.

31. "Alexander's Tent." Livius.org. March 13, 2019. https://www.livius.org/sources/content/polyaenus/alexanders-tent/.

32. Strong, James. "G2078: eschatos." *A Concise Dictionary of the Words in the Greek Testament and the Hebrew Bible*. Faithlife, 2019.

33. Strong, James. "G3048: logia." *A Concise Dictionary of the Words in the Greek Testament and the Hebrew Bible*. Faithlife, 2019.

34. Alcorn, Randy. *Heaven*. Tyndall Momentum, 2011.

35. There's a continuum of "7 Spheres" or "7 Mountains" theology and practice that ranges from harmless to dangerous. Not all leaders in this theological stream warrant red flags of caution. But when pushed to extremes, Dominionism has cultic qualities. Many teachers in the "New Apostolic Reformation" claim to be modern Apostles and

Prophets with authority approaching the level of Paul or Isaiah, in order to take over the spheres of society. This author is not cessationist and does not deny the modern use of apostolic or prophetic gifting. But let's keep the "a" lower case in the title "apostle" and the "p" lower case before "prophet." Upper-case Apostles and Prophets are reserved exclusively for the original establishment of the canon of Scripture. For a more in-depth treatment of these topics, see Holly Pivec, *A New Apostolic Reformation?: A Biblical Response to a Worldwide Movement*, Weaver Book Company, 2014. Pivec's companion book is also instructive: *God's Super-Apostles: Encountering the Worldwide Prophets and Apostles Movement*, 2014, Weaver Book Company, 2014.

36. Wright, N. T. "Imagining the Kingdom: Mission and Theology in Early Christianity." NTWrightPage. October 26, 2011. http://ntwrightpage.com/2016/07/12/imagining-the-kingdom/.

See also N. T. Wright, *Surprised by Scripture*, HarperOne, 2014.

37. Chesterton, Gilbert Keith. *Orthodoxy*. Moody Publishers, 2013.

38. "Confronting a Crisis of Christology: Q and A with David Bryant." Tri-State Voice. December 17, 2017. https://www.tristatevoice.com/2017/12/17/confronting-a-crisis-of-christology-david-bryant-pillar-college-develop-unique-course/.

39. Although, I argue later in the book that the kingdom story is written into our DNA and we innately understand kingdom narratives because God created us to live in his eternal kingdom.

40. Photo credit: Brian Steele, July 2, 2014.

41 Bates, Matthew. *Salvation by Allegiance Alone*. Baker Academic, 2017

42. Grenny, Joseph, Kerry Patterson, Ron McMillan, and Al Switzler. *Crucial Conversations: Tools for Talking When Stakes Are High.* McGraw-Hill Education, 2011.

43. Wright, N. T. "N. T. Wright on Scripture and the Authority of God." Biologos. October 3, 2018. https://biologos.org/articles/n-t-wright-on-scripture-and-the-authority-of-god.

44. Reimer, David. "Introduction to the Poetic and Wisdom Literature." *English Standard Version Study Bible.* Crossway, 2008, p. 866.

45. Wilson, Timothy. *Redirect: Changing the Stories We Live By.* Back Bay Books, 2015.

46. Loehr, Jim. *The Power of Story: Rewrite Your Destiny in Business and Life.* Free Press, 2008.

47. Thompson, Curt. *The Anatomy of the Soul: Surprising Connections Between Neuroscience and Spiritual Practices That Can Transform Your Life and Relationships.* Tyndale Momentum, 2007.

48. Peterson, Jordan, Daniel Higgins, and Robert Pihl. Self Authoring. https://selfauthoring.com/.

49. Walsh, Jerome T. *Old Testament Narrative: A Guide to Interpretation.* Westminster John Knox Press, 2010.

50. Fleming, David L. "Pray with Your Imagination." IgnatianSpirituality.com. Loyola Press. https://www.ignatianspirituality.com/ignatian-prayer/the-spiritual-exercises/pray-with-your-imagination.

51. Fisher, Fred L. "The New and Greater Exodus: The Exodus Pattern in the New Testament." *Southwestern Journal of Theology* 20

(1977). http://preachingsource.com/journal/the-new-and-greater-exodus-the-exodus-pattern-in-the-new-testament/.

52. Bartholomew, Craig, and Michael Goheen. *The Drama of Scripture: Finding Our Place in the Biblical Story*. Baker Academic, 2014.

53. Photo credit: Alison Gorum, 2019. Used with permission.

54. Gentry, Peter J., and Stephen J. Wellum. *Kingdom Through Covenant*. Crossway, 2012, p. 101.

55. There are arguably more than four covenants in the Bible. Other covenants include the Noahic covenant (Genesis 9:8–17) and the less explicit "covenant with Creation" (Jeremiah 33:20, 25; Psalm 19, 74) and "Adamic covenant" (Hosea 6:7). But these additional covenants likewise serve specific purposes to advance God's kingdom agenda.

56. For example, see: James S. Diamond, *Stringing the Pearls: How to Read the Weekly Torah Portion* (Jewish Publication Society, 2008).

57. Scazzero, Peter. *Emotionally Healthy Spirituality*. Thomas Nelson, 2011.

58. We use the masculine term *son* without reference to gender since all of Israel corporately, male and female, was considered the son of God, in the same sense that all of the church is considered the "bride of Christ" without reference to gender.

59. Gentry, Peter J., and Stephen J. Wellum. *Kingdom Through Covenant: A Biblical-Theological Understanding of the Covenants*. Crossway, 2012, p. 217.

60. The Prayer Covenant is a discipleship tool you use to pray with people as you follow Jesus together. For more information, see Dr.

Kirk's website (https://theprayercovenant.org/) and the book *The Prayer Covenant: Following Jesus Together* by Dr. Jerry Kirk and Stephen Eyre (2013).

61. This isn't an argument for pacifism. I believe that the Christian faith can be honorably exercised in a professional military career.

62. Gesenius, Friedrich Wilhelm. *Gesenius' Hebrew-Chaldee Lexicon to the Old Testament Scriptures*. Translated by Samuel Prideaux Tregelles. S. Bagster, 1846.

63. Louw, Johannes P., and Eugene Nida, eds. *Greek-English Lexicon of the New Testament Based on Semantic Domains*. 2nd edition. United Bible Societies, 1989.

64. "Working for Us: Current Vacancies." The Royal Household. https://theroyalhousehold.tal.net/vx/candidate/jobboard/vacancy/4/adv.

65. *Encyclopaedia Britannica*, "Elizabeth II: Queen of United Kingdom." April 17, 2020. https://www.britannica.com/biography/Elizabeth-II.

66. Photo Credit: Brian Steele, 2012.

67. Photo credit: Scott Sayers, 2014. Used with permission.

68. Wright, N. T. *The Day the Revolution Began: Reconsidering the Meaning of the Crucifixion*. HarperOne, 2016, p. 76–77.

69. Smith, K. A. *You Are What You Love: The Spiritual Power of Habit*. Brazos Press, 2016, p. 40–46.

70. Spheeris, Penelope, dir. *Wayne's World*. NBC Films, 1992.

71. Willard, Dallas. *Life Without Lack: Living in the Fullness of*

Psalm 23. Thomas Nelson, 2019.

72. There are legal restrictions for how a bill can be marked. Please read carefully the instructions at the "Where's George" website for what's appropriate. Illegal marking makes a bill "unfit to be re-issued."

73. "Top Users." Where'sGeorge.com. 2020. https://www.wheres george.com/state-profiles-detail.php?st=top#.

74. Chesterton, *Orthodoxy*, p. 91.

75. Barton, Ruth Haley. *Strengthening the Soul of Your Leadership: Seeking God in the Crucible of Ministry*. InterVarsity Press, 2018, p. 161.

About the Author

Brian C. Steele is a pastor, speaker, and author. His work has focused on discipleship, leadership development, and small groups. After spending eight years studying Jesus' parable of the hidden treasure, he loves helping people to find God's kingdom right beneath their feet. His teaching venues have ranged from thousands of people in megachurch sermons to conferences, retreats, workshops, and one-on-one coaching. He is also a professional geologist and is in (partial) recovery from a bird-watching addiction. He delights in exploring the alpine wilderness of the Pacific Crest Trail with his wife, Katie, and dog, Banner. Find more at www.kingdomfieldguides.com.

Made in the USA
Columbia, SC
16 May 2021

37386681R00196